C000156969

Africa, Asia, and the History of Philosophy

SUNY series, Philosophy and Race

Robert Bernasconi and T. Denean Sharpley-Whiting, editors

Africa, Asia, and the History of Philosophy

Racism in the Formation of the
Philosophical Canon, 1780–1830

Peter K. J. Park

Cover image © Zsolt Ercsei / Bigstockphoto

Published by State University of New York Press, Albany

© 2013 State University of New York

All rights reserved

Printed in the United States of America

No part of this book may be used or reproduced in any manner whatsoever without written permission. No part of this book may be stored in a retrieval system or transmitted in any form or by any means including electronic, electrostatic, magnetic tape, mechanical, photocopying, recording, or otherwise without the prior permission in writing of the publisher.

For information, contact State University of New York Press, Albany, NY
www.sunypress.edu

Production by Diane Ganeles
Marketing by Kate McDonnell

Library of Congress Cataloging-in-Publication Data

Park, Peter K. J.
    Africa, Asia, and the history of philosophy : racism in the formation of the philosophical canon, 1780–1830 / Peter K. J. Park.
        p. cm. — (SUNY series, Philosophy and Race)
    Includes bibliographical references (p.   ) and index.
    ISBN 978-1-4384-4641-7 (hc : alk. paper)—978-1-4384-4642-4 (pb : alk. paper)
    1. Philosophy—History—18th century.   2. Philosophy—History—19th century.   3. Continental philosophy—History.   4. Philosophers—Europe—Attitudes.   5. Racism.   6. Philosophy, African.   7. Philosophy, Asian. I. Title.

B802.P27 2013
190.9'033—dc23   2012019188

10 9 8 7 6 5 4 3 2 1

Contents

Contents

Figures

Acknowledgments

One agency, two foundations, and many, many people made this book possible. I would like to thank first my teachers: Peter Reill, Margaret Jacob, Richard Popkin, and James Wald. I would like to thank the people who helped me to improve the manuscript of this book with their criticisms, questions, answers, suggestions, and practical aid. They are Sunil Agnani, Ali Anooshahr, Charles Bambach, Robert Bernasconi, Thomas A. Brady, Jr., Zoltan Biedermann, Neilesh Bose, Susan Briante, Matthew J. Brown, Stephen Chappell, Alexandra Cook, Sean Cotter, Jon Daniel, Tobias Delfs, Wendy DeSouza, Gita Dharampal-Frick, Thomas Douglas, Douglas Dow, Reem Elghonimi, J. Michael Farmer, Micah Forbes, Amy Freund, Diane Ganeles, Kimberly Garmoe, Frank Garrett, Bryan Givens, John Gooch, Pamela Gossin, John Grever, Dragana Grbić, Simon Grote, Ming Dong Gu, Knud Haakonssen, Charles Hatfield, Joseph Holt, Pia Jakobsson, Eric F. Johnson, Andrew Kenyon, Sigrid Koepke, John Christian Laursen, Corinne Lefèvre, Nancy E. Levine, David Luft, Jürgen Lütt, Megan Lynch, Anne MacLachlan, Benjamin and Marianne Marschke, Farid Matuk, Kelly Maynard, Kate McDonnell, Angelo Mercado, Jessica Murphy, Cihan Yüksel Muslu, Michelle Nickerson, Zsuzsanna Ozsvath, Charlton Payne, Jared Poley, Clark Pomerleau, Jeremy Popkin, Julie Popkin, Jeremy Prince, Stephen Rabe, Courtenay Raia, Gita Rajan, Monica Rankin, Cindy Renker, Natalie Ring, Nils Roemer, Mark Rosen, Axel Rüdiger, Hartmut Scharfe, Eric Schlereth, Rainer Schulte, Linda Snow, Jerry and Elke Soliday, Sabrina Starnaman, Deborah Stott, Mikiko Tanaka, Brent Thorn, Claudia Verhoeven, Han Vermeulen, Brent Vine, William Weber, Georg Werther, Daniel Wickberg, Jeffrey L. Wilson, Michael L. Wilson, Gabriel Wolfenstein, Victor Wolfenstein, Amy Woodson-Boulton, Johan van der Zande, and the staff of the Center for 17th and 18th-Century Studies at UCLA and of the McDermott Library at the University of Texas at Dallas.

My project benefited from the research work that others shared with me on the history of Orientalism, language sciences, and race science. For this, I thank Tuska Benes, Robert Bernasconi, Sai Bhatawadekar, Robert Cowan, Nicholas Germana, Wilhelm Halbfass, Bradley Herling, David Hoyt, Hanco Jürgens, Roland Lardinois, Kris Manjapra, Suzanne Marchand, Douglas McGetchin, Frank Neubert, Karen Oslund, Pascale Rabault-Feuerhahn, Saverio Marchignoli, and Indra Sengupta. I am fortunate to have Doug as my most constant companion in research. I thank Brad for being a careful critic of my manuscript at a late stage of development.

I began the research for this book in 2000–2001, when I was a doctoral fellow funded by the German Academic Exchange Service (DAAD). I thank the Service and my colleagues at the South Asia Institute at Heidelberg University: Dietmar Rothermund, Tilman Frasch, and Harald Fischer-Tiné. In 2009, I spent several months reading in the libraries of Halle an der Saale with the support of a Fritz Thyssen Fellowship from the Francke Foundations. I thank the Foundations and my hosts at the Interdisciplinary Centre for Pietism Research and the Interdisciplinary Centre for European Enlightenment Studies: Daniel Fulda, Rainer Godel, Frank Grunert, Erdmut Jost, Britta Klosterberg, Thomas Müller-Bahlke, Axel Rüdiger, Christian Soboth, Jürgen Stolzenberg, Udo Sträter, Sabine Volk-Birke, and Andrea Thiele. I must also thank the dedicated staff of the Archive and Library of the Franke Foundations. I would not have been able to take up the Thyssen Fellowship without the leave granted by my dean, Dennis Kratz.

I would never have finished writing this book without the emotional support of Rafael Alanis, Johnny Armijo, Gwen Camacho, Shane Chang, Howard Chin, Kristian Craige, Micah Forbes, Rita Joye Gray, Gus Heard-Hughes, Kate Hugh-Jones, Peter Hornick, Richard E. Jones, Jin Kim, Annette Korbin, Uwe Küchler, Richard Kwon, Brandyn Lee, Lucy McCauley, Scott B. Morgan, Craig Navarro, Spenser Nicholas, Paul Nogler, Jena Pincott, Coryn Prince, Jesse Rossa, Emily Sandor, David Schonfeld, Julianne Scott, Luis Selva, Shawn Suarez, Thomas and Mahwish Syed-Mangan, Sergey Trakhtenberg, and Benjamin Vogler.

Yungsuhn, David, Simon, Mom, and Halmoni, this book is dedicated to you.

Preface

When I began this project more than a decade ago, I did not consider that racism could have been involved in the formation of the modern canon of philosophy. Having paid little attention to Christoph Meiners, I could not have suspected that the racist arguments of this half-forgotten anthropological writer of the late eighteenth century lay at the origin of the exclusion of Africa and Asia from modern histories of philosophy. Two developments since the completion of my dissertation in 2005 affected my thinking. The first was that I read the dozen articles by the philosopher Robert Bernasconi on race concepts and racism in the thought of Kant and Hegel. The second was that I read more extensively in Meiners's corpus.

Christoph Meiners (1747–1810) was a professor of philosophy at the University of Göttingen and the author of more than forty books and one hundred and eighty journal articles on psychology and aesthetics; the history of science, philosophy, and universities; and early anthropology. Meiners is included in Johann Gustav Droysen's account of the "Göttingen Historical School," which is credited with the development of the modern historical sciences. There is evidence to suggest that Meiners shaped the human sciences in Germany and France through his numerous publications and that he continued to influence historical and anthropological thought in the nineteenth century.[1] In this book, I argue that Meiners was the first agent of a successful campaign to exclude Africa and Asia from the history of philosophy and that this campaign was carried forward by Wilhelm Tennemann, who was the most important Kantian historian of philosophy at the turn of the nineteenth century, and Hegel. Meiners's direct influence on them is evident in their arguments for excluding the Orient from the history of philosophy. The central arguments that cut across both Kantian and Hegelian histories of philosophy were racial-anthropological ones, imported from Meiners's publications and repeated without much change. Kant never produced a work of history of philosophy, but he sketched the outlines of one in his logic lectures. There, one can behold Kant's own words authorizing the exclusion of the Orient from the history of philosophy. His reasons for the exclusion were ones he got from Meiners, whose influential *Geschichte des Ursprungs, Fortgangs und Verfalls der Wissenschaften in Griechenland und Rom (History of the Origin, Progress, and Decline of the Sciences in Greece and Rome)* appeared in 1781.[2]

I should note that Meiners remains a conspicuously under-researched *Aufklärer*. The exact nature of his contribution to the human or social sciences, the kind and degree of his influence on his contemporaries and on posterity is still mostly unknown. Historians, including literary historians, of the German Enlightenment either have completely passed over him or have discussed him without address-ing his racism.[3] A couple of historians have described his work just enough to denounce it as racist.[4] More recently, one historian of the German Enlightenment has attempted to treat Meiners's "science of culture" without discussing his science of race.[5] Studies that confront his racism with analysis are few.[6] I believe that the position of Mein-ers, always on the periphery of historical accounts of the eighteenth-century "science of man," is a result of the shock and revulsion that historians in the wake of World War II and the Holocaust have felt for his racist ideas. Meiners is not the face of the German Enlighten-ment that the historians can countenance.

The present work is not a history of scientific racism in the German Enlightenment. That history still awaits to be written. And when that history comes out, it will provide a vital context for read-ers of my work. That history will show that racism of the modes or types identified by our contemporary social scientists existed in the eighteenth century. According to the sociologist Michael Banton, there are three types of racism: racist ideology, racial prejudice, and racial discrimination.[7] All three describe eighteenth-century phenomena. It was racial prejudice that animated David Hume to write the footnote to his essay "Of National Characters" (1753), where he states that non-whites, especially negroes, are naturally inferior to whites.[8] Racial prejudice is the substance of Kant's comments about blacks in "Obser-vations on the Feeling of the Beautiful and Sublime" (1764).[9] Racial discrimination was embodied in the electoral laws in France (before and after the Revolution), the Dutch Republic, and much of the rest of Europe, which denied political rights to persons with the slightest trace of African blood.[10] Finally, eighteenth-century racist ideology is exemplified by Meiners's anthropological work.

In the 1780s and 1790s, Meiners published several essays in which he argued against the abolition of slavery, defended aristocratic privilege and rule, and gave moral justifications for European colonialism. He argued from racial-anthropological grounds. If, according to Banton, racist ideology is "the doctrine that a man's behavior is determined by stable inherited characters deriving from separate racial stocks having distinctive attributes and usually considered to stand to one another in relations of superiority and inferiority," then what we have in Meiners's publications is racist ideology. Indeed, Georg Forster was able to recognize the ideological function of Meiners's anthropology. One of the most effective arguments that he could bring against Meiners was the charge that the latter abetted the pro-slavery camp with his claims about the "nature" of black Africans.

Racist ideology presupposes a theory of races.[11] What we know about the eighteenth century is that the thesis of naturally distinct races was being theoretically and empirically elaborated by some of the most prominent natural historians and medical and anthropological thinkers of the European Enlightenment. Their names were Linnaeus, Buffon, Voltaire, Henry Home, Kant, Blumenbach, Georg Forster, and Meiners.

It is not so problematic for my claim of racism in Kantian and Hegelian histories of philosophy that the words *race* and *racism* do not appear in them. (It is a fact that the word racism does not appear in any European language until the early part of the twentieth century.[12]) But as Pierre-André Taguieff notes, racial prejudice, racial discrimination, and racist ideology do quite well without the word race.[13] The German Enlightenment's most notable racist, Meiners, seldom used the word. Herder explicitly rejected the word, but it would be a mistake to conclude from this that there is nothing racist in his thought. Taguieff is right that "the word race can no longer be taken for the exclusive (or best) indicator of the modes of racialization."[14]

The decisive role that Meiners played in the exclusion of Africa and Asia from modern histories of philosophy is documented below. Historians would do well to investigate the extent to which Meiners is also responsible for the exclusion of Africa and Asia from modern histories of the sciences—astronomy, mathematics, and medicine or biology in particular—and from modern histories of the arts. The results of such investigation may well challenge the opinion of some historians that the eighteenth-century science of man dissipated and left no epistemic foundations for the human and social sciences of the nineteenth and twentieth centuries.[15]

Abbreviations

AA   *Kants gesammelte Schriften*. Edited by the Königliche
            Preussische (later Deutsche) Akademie der Wissen-
            schaften. 29 vols. to date. Berlin: Georg Reimer (later
            Walter de Gruyter), 1900–.

KFSA   *Kritische Friedrich-Schlegel-Ausgabe*. Edited by Ernst
            Behler, Jean Jacques Anstett, and Hans Eichner. 35 vols.
            projected. München: F. Schöningh, 1958–.

Vorlesungen   Hegel, G. W. F. *Vorlesungen: Ausgewählte Nachschriften
            und Manuskripte*. Multiple editors. 17 vols. Hamburg:
            Felix Meiner, 1983–2007.

Introduction

In the modern university, courses on the history of philosophy introduce students to philosophy as a discipline.[1] History of philosophy courses alternate with logic courses as ways to teach students the canon of philosophy in more than one sense of the word *canon*. By recounting philosophy's past (what philosophy was), the history of philosophy teaches what philosophy is (the concept of philosophy). The history of philosophy teaches the goals, rules, and language of proper philosophical reasoning. Teachers of philosophy do not merely recount the history of philosophy, they use it to define philosophy in exact terms and set its epistemic boundaries, differentiating it from other fields of knowledge such as mathematics, natural sciences, social sciences, and theology. Philosophers use the history of philosophy to reaffirm the canon of philosophy in the sense also of the authors and texts that define the discipline and to show philosophy's coherent and progressive development. "History of philosophy research reveals clearly that its ultimate goal is never only a historical knowing, but always at the same time an understanding that puts itself in the service of philosophy."[2] The history of philosophy can do all this work, however, only by performing massive exclusions.

The present work is a historical investigation of the exclusion of Africa and Asia from modern histories of philosophy. It is an account of the events that led to the formation within German philosophy of an exclusionary, Eurocentric canon of philosophy by the first third of the nineteenth century.

The exclusion of Africa and Asia from histories of philosophy is relatively recent. It was no earlier than the 1780s that historians of philosophy began to deny that African and Asian peoples were philosophical. Also beginning at that time, they segregated religion from philosophy and argued that Africans and Asians had religion, but not philosophy.[3] Stated more simply, historians of philosophy

1

began to exclude peoples they deemed too primitive and incapable of philosophy.

There is, however, an older tradition of history of philosophy writing. From the time of Marsilio Ficino (1433–99) to the death of Étienne Bonnot de Condillac (1715–80), the prevailing convention among historians of philosophy was to begin the history of philosophy with Adam, Noah, Moses (or the Jews), or the Egyptians. In some early modern histories of philosophy, Zoroaster, the "Chaldeans," or another ancient Oriental people appear as the first philosophers. The great majority of early modern historians of philosophy were in agreement that philosophy began in the Orient. It was in the late eighteenth century that historians of philosophy began to claim a Greek beginning for philosophy.[4]

Historians have established that from the eighteenth century onward Europeans had ever greater access to the languages and literatures of Asia and that the stream into Europe of manuscript sources and source-based information on Asian philosophies only increased over the course of the modern centuries.[5] Prominent names in European cultural and intellectual history are associated with the late eighteenth- and early nineteenth-century "Oriental Renaissance."[6] Some historians pinpoint this rebirth to the time when officials of the British East India Company acquired the knowledge of Sanskrit and then intensified the collection and transport of Sanskrit manuscripts to Europe. A key activity of the Oriental Renaissance was the translation of Asian texts into European languages, which cleared the way for their literary and scientific appropriation by Europeans.[7] This led to reevaluations—even radical reorderings—of the perceived historical origins of European peoples and civilization. In 1786, the Chief Magistrate for the Supreme Court of British Bengal, Sir William Jones, spread the news that Sanskrit and Persian appeared to be descended from the same mother language as that of Greek, Latin, Gothic, and Celtic languages.[8] Jones formulated the thesis of the family relation between these languages. The names Indo-Germanic, Indo-European, and Aryan were coined in the nineteenth century to signify this relation.

The excitement generated by the European discovery of Sanskrit and Persian literatures led to efforts in Europe to establish institutions for the study of them. The first professorial chair of Sanskrit in Europe was created at the Collège de France in 1814.[9] Paris in the early nineteenth century was Europe's center of Oriental philology. The Schlegel brothers traveled to Paris to learn Sanskrit. The older brother, August Wilhelm, went on to become the first professor at a German university to offer courses in Sanskrit language and literature, which he did starting in the summer of 1819 at the newly founded Prussian university in Bonn.[10] The Prussian government provided the funds for the manufacture of the printing press that August Wilhelm used to produce his Sanskrit-Latin edition, with commentary, of the *Bhagavadgītā* in 1823.[11] Also in 1819, the Kingdom of Bavaria sponsored two of its subjects to study Oriental languages in Paris. One of them, the exceptionally talented Franz Bopp, acquired enough technical expertise to establish the Indo-European linguistic relationship on hard grammatical evidence. In 1821 he was given a professorship in Oriental languages at the University of Berlin. His efforts culminated in an extensive comparison of the grammar of Sanskrit, Persian, and several European languages. His work was published as *Vergleichende Grammatik des Sanskrit, Zend, Griechischen, Lateinischen, Litthauischen, Gothischen und Deutschen,* appearing in six volumes between 1833 and 1852.[12] Intellectual historians as well as practicing linguists of today regard Bopp as one of the founders of modern linguistics.

Sanskrit philology and comparative grammatical studies spread to other German and Central European universities. By 1903, there were forty-seven professors, including twenty-six full professors, of Sanskrit and comparative Indo-European philology in German-speaking Europe.[13] The multiplication of professorial chairs resulted in piles of journals, philological treatises, grammars, dictionaries, and translated editions of Asian texts. In the nineteenth century, German scholarly production in these fields exceeded that of the rest of Europe and America combined.[14] By the second half of the century, the overproduction of German, university-trained Orientalists led to their exodus. Some were able to find work in the British Empire.[15]

Given this history, one may suppose that Asian philosophical ideas had a presence in modern German thought and that some German philosophers may have regarded Indian philosophy as part of their Indo-European or Aryan heritage. Certainly, Friedrich Max Müller, the famous Sanskritist and comparative philologist at Oxford, thought precisely in these terms. In the introduction to his English translation of Kant's *Critique of Pure Reason*, he states, "While in the Veda [Hindu sacred scriptures] we may study the childhood, we may study in Kant's Critique the perfect manhood of the Aryan mind."[16] Müller was not a professor of philosophy, and so one cannot say that he represented the view of the academic philosophers. What then did academic philosophers think of Asian philosophies?

The following quotations are taken from histories of philosophy published during the last two centuries. Julius Bergmann states in his *Geschichte der Philosophie* (1892): "Just as its name, so philosophy itself is originally Greek."[17] Friedrich Michelis states in his *Geschichte der Philosophie von Thales bis auf unsere Zeit* (1865): "No Asian people . . . has lifted itself to the heights of free human contemplation from which philosophy issues; philosophy is the fruit of the Hellenic spirit."[18] Albert Schwegler's *Geschichte der Philosophie im Umriss* (1863) states: "When and where does philosophy begin? . . . Obviously at that point when the first search for the final philosophical principle, for the ultimate reason for Being, was made in a philosophical manner. In other words, with Greek philosophy."[19] In the fifth edition of his history of Greek philosophy (1892), Eduard Zeller offers this comment: "All the same, we do not need to search for any foreign sources: the philosophical science of the Greeks may be completely explained by recalling the spirit, the devices, and the educational status of the Hellenic tribes. If there has ever been a people which was suited to generate its sciences on its own, it was the Greek."[20] In the eighth edition of *Grundriss der Geschichte der Philosophie* (1894–1902), Friedrich Ueberweg claims that neither the Nordic peoples nor the Orientals, but only the Greeks had the capacity to invent philosophy: "Philosophy, as a science, could not originate among the Nordic peoples, who are distinguished through their strength and courage, but do not have culture, nor among the Orientals, who are indeed capable of producing the elements of a higher culture but who tend more to passively preserve such elements rather than improve them through mental activity, but solely among the Hellenes, who harmoniously unite mental power and receptivity within themselves."[21] *The History of Philosophy from Thales to Comte* (1871) by George Henry Lewes similarly states: "It is the distinguishing peculiarity of the Greeks, that they were the only people of the ancient world, who were prompted to assume a scientific attitude in explaining the mysteries which surrounded them."[22] Seymour Guy Martin et al. in *A History of Philosophy* (1941) is more terse: "Philosophy originated in the ancient world among the Greek people."[23] Bertrand Russell's *A History of Western Philosophy* (1945) states, "Philosophy begins with Thales."[24] Martin Heidegger said in a lecture at Cerisy-la-Salle, France, in 1955: "The often heard expression 'Western-European philosophy' is, in truth, a tautology. Why? Because philosophy is Greek in its nature; Greek, in this instance, means that in origin the nature of philosophy is of such a kind that it first appropriated the Greek world, and only it, in order to unfold."[25]

Reflecting the disciplinary opinion, the great majority of nineteenth- and twentieth-century histories of philosophy either completely pass over non-European thought or relegate it to the "pre-history" of philosophy, in which case it still was not accorded the status of "philosophy." Moreover, some of these histories present no reasons for the exclusion of Asia and Africa, taking a Greek origin of philosophy for granted.

The development of the modern discipline of philosophy and the exclusion of non-European philosophies from the history of philosophy are related phenomena, but scholarly inquiry into their connection so far has yielded little explanation. The history of the history of philosophy (historiography of philosophy) is already a small field occupied by a handful of scholars. In the classic works of historiography by Lucien Braun and Lutz Geldsetzer, passing reference is made here and there to debates on the origins of philosophy, but that is all.[26] Martial Guéroult's three-volume *Histoire de l'histoire de la philosophie,* which was to be part of a larger philosophical project called *Dianoématique,* does not thematize the historical origin of philosophy, but does assume that it is Greek.[27] More recent research by the team of scholars led by Giovanni Santinello and the "archaeology of the history of philosophy" by Ulrich Johannes Schneider investigate the theory and practice of history of philosophy but without investigating its Eurocentrism.[28]

I am aware of only three philosophers who have published essays on the exclusion of non-European thought from the history of philosophy as a problem for philosophical and historical inquiry. They are the U.S.-based philosophers Wilhelm Halbfass and Robert Bernasconi and the British scholar Richard King.[29] Halbfass surveyed two dozen works of history of philosophy and found that, starting in the late eighteenth century, historians of philosophy tended overwhelming to exclude Asian philosophies.[30] His explanation was that a restrictive definition of philosophy came to narrow the scope of the history of philosophy with the result that Indian and other non-European philosophies fell out of this scope. Although most of the historians of philosophy that Halbfass surveyed viewed reason as a universal human faculty, they seemed to regard the proper development and use of reason as something else—indeed, as something *not* universal. Criteria were established for what counted as "proper," "actual," or "real" philosophy.[31]

Bernasconi has called the dual claim of the universality of reason and the Greek origin of philosophy "the paradox of philosophy's parochialism." He asks, "What is one to make of the apparent tension between the alleged universality of reason and the fact that its upholders are so intent on localising its historical instantiation?"[32] When and how did the history of philosophy become the story of Europe, of the West, of Greeks and Germans? Bernasconi had to delve into the historiography of philosophy, his focus trained on developments during the late eighteenth century. He identified two historians of philosophy who claimed that philosophy's origin was Greek: Dieterich Tiedemann, the author of *Geist der spekulativen Philosophie von Thales bis Sokrates* (1791–7), and Wilhelm Gottlieb Tennemann, who claimed a Greek origin for philosophy in the first volume of his *Geschichte der Philosophie* (1798).[33] To explain the claim of the Greek origin of philosophy, Bernasconi considered the thesis in the first volume of Martin Bernal's *Black Athena* that, starting in the late eighteenth century, racist ideas and attitudes induced major revisions in historiography.[34] He concluded, however, that better arguments than Bernal's were needed "before it [could] be established that the history of philosophy as a modern academic discipline was from the outset dominated by racist considerations."[35]

Bernasconi has also probed Hegel's and Heidegger's denial of Asian philosophy.[36] Both philosophers explicitly denied that Chinese or Indian philosophy was philosophy.[37] In the case of Heidegger, the claim of the Greek origin of philosophy seems tied up with the quest for a German identity and future.[38] Hegel used the distinction between religion and philosophy to more narrowly delimit philosophy and exclude Asian thought from it, but this landed Hegel in perplexity after 1827, when he acknowledged the existence of philosophy, autonomous from religion, in India.[39] Despite this acknowledgment, Hegel's assessment of Indian thought is so negative, his regard for Indian civilization so contemptuous, that Bernasconi wonders whether contemporary debates (in Germany) about pantheism were a factor in Hegel's thinking about India.[40] Through yet other essays analyzing Hegel's judgments of Africa and Asia in world history, Bernasconi has confronted the issue of racism—Hegel's racism.[41]

Beyond any historian, it is a philosopher, Bernasconi, who sets the stage for my investigation. I approach my problem by analyzing changes in the writing of history of philosophy based on actual histories of philosophy published in the early modern centuries up to the early nineteenth century. I uncover racial ideas in these histories and track them down to their sources. I then tell the history of the history of philosophy with the thread of racism intact.

My account begins in the 1790s, when Kantian philosophers began a coordinated campaign to reform the history of philosophy. In journal articles, longer treatises, and in the introductions to the histories of philosophy that they themselves authored, the Kantians formulated the method of *a priori* construction in historical writing. According to the principles of *a priori* construction, the history of philosophy was to be organized under a ruling definition of philosophy, which also established criteria for what qualified as philosophy. This definition the Kantians took from the master as they were convinced that Kant had presented the one true system of philosophy. If Kant's philosophy provided a definition of philosophy and principles by which the history of philosophy could now be organized, it also provided principles of exclusion. In *Geschichte der Philosophie*, written by Wilhelm Tennemann (1761–1819) in the Kantian mode, Egyptian and Asian philosophies are excluded. In Chapter 4, I examine more closely to what extent Tennemann's exclusion of Egypt and Asia conforms to Kant's own thought.

Historiographers of philosophy have tended to see the Kantian "revolution" in the writing of history of philosophy as one of those great moments in philosophy's scientization (*Verwissenschaftlichung*), but a contemporaneous development in France suggests a different narrative. Joseph-Marie de Gérando (1772–1842) and Friedrich Schlegel (1772–1829) pioneered the comparative history of philosophy, the methodological principles for which they derived from the emerging sciences of comparative anatomy and comparative physiology. With a comparative-historical approach to problems of philosophy, de Gérando was able to show that Locke's (eclectic) philosophy succeeded in fulfilling the promise of philosophy while other philosophical systems failed, Kantianism being a spectacular example.

Schlegel's comparative history of philosophy revealed the flaws in kind and degree of each of five classes of philosophical systems. The comparative history of philosophy seemed to disclose the erstwhile existence of man's perfect intelligence, which Schlegel conceived as the knowledge of divine revelation. In relation to it, the systems of philosophy were historical degenerations—the products of human intelligence in decay. In his 1808 publication, *Ueber die Sprache und Weisheit der Indier*, Schlegel presented more evidence, which he took from Indian textual sources, for the existence of divine revelation. He extended the comparative-historical analysis of philosophical systems to Oriental philosophies, putting them on par with European philosophies and radically affirming the reality of Oriental philosophy. Schlegel's and de Gérando's comparative histories of philosophy are included in my account so as to disrupt the Kantian paradigm which drives the *a priori* and teleological constructions of the history and historiography of philosophy such as we find in the works of Geldsetzer and Braun.[42]

That philosophy is exclusively of Greek origin was an opinion held by only three published historians of philosophy in the eighteenth century. All three were active late in the century. Christoph Meiners (1747–1810), Dieterich Tiedemann (1748–1803), and, as already mentioned, Tennemann excluded the Orient. Tiedemann tersely stated his reasons for the exclusion. These can be summed up by the following: the so-called philosophical ideas of the Chaldeans, Persians, Indians, and Egyptians "contain mere poetry of times still half-brutish" or are based on revelation.[43] He urged that such ideas be barred from the history of philosophy. Meiners, a friend of Tiedemann's ever since their days at the same *Gymnasium*, elaborated his reasons over copious pages in several of his books and articles. He is the key to explaining the exclusion of Asia and Africa from the history of philosophy.[44]

Tennemann, whose first volume of *Geschichte der Philosophie* appeared in 1798, was immediately criticized for *not* including any account of Oriental philosophies. His critics sided with historiographical tradition, which regarded the Orient (e.g., Egypt or India) as the birthplace of Greek learning. Even as they were confronted by recent and growing information on the civilizations of the ancient Persians and Indians, Kantian historians of philosophy remained very ambivalent about Asia. This ambivalence was perfectly expressed in the compromise position struck by Friedrich August Carus (1770–1807), an idealist philosopher at the University of Leipzig. He proposed that non-European thought be discussed, but *not* in connection to the historical development of Greek philosophy. This became the solution adopted by the later Tennemann and Hegel (1770–1831).

Hegel explicitly excluded the Orient from the history of philosophy, although he was compelled to give an account of what Oriental philosophy is and why it should be excluded. In 1825, Hegel said in his history of philosophy lecture, "The first is Oriental philosophy, but it does not enter into the body of the whole presentation; it is something only preliminary, of which we speak in order to account for why we do not occupy ourselves with it further and what relation it has to thought, to true philosophy."[45] That Oriental philosophy is in ways preliminary to Greek philosophy was not disputed by either Friedrich Ast (1778–1841) or Thaddä Anselm Rixner (1766–1838), who taught the history of philosophy at the University of Landshut and at the Lyceum in Amberg, respectively. This, however, presented them no reason to deny that Oriental thought was philosophy and deserving of a place in the history of philosophy. Ast and Rixner, who became idealists in the wake of Schelling's *System of Transcendental Idealism*

(1800), designated Indian philosophy as the primeval philosophy (*Urphilosophie*), placing it in the first major period of history along with the philosophies of the Chinese, Tibetans, Chaldeans, Persians, and Egyptians. They placed Greek philosophy in the second major period and medieval and modern philosophies in the third and fourth periods, respectively.

That Hegel had a choice between two positions on Oriental philosophy becomes visible in the context of the standing debates over Oriental philosophy among historians of philosophy. It is surprising that Hegel sided with Tennemann and Meiners, adopting their arguments as his own. Hegel's position on Oriental philosophy is a reversion from the position of Ast and Rixner and, thus, cries out for explanation.

Hegel's view of the Orient, his statements about "the Oriental character," his refusal to compare Asian to European systems or schools of philosophy can be explained more fully in the context of the theological controversies in which he was embroiled. In the 1820s, Christian polemicists stepped up their attacks on Hegelianism, denouncing it as "pantheism," un-Christian, and morally repugnant. In both scholarly and polemical publications, the theologian and Orientalist August Tholuck (1799–1873) compared Hegel's philosophy to certain speculative systems from the medieval Middle East and more generally classified his philosophy as "conceptual pantheism" along with the systems of the Eleatics, Spinoza, and Fichte. In one of these polemical works, Tholuck presented the history of philosophy as a long succession of pantheistic systems starting with the "pantheistic religions" of China and ending with the systems of Schelling and Hegel.

In my final chapter, I argue that Hegel's elaboration, over the course of the 1820s, of the reasons for excluding Asia from the history of philosophy was a defensive maneuver against Tholuck's polemical attacks. In the end, Hegel was able to ward off the danger of comparisons made between his philosophy and Oriental speculation. Through his own telling of the history of philosophy, Hegel could show students that the history of philosophy was not a repetition of empty speculation, but a progressive or true development.

When the debates over Oriental philosophy ended in the period after Hegel's death, the absence of Africa and Asia from the lecture halls and seminar rooms of philosophy had become normal. Within one generation, academic philosophers succeeded in excluding the non-European world and in consolidating a canon of philosophy that powerfully legitimized their discipline.

1

The Kantian School and the Consolidation of Modern Historiography of Philosophy

> The history of philosophy presents to us reason in its sublime aspect, in its divine striving after truth without concealing its weaknesses, since it shows us its aberrations and entanglements in vain whimsy; it gives us a faithful painting of the transience of human opinions and of the ever more victorious struggle of reason against error and superstition.
>
> —Wilhelm Tennemann (1798)[1]

In 1791, Karl Leonhard Reinhold (1758–1825), the important early exponent of Immanuel Kant's philosophy, decried the lack of agreement among philosophers on what constitutes the proper object of the history of philosophy.[2] There was no agreement on even a concept of philosophy.[3] It remained an unresolved question whether the scientific study of nature, for instance, came under the domain of philosophy. None of the existing concepts of philosophy satisfied Reinhold, who was compelled to give his own definition: Philosophy is the "science of the determinate interrelation of things, independent of experience."[4] He elaborated this definition term by term: Philosophy is "scientific" as opposed to that which is "common, unordered" or "irregular."[5] The "philosophy of the common man" consists of accidental knowledge as means toward the satisfaction of sensual needs and does not qualify as philosophy.[6] If philosophy is to fulfill its

11

intended purpose, it should satisfy the need of consciousness only, the need of reason itself. Philosophy is the science of the "determinate" or "necessary," as opposed to the accidental, interrelation of things.[7] Things accidentally related to each other come under the domain of history and not philosophy.[8] Philosophy is "independent of experience" since the forms by which reason arrives at the interrelation of things are determined by the nature of human consciousness, the human faculty of representation, which does not originate in experience, but rather makes experience possible.[9]

Due to a "completely indeterminate" concept of philosophy, the idea of the history of philosophy has been equally indeterminate. This is the reason why one commonly confused the "actual" history of philosophy with intellectual history (the history of the sciences in particular) and with the "lives and opinions" of the philosophers. Reinhold also drew a distinction between the history of philosophy and the special histories of particular subfields of philosophy; such as metaphysics, which was often confused with philosophy in general.[10] Reinhold considered the history of philosophy as separate and distinct also from the history of the literature of philosophy.[11] This traditional confusion of genres gave him cause to strictly define the history of philosophy as "the portrayed quintessence of the changes that the science of the necessary interrelation of things has undergone from its [first] emergence to our times."[12]

Reinhold also wanted to exclude from the history of philosophy biographical details of the philosophers, excerpts of their writings, and reports by others of their contents. He wanted to exclude even historical information derived from the philosophers' own writings.[13] However, he did concede—but only barely—that in the special cases in which the psychological or moral character of a man, or certain circumstances of his life, had a decisive impact on his philosophical system—indeed, if his philosophical system was a peculiar one; that in these rare cases, the history of philosophy may take such historical data (e.g., biographical details) into consideration.[14] However, even the most accurate historical information could supply at best "nothing more than materials for the history of philosophy and not this history itself."[15] Notwithstanding rare exceptions, recounting the life circumstances of a philosopher would be a "useless waste of time" in the lecture hall and, Reinhold added, would even excuse the lecturer as well as the students from thinking.[16]

In this chapter I argue that, in distinguishing between what the history of philosophy had been previously and what it ought to be, Reinhold was calling for reform in this field of knowledge. He inaugurated a movement in the writing of history of philosophy that would span the rest of the decade and spill into the nineteenth century. As never before, German university philosophers would explicitly discuss the concept, content, form, purpose, method, scope, types, and value of the history of philosophy. Greater space was allotted to the discussion of these themes in the introductions and prefaces to a growing number of student handbooks on the history of philosophy as well as full-scale works on the same. These appeared alongside a dozen separate theoretical treatises on history of philosophy in this period.[17] That issues relating to the history of philosophy drew more attention in the 1790s than at any other time in the eighteenth century was due partly to the radical changes in the political and social order of Europe then occurring and philosophical reflection in Germany (as elsewhere) on the meaning of these changes for the history and destiny of humanity. During these years, Kant posed the question, "Whether the human race is constantly progressing?"[18] Interest in the history of philosophy received a concrete stimulus in 1790 with the announcement of the Berlin Royal Academy's prize question: "What real progress has metaphysics made in Germany since the time of Leibniz and Wolff?" After looking through German philosophical journals of this period, the historiographer Lutz Geldsetzer reported that "the overwhelming portion of the philosophical research is devoted to historical themes."[19] One should note that Reinhold's essay, "Ueber den Begrif der Geschichte der Philosophie" ("On the Concept of History of Philosophy"), was published in a journal wholly devoted to the theoretical discussion of the history of philosophy: *Beyträge zur Geschichte der Philosophie*, edited by Georg Gustav Fülleborn. Seven volumes of this journal appeared from 1794 to 1799.[20] That there was increased interest in the history of philosophy among academic philosophers is more than plausible if one considers that the discussion of the history of philosophy was philosophical in nature, beginning with the very concepts of history and philosophy.[21] "It is above all in Germany and in the northern countries that the most important works of history of philosophy were conceived and executed," states Joseph-Marie de Gérando in *Histoire comparée des systèmes de philosophie* (Paris, 1804).[22] Wilhelm Tennemann, the leading German historian of philosophy at century's end and de Gérando's translator, declared with some self-conceit: "The German nation has done far more for the reclamation and culture of the field of history of philosophy than any other nation." He added, "This is a fact that needs no proof."[23] More recently, Lucien Braun has commented, "The history of philosophy is, at the moment of its radical modification, a German thing, a Protestant thing."[24] All elements of the history of philosophy were subject to debate, and opinions were so varied that in 1800 one internal observer remarked, "Among the writers of history, no type is more disunited than the writers of the history of philosophy."[25]

I view Reinhold, Kant's greatest early exponent, as leading a movement to overthrow the long tradition of history of philosophy writing in the West.[26] This tradition has its beginnings with Diogenes Laërtius, the third-century author of *Lives and Opinions of Eminent Philosophers*, which has been one of the most frequently consulted sources on ancient philosophers since its Latin translation and printing in 1475.[27] The work organizes philosophers into schools, following their chronological succession and beginning with the biographical details and philosophical views of each school's founder. As late as the eighteenth century, "lives and opinions," a combination of doxography and biography, was the dominant mode of history of philosophy writing.[28] The "lives and opinions" mode is characteristic of several successful works of history of philosophy of the seventeenth and eighteenth centuries. One such work is Thomas Stanley's *The history of philosophy: containing the lives, opinions, actions and discourses of the philosophers of every sect* (1655–62), which draws its material heavily from Isaac Casaubon's Latin edition of Diogenes's text.[29] Another example is Pierre Bayle's *Dictionnaire historique et critique*, expanded and republished several times since the first edition of 1697.[30] (Bayle ordered his articles alphabetically by philosopher's name.) An early eighteenth-century example is Gerhard Johannes Voss's *De philosophia et philosophorum sectis* in the enlarged edition of 1705.[31] History of philosophy was offered in *Acta philosophorum*, a journal edited by Christoph August Heumann from 1715 to 1726.[32] André-François Boureau-Deslandes' *Histoire critique de la philosophie, où l'on traite de son origine, de ses progres et des diverses revolutions qui lui sont arrivées jusqu'à notre temps*, published in 1737, is another work of "lives and opinions."[33] These were all eclipsed by the *Historia critica philosophiae*, written by the Lutheran theologian Jacob Brucker.[34] Its five volumes (the fourth volume was issued in two parts) appeared between 1742 and 1744; a sixth volume appeared with the second edition of 1766–7.[35] It would not be an exaggeration to say that the eighteenth century consulted Brucker. Several generations of philosophers learned the history of philosophy from his work. After finishing his own six-volume history of philosophy, Dieterich Tiedemann complained that his contemporaries still used Brucker as if no new work in the history of philosophy had been done since.[36] Johann

Gottlieb Gerhard Buhle, another end-of-century historian of philosophy, considered Brucker the true founder of the history of philosophy.[37] Goethe learned his history of philosophy from Brucker. Kant,
Hegel, and Schopenhauer referred to Brucker.[38] The great bulk of the
articles on philosophers and topics in the history of philosophy in
Denis Diderot's *Encyclopédie* are not much more than translations of the
relevant parts of Brucker's Latin work.[39] (Denis Diderot and his col-
laborators used Boureau-Deslandes' *Histoire critique* secondly.[40]) There
were yet other foreign imitators.[41] De Gérando wrote that the *Historia
critica philosophiae* was "the vastest composition of this genre that still
[sees] the light of day."[42] With Brucker's work, the history of philosophy attained new heights of erudition through the study and criticism
of an array of sources and with attention paid to the historical and
cultural context of the philosophers' ideas.

Nonetheless, Reinhold charged that historians of philosophy,
Brucker not exempted, had devoted more space to the lives of philosophers than to their philosophical ideas. Thoroughly dissatisfied
with the existing works of history of philosophy, he declared,

> The man who has in his possession and power not only
> the old monuments and sources of the history of philoso-
> phy, but all necessary and useful historical, philological,
> grammatical and logical aids is nevertheless called a mere
> compiler and mechanical handler of the materials for a
> future history of philosophy, not inventor of its plan, not
> architect of its structure.[43]

If all previous authors of history of philosophy were compilers and
mechanical handlers, what new requirement did Reinhold set for a
man to deserve the title of historian of philosophy? He required that
he have "an acquaintance with the nature of the human faculties of
representation, knowledge, and desire."[44] That is, he required them to
be acquainted with the philosophy of Immanuel Kant. Reinhold was
not happy and would not be happy until a Kantian thinker wrote
the history of philosophy. Until this future event, the history of philosophy was condemned to read like Bayle's unrelentingly skeptical
account of philosophy in *Dictionnaire historique et critique*, one of the
more widely known sources on the history of philosophy circulating
in the eighteenth century in which, Reinhold bewailed, "the most
famous and worthy autonomous thinkers [*Selbstdenker*]" are treated
"in the most unworthy manner." By the end of the eighteenth century,

eleven editions of Bayle's *Dictionnaire*, including the German edition of 1741–4, existed.[45]

Georg Goess, *Privatlehrer* at Erlangen, agreed perfectly with Reinhold: The history of philosophy should be something distinct from the existing genres of "history of the human intellect," history of sciences, and "lives and opinions."[46] Goess also wanted to separate the history of philosophy from the history of mathematics, natural history, and the history of mankind and its religion.[47] Similarly, the forementioned Buhle, a professor *ordinarius* of philosophy at Göttingen (and a Kantian), taught that the history of philosophy was separate and distinct from other historical sciences, e.g., intellectual history, the history of arts and sciences, and history of religions.[48] For Buhle, too, a collection of literary and biographical notes ("lives and opinions") relating to the texts of philosophers or philosophical schools did not qualify as history of philosophy.[49] The history of philosophy as presented by Johann Heinrich Alsted, Gerhard Johannes Voss, and Daniel Georg Morhof, "for whom philosophy itself . . . was in the first instance a form of literature," would not be acceptable.[50] Morhof's concept of history of philosophy encompassed exactly those things that Goess wanted to exclude: natural philosophy, mathematics, astrology, and magic.[51] Brucker's approach was also unacceptable because the *Historia critica philosophiae* was, at a certain level, a history of natural philosophy concerned centrally with the theory of matter.[52]

Morhof's *Polyhistor*, a fine example of the genre *historia literaria*, which flourished in the late seventeenth and early eighteenth centuries, consists of three parts: *literarius, philosophicus* and *practicus*.[53] The *Polyhistor literarius* is divided into seven sections: libraries, method, excerpting, grammar, criticism, rhetoric, and poetics. The *Polyhistor philosophicus* is divided into the history of philosopy (*Polyhistor philosophicus-historicus*), covering the ancient schools, the Scholastics, and the *Novatores* as well as the history of natural philosophy (*Polyhistor physicus*) including metaphyics (in the Aristotelian sense), the *artes divinatoriae*, magic, mathematics, and, finally, the theory of knowledge. The third part, *Practicus,* covers ethics, politics, economy, history, theology, jurisprudence, and medicine. Like its predecessor, the Humanist encyclopedia, the *Polyhistor* disclosed the contents of the great philosophical, poetical, rhetorical, and historical texts of antiquity, but in addition gave a historical account of each field through an account of the literature relating to it. The *Polyhistor* was in this sense "literary history" in that knowledge of any discipline is intimately tied to knowledge of books and libraries.[54]

In the early pages of the first edition of the *Polyhistor*, Morhof claims the glory of being the first to write a work of *historia literaria* as outlined by Francis Bacon in *De augmentis scientiarum* (1623).[55] There, Bacon proposes the idea of collecting philosophical systems and opinions from the writings of the ancients, whether they dealt directly with philosophical matters or not.[56] *Historia literaria* combined Baconian methods of attaining knowledge with the older, Humanist methods of attaining knowledge through texts.[57] Therefore, when the Kantians moved to separate the history of philosophy from the history of all other fields of knowledge; when they insisted on a distinction between the history of philosophy on the one hand and the history of literature on the other, they were rejecting both Humanist and Baconian modes of historical writing, which were by then two-hundred- and three-hundred-year-old practices.

Reinhold, Goess, and Buhle wanted the history of philosophy to become an autonomous field of knowledge and hoped to set its boundaries with a Kantian definition.[58] To them, it was necessary to have a definition and to base the definition on a precise concept of philosophy. "*Philosophy* is the science of the nature of human mind in and for itself, and of its pure relation to objects outside itself. The *history of philosophy* is a pragmatic account of the most important attempts made by the most preeminent minds of antiquity and modern times to bring about this science."[59] That previous historians "did not correctly, precisely, and distinctly establish . . . the concept of philosophy and . . . the purpose of the history of philosophy and mistook its true domain" is why the discipline, in its current state, is more "literary" or "cultural history" than history of philosophy.[60]

In the same year that Reinhold called for the reform of the history of philosophy, another essay appeared, bearing a remarkable title: "A Few Ideas on the Revolution in Philosophy Brought About by I. Kant and Particularly on the Influence of the Same on the Treatment of the History of Philosophy."[61] The author, Carl Heinrich Heydenreich, claimed that Kant's philosophy necessitated a "complete transformation of the method of treatment of philosophical history" just as it necessitated a revolution in philosophy itself; and that even the best of the existing histories must appear as mere compilations in relation to a (yet to be realized) history of philosophy composed according to Kantian principles.[62] Now that Kant presented the one true system of philosophy, in Heydenreich's opinion, it was now possible to give an account of philosophy that could present its development toward its true end. The term he used for such an account was "pragmatic history."[63] He also argued that, since Kant had sized up the whole field of pure reason, a pragmatic history of metaphysics was now possible as well. Furthermore, a pragmatic history of practical philosophy could now be written since the "path to the true principles of morality" had been established.[64] A pragmatic history of religion was likewise for the first time feasible now that Kant had arrived at the true principles of rational religion.[65]

Heydenreich published an expanded version of his essay under a different title, *Originalideen über die Kritische Philosophie* (1793), which poses these questions: "Is there one philosophy? What is its essence? From when can one recount its existence? In what sense and to what extent can one call Kant the creator of philosophy? What kind of influence do his investigations have on the treatment of philosophical history?"[66] More boldly than in the earlier version, Heydenreich claimed that Kant's Critical Philosophy provided a universally valid concept of philosophy. Believing that he was in possession of this true concept, he defined philosophy as

> [t]he science of human nature, to the extent that its powers are determined by the original, essential, universally valid forms, rules and principles and to the extent that the efficacy of these (powers) can be grasped through the pure consciousness of these (forms, rules, principles) individually and as a whole.[67]

Original sources and the careful scrutiny of the same, so essential to humanist and modern-historical practice, were thought more or less superfluous if one may judge by Heydenreich's assertion that "[t]he only source of knowledge for all philosophy is consciousness itself," the purpose of philosophy being the investigation of "the faculties of human nature." He also claimed that the form and function of these faculties were a design of nature and that one should understand them "through pure consciousness of the natural laws" that rule their operation.[68]

For Heydenreich, the most conspicuous sign of the incomplete state of philosophy before Kant's arrival was the absence of a universally valid concept of this science—a point that Reinhold had also made. One was faced with a choice among a dozen concepts of philosophy. Heydenreich noted that it was actually a position taken by certain "skeptical" opponents of the Critical Philosophy that, due to the existence of several competing concepts of philosophy, one should withhold assent to any one concept. For them, the purpose of the history of philosophy was to show the strengths and weaknesses of existing systems of philosophy and to demonstrate especially the inherent limitations or defects of systematic philosophy in general. They compared systems of philosophy and allowed themselves to take the best aspects of two or more systems if, in doing so, it should prove useful to their ends. These unnamed opponents of Kantian philosophy were Johann Georg Feder, Christoph Meiners, and Christian Garve, known to the learned German public as "common sense philosophers" and known to today's historians as *Popularphilosophen*.

As Feder explained, "[i]n order to protect myself from the delusions of one-sided representations and to reach well-founded insights it is necessary to compare different ways of representation and to study several systems."[69] The method of *Popularphilosophie* is exhibited in Feder's textbook history of philosophy, *Grundriss der philosophischen Wissenschaften, nebst der nötigen Geschichte, zum Gebrauche seiner Zuhörer* (1767; 2nd ed. 1769).[70] Kantians ridiculed Feder and other *Popularphilosophen* for their concept of philosophy, which they derided as "syncretism."[71]

Although the *Popularphilosophen* received training in Leibnizio-Wolffian philosophy, it was not their intention to produce systematic philosophy. They were not interested in finding the rational foundations of human knowledge and morality and were not persuaded by the recent claims of the Kantians to having done so. Johan van der Zande has described them as moderate or "methodical" skeptics who settled for probabilites in knowledge and not certainties.[72] The Kantians may have claimed that Kant had strictly shown the limits of the human faculties of knowledge, but the *Popularphilosophen* claimed that they had always assumed these limits as a given.

Heydenreich complained of the "skeptics" who "cannot persuade themselves that Kant's critical system is new and singular, the first and last of its kind. They refer to history and accuse all those of ignorance who claim that no attempt of a philosopher before Kant can be compared . . . to the latter's enterprise."[73] Here, Heydenreich was echoing Kant's irritation with the "scholars for whom the history of philosophy (ancient as well as modern) is itself their philosophy":

> [I]n their opinion nothing can be said that has not already been said before; and in fact this opinion can stand for all time as an infallible prediction, for since the human understanding has wandered over countless subjects in various ways through many centuries, it can hardly fail that for anything new something old should be found that has some similarity with it.[74]

Like Kant, Heydenreich did not say who these critics were or what they argued exactly, but he could well have been referring to the first reviewer of the *Critique of Pure Reason*. The anonymous review appeared on January 19, 1782 in a supplement to the *Göttingische Anzeigen*.[75] The reviewer, who would later reveal himself as Christian Garve, summed up Kant's philosophy as a "system of higher or transcendental idealism" *not* unlike that of George Berkeley.[76]

Bishop Berkeley claimed that objects in the world were mere representations or "modifications" of ourselves.[77] To the extent that this seemed true of Kant's philosophy, it invited comparisons to Berkeley's.[78] Others compared Kant to David Hume. Johann Georg Hamann, for instance, called Kant the "Prussian Hume."[79] Late eighteenth-century critics pegged Kant's philosophy as a skeptical idealism, which common sense philosophers regarded moreover as a form of solipsism or "egoism," i.e., doubt of the reality of everything except one's own self.[80]

Heydenreich also did not mention Johann August Eberhard at Halle, who referred readers to the history of philosophy, specifically to the achievements of Leibniz, in arguing for the *unexceptionality* of Kant's work.[81] Eberhard claimed that whatever was true in Kant's philosophy was already discovered by Leibniz and that wherever Kant differed from Leibniz, Kant was wrong.[82] Eberhard carried out his polemic in a journal founded specifically to combat Kantianism, *Philosophisches Magazin*, edited by himself and J. G. Maass and J. E. Schwab.[83] In an article appearing in the first volume (1788–9), Eberhard wrote,

> The Leibnizian philosophy contains just as much of a critique of reason as [the Kantian philosophy], while at the same time it still introduces a dogmatism based on a precise analysis of the faculties of knowledge. It therefore contains all that is true in the new philosophy and, in addition, a well-grounded extension of the sphere of the understanding.[84]

If this were true, the Kantians could not claim that Kant's philosophy represented a real advance over the Leibnizio-Wolffian system. Claims of a "Copernican revolution" effected by the new philosophy would be unfounded. In Eberhard's view, there was no real progress in philosophy since the time of Leibniz and Wolff.

The first counterattacks came from Reinhold and another Kantian, A. W. Rehburg, through articles and reviews that appeared in the Jena-based *Allgemeine Literatur-Zeitung*, but the Wolffians' provocation was too great: Kant broke a personal vow not to engage in controversies with his critics and wrote a rare polemical piece, *On the Discovery According to Which Any New Critique of Pure Reason Has Been Made Superfluous by an Earlier One?* (1790).[85] Here, he reiterates, but in clearer terms, the central theses of his *Critique of Pure Reason* and accused Eberhard of misinterpreting—indeed, misrepresenting—his philosophy to the public. Thus, in 1793, with no sign of this controversy relenting, Heydenreich came to Kantianism's defense by arguing that those who denied the originality of Kant's philosophy by referring to history betrayed an inability to judge that philosophy. He contended that history showed the novelty and singularity of the Kantian system.[86]

From Heydenreich's (Kantian) perspective, philosophy was in a woeful state before Kant, when all systems "without exception" were "groundless and inconsequential" by virtue of the fact that they were not "Critical" (not Kantian). He likened this state of philosophy to a state of war, which the *Critique of Pure Reason* brought to an end.[87] Heydenreich would not altogether deny the usefulness of previous philosophical work, but what could one expect from eras that did not know Kantian philosophy?[88] In a Kantian era, a history of philosophy was at last possible. The "pragmatic historian" could now show the progressions and revolutions of philosophy in their coherent totality and describe the development of a system or opinion of a philosopher in connection to the nature of the faculties of the human mind. The author of such a history should be able to judge the diversity of opinions and systems by applying firm principles. He should be able to explain why the human mind took this and that turn, leading ultimately to the most recent revolution in philosophy. It was as if Kantian philosophy bestowed on the historian special powers of divination, enabling him to see the past and future course of philosophy. Heydenreich called Kantian philosophy the "light" that reveals the link between one moment in philosophy to the next. He even stated that the historian of philosophy was to show the "goal" to which philosophy was directed.[89] Finally, as if to forestall criticism that an application of Kantian principles to the history of philosophy would skew that history and result in one-sidedness, Heydenreich assured the reader that "the rules of critique and hermeneutics" were not to be discarded; that no inappropriate meaning would be imposed on this history but, rather, its "actual" meaning would be strengthened.[90]

Possibly the most rigorous theorist to tackle these questions was Johann Christian August Grohmann, a Kantian philosopher at Wittenberg.[91] In an essay *Über den Begriff der Geschichte der Philoso-*

phie (1797), Grohmann defined the history of philosophy in stricter terms than even Reinhold or Goess: "The history of philosophy is the systematic exposition of the necessary and effective systems of philosophy considered as science of *a priori* knowledge."[92] Philosophy is concerned with knowledge that is neither empirical nor temporal.[93] The chronology of history can contradict the progress of philosophy since the latter "proceeds systematically according to the laws of thinking itself."[94] Grohmann warned that the historian who sticks to chronology is apt to do so at the expense of reason. The history of philosophy did have some sort of order, but, for Grohmann, this order was not chronology.

Does the Kantian theory of history of philosophy actually conform to Kant's own thought? Kant never offered a lecture course on the history of philosophy. He never produced a formal work of history of philosophy nor did he publish theoretical views on the history of philosophy, but, as I have shown, the converts to his philosophy published in this area and sometimes with his approval. In their responses to the Berlin Academy's prize question on the progress of metaphysics, K. L. Reinhold, Johann Heinrich Abicht, and Christian Friedrich Jensch argued that Kant's philosophy was a decisive step forward from Leibniz's and Wolff's.[95] Kant himself drafted a response to the Academy's question.[96] In "Lose Blätter zu den Fortschritten der Metaphysik" ("Loose Papers on the Progress of Metaphysics"), published in Kant's *Gesammelte Schriften*, there is a fragment "on a philosophical [*philosophirende*] history of philosophy"[97]:

> All historical knowledge is empirical and thus knowledge of things as they are, not as they must necessarily be. . . . A historical account of philosophy relates how and in what order one has philosophized until now. However, to philosophize is a gradual development of human reason, and this could not have gone on or have even begun empirically, but, indeed, by concepts only. What reason compelled through its verdicts on things . . . must have been a (theoretical or practical) need of reason to climb toward the grounds [of things] and further toward the first grounds; from the very beginning through common reason. . . .[98]

Unlike ordinary history, the history of philosophy is not empirical; it is not characterized by chance or accident. The history of philosophy as "a gradual development of human reason" has a logical necessity. Kant continues:

> A philosophical history of philosophy is itself not histori-
> cally or empirically possible, but rationally, that is, *a priori*
> possible. For when it selects the *facta* of reason, it does not
> borrow them from historical narrative, but draws them from
> the nature of human reason; as philosophical archaeology.[99]

For Kant, the terms "historical" and "empirical" do not describe the
work of the historian of philosophy.[100] So different is the history of
philosophy from ordinary history that Kant suggested to rename it
"philosophical archaeology."

"How is an *a priori* history possible?" Kant posed this question
in 1794 and alluded to the traits of a prophet.[101] In a letter of August
14, 1795 to Carl Morgenstern, Kant flatters his friend, writing that he
is a man capable "of composing a history of philosophy that does not
follow the chronological order of books relating to it, but the natural order of the ideas which must successively develop themselves
according to human reason."[102] In "Lose Blätter," Kant describes the
history of philosophy as "so special a kind that nothing of what is
recounted therein could happen without knowing beforehand what
should have happened and therefore also what can happen."[103] Thus,
Kant himself seems to prescribe the *a priori* construction of the history
of philosophy.

In another of Kant's manuscripts, one finds this passage:

> There are thus three stages that philosophy had to go
> through with respect to metaphysics. The first was the
> stage of dogmatism; the second was that of skepticism; the
> third was that of the criticism of pure reason. This temporal
> order is grounded in the nature of the human faculty of
> knowledge.[104]

Not only do Kant's words authorize the *a priori* construction of the
history of philosophy; they also prescribe the narrative: Metaphysics
was dogmatic; skepticism falsified it; and then true metaphysics was
achieved by Kant. The history of philosophy culminates in Kant's
philosophy.[105]

Attacks against Kantianism grew more intense in the 1790s.
Critics renewed the charge of Humean skepticism even as Kant and
Reinhold maintained that Kantian philosophy refuted Hume's skep-
ticism. Salomon Maimon thought that Kant succeeded in refuting
the dogmatism of School Philosophy, but he was not persuaded that
Kant succeeded in refuting skepticism. Indeed, Maimon interpreted

Kantianism itself as a variety of skepticism. This was also the view of Kant's friend in Göttingen, Carl Friedrich Stäudlin, the author of *Geschichte und Geist des Skepticismus, vorzüglich in Rücksicht auf Moral und Religion* (1794).[106] Stäudlin was aware of Kant's claim that he had defeated skepticism, but he pointed out that, to some readers, Kant's philosophy seemed as harmful to religion and morality as the works of the greatest skeptics.[107] In the introduction to *Geschichte und Geist des Skepticismus*, Stäudlin disapproved of popular disruptive kinds of skepticism, while approving of the "philosophical skepticism" that he, during the 1780s as a student at Tübingen, found in Kant's work. He related further how, after studying the *Critique of Pure Reason*, he and fellow-students became more skeptical, doubting everything that they had been taught, including their religion.[108] Despite Kant's and Reinhold's statements to the contrary, Kant's *Critique of Pure Reason* was interpreted from the moment of its first appearance as the newest incarnation of skepticism. Kant was a skeptic *malgré lui.*

Kant's philosophy was attacked continually since 1781. Among the battery of arguments used by the *Popularphilosphen* and orthodox Wolffians were arguments from history. As Heydenreich noted, the history of philosophy, as it stood, did not do justice to Immanuel Kant. History was used not infrequently to indict Kant on a variety of charges, including Berkeleyan subjectivism and Humean skepticism. Historical precedents, the failures or successes of past systems, were facts brought up in arguing that Kant's philosophy did not represent real progress in philosophy.

If the history of philosophy could be used to confute Kant's claims, it could be used also to defend them. In the 1790s, the rival philosophical schools moved the battle into the field of history of philosophy, with the Kantians hoping to usurp the writing of the history of philosophy from those empiricists, eclectics, and other pre-Critical writers whose job it had been previously.[109] Within a decade of the completion of Kant's philosophical project, there arose a coordinated effort among Kantian philosophers to rewrite the history of philosophy so as to remake it into the unfolding of the Critical Philosophy. The break from historiographical tradition could not have been more complete: The Kantians favored *a priori* construction in historical writing and insisted on a definition and criteria for philosophy derived from Kant's system.

While there were a half-dozen Kantians who contributed to the theory of history of philosophy, there were just two Kantians who actually dedicated labor to writing histories of philosophy of any length: Buhle and Tennemann. Buhle authored an eight-volume *Lehrbuch der Geschichte der Philosophie* (1796–1804) and a separate six-volume work, *Geschichte der neuern Philosophie seit der Epoche der Wiederherstellung der Wissenschaften* (1800–1804).[110] Tennemann, a professor of philosophy at Jena and later at Marburg, produced the lengthiest history of philosophy written in the Kantian mode: the eleven-volume, unfinished *Geschichte der Philosophie* (1798–1819).[111] He also published a single-volume history, *Grundriss der Geschichte der Philosophie* (1812; later editions of 1816, 1820, 1825, and 1829).[112] Given the scale of Tennemann's project and the reforms he hoped to institute, *Geschichte der Philosophie* was positioned to displace Brucker's *Historia critica philosophiae* as the standard work of history of philosophy.[113]

In the introduction to his *Geschichte der Philosophie*, Tennemann detailed the flaws of previous histories of philosophy. They were mainly collections of reports on the lives and opinions of philosophers. They made incomplete use of sources or used inappropriate sources. They were poorly organized and lacked an overall plan.[114] Like the other Kantians, he charged that previous histories of philosophy were simply copied out of earlier works "without critique, taste, discriminations" and "without philosophical spirit."[115] They perpetuated "a mass of historical errors" and the prejudices of the Church Fathers, who unfortunately relied on revelation and were biased in favor of the Jews. Subsequent historians of philosophy, the majority of them theologians, introduced the dubious notion of "antediluvian philosophy" and theological polemics into the history of philosophy.[116] In brief, Tennemann regarded most previous histories of philosophy as unphilosophical compilations and chronicles.[117]

Tennemann was able to concede that Brucker's work was a great achievement, but he made the qualification that its greatness lies in the scale of the compilation and not in any transformation of the way in which sources were studied. In Tennemann's view, Brucker, too, is guilty of giving greater description to the lives than to the systems of the philosophers, and even where he gives greater description to the latter, the result is fragmentary. In addition to these weaknesses, there are "many investigations that do not belong in there." As sharp as he was, Brucker could have possessed more "philosophical spirit"; his concept of philosophy was "too vacillating and indeterminate"; and he did not proceed from "a fixed point of view and plan."[118] Yet, despite these many flaws, Tennemann fully acknowledged that Brucker deserved praise for "the first complete work on the history" of philosophy.[119]

Tennemann recognized that the history of philosophy shared certain characteristics with other genres of history, but he still held that it was an autonomous genre separate from the history of nations, scholarship, and other sciences. In agreement with Reinhold and Goess, Tennemann cautioned against mistaking the history of the literature of philosophy for the history of philosophy itself.[120] In his *Grundriss der Geschichte der Philosophie* (1816 edition), Tennemann differentiated between, on the one hand, the history of philosophy and, on the other, the history of mankind, intellectual history, history of the sciences, biography, literary history, analysis of works, and compilations of opinions. He assigned to these latter the status of "either background knowledge or materials useful to the history of philosophy."[121] No less importantly, the history of philosophy should not be a mere exposition of philosophical systems with the historical dimension omitted.[122]

Regarding kinds of sources, Tennemann permitted philosophers' own writings, other literary works by them, reports and investigations of observers, and other historical data.[123] "Philosophemes" (*Philosopheme*) should in any case be taken only from the writings of the philosophers. Their extra-philosophical writings should be treated as supplementary sources.[124] Since all the information from such a fund of sources cannot be incorporated into a history, it was important to decide what should be included. Tennemann presented some rules: That which has "a relation to and influence on the formation of this science [philosophy]" may be included. That which "disrupts the coherency and overview of the history" should not be included.[125] Detailed biographies of philosophers should not be included as these would "injure the unity of the history" and inappropriately connect the actual object of inquiry, philosophy, to the personal histories of the philosophers. Details of the life of a philosopher may still be woven into the history of philosophy, but only if doing so enhances the coherency of philosophy's development.[126]

As a philosopher practicing history of philosophy, Tennemann had no use for the fanatical precepts put forward by Reinhold and Grohmann. In the introduction to his *Geschichte der Philosophie*, Tennemann works methodically toward a definition for the "history of the discipline of philosophy":

> History in the broad sense is the recounting of past events. History in a narrower sense is the recounting of a succession of events that composes a whole. A mere chronology does not compose this whole. These events must stand in mutual relation to each other as changes, effects, or causes

with respect to an object; or their mutual relation must consist in their being directed toward a purpose.[127]

The history of a people, the biography of an individual, and the history of philosophy itself were given as examples of history in the narrower sense. *Contra* Grohmann, Tennemann held that chronology is essential to every kind of history, including the history of philosophy. He would observe chronology as "the first law of history."[128] *Contra* Reinhold, who had argued that the history of philosophy had nothing to do with events in time and space, Tennemann held a heterodox position. He stated that events in the history of philosophy related both internally to human consciousness and externally to the world. "The development of reason occurs through external stimulation and thus depends on external causes" that advance, impede, or hold it in place.[129] "The efforts of reason are inner events of the mind." "There is thus an internal and external connection among events in time. Events have their external causes and results, and they have their internal grounds in the organization and laws of human consciousness."[130] Lastly, these events have a relation to reason's purpose.[131] Unlike simple annals and chronicles, history as conceived by Tennemann can claim to present events "according to their real interrelation in time" as causes and effects.[132] "This concrete relation among events is the foundation of all history, the condition of fidelity and truth, without which history would no longer be history."[133]

"Science," as defined by Tennemann, is a "system of knowledge."[134] "[R]eason is the only source of all science; for every science is an architectonically rendered structure for which reason draws up the idea and guides the completion."[135] The "idea of science" is a "necessary expression of reason," subsisting through all the changes of the science's history.[136] Tennemann thus reasoned that the idea of science is at the same time an *ideal* of science, but in this case, the events relating to that science, taken together, constitute a history whose course runs from what is consummate in philosophy to what is defective. Since he considered such a course "unnatural," contradicting "every analogy of human nature," he recommended that one view the idea or ideal of the science as the "goal." As such, "all events . . . now appear not as changes of the science, but rather as exertions and activities of reason on behalf of science."[137] Through such reasoning, Tennemann was able to arrive at a complete definition: "History of philosophy is exposition of the successive development of philosophy or exposition of the exertions of reason to realize the idea of the science from the final grounds and laws of nature and freedom."[138] Even before the turn of the nineteenth century, the first Kantian historians self-consciously set themselves on the path of teleology.

But not all students of philosophy were persuaded that a revolution had taken place in philosophy and that a corresponding revolution in historiography was necessary. Certainly, the opponents of Kantian philosophy remained unconvinced. One such opponent was Friedrich Nicolai (1733–1811), the literary critic and editor of *Briefe, die neueste Literatur betreffend*, his collaboration with Gotthold Ephraim Lessing and Moses Mendelssohn from 1759 to 1765. He edited the *Allgemeine deutsche Bibliothek* from 1765 to 1792. Near the end of his life, this pillar of the Berlin Enlightenment and member of that city's Academy of Sciences noted that esteemed German authors still did not agree on what belongs in the history of philosophy or how this history was to be organized and made practical.[139] He was well aware that Tennemann thought that the purpose of the history of philosophy was to cultivate the science of the final grounds and laws of nature and freedom and their interrelation.[140] He related that Reinhold, as early as 1781, wanted to remove all references to "opinions" from the history of philosophy. For Nicolai, these were enough clues to indicate that Tennemann and Reinhold believed that this "science of the final grounds of nature and freedom" was already discovered; that the project of philosophy was completed through Kant's critique of theoretical and practical reason and Reinhold's theory of the faculty of representation. Or in any case, this was the tone of many followers of Kant.[141] Nicolai continued,

> They believed that philosophical science has been fully discovered and secured; that knowledge has reached its conclusion with Kant and Fichte; and that it has fulfilled what philosophers had sought since millennia. Thus, Goess, Buhle, Grohmann, and Reinhold all at the same time viewed philosophical history from the perspective that all philosophers of ancient and modern times should be represented, and be accepted or rejected, according to how much they had in common with the *Critique of Pure Reason*.[142]

Buhle came in for harsher criticism. What made both of his works "completely useless," in Nicolai's judgment, was "his slavish adherence to the Kantian system, by which he subordinates to this system the whole history of philosophy and wants to discover almost everywhere traces of Kantian ideas . . . he judges many objects all too one-sidedly; indeed, sometimes distorts the true perspective of the doctrines of ancient philosophers."[143] Nicolai found that this was especially apparent in Buhle's account of Aristotle, in which constant agreements are discovered between Kant and Aristotle through, Nicolai alleged, Buhle's arbitrary translation. He did this even if the method and system of these two philosophers were essentially different. Nicolai pointed out that Tennemann, too, proceeded mainly from Kantian perspectives, although he was nowhere near the same degree a partisan as Buhle. He compared Tennemann to another historian of philosophy, Dieterich Tiedemann. While it could be said that both Tennemann and Tiedemann carefully studied sources and exercised good judgment, "Tiedemann [was] attached to no system" and was free of biases.[144]

Nicolai, too, had no attachment to any particular system. This eclectic philosopher was not deterred, throughout the years of Kantianism's ascendancy, from thinking that "the best philosophy" was "the one that examines all systems impartially"; the one that distinguishes "disputes over words from truly different opinions"; the one that does not separate systems, but "seeks to unite them as it selects the best from each."[145] In 1808, when Nicolai published these criticisms, eclecticism was already an endangered philosophy in Germany as increasingly only one system was being presented to students.[146]

We shall see in Chapters 5 and 6 that the Kantian School changed the conventions of writing the history of philosophy for later historians of philosophy. The Kantians discarded the old rules of composition, which had defined the genre for centuries, and embraced the rules of *a priori* construction. They (re)wrote the history of philosophy so that it read as the unfolding of Kantianism and demonstration of its truth. We shall see in Chapter 4 that they also excluded Africa and Asia from the history of philosophy, which they justified with racial-anthropological arguments learned from Christoph Meiners. This combination of *a priori* construction and racial Eurocentrism would become enduring features of modern histories of philosophy starting from the era of Kant's *Critiques*.

2
_____

The Birth of Comparative
History of Philosophy

Joseph-Marie de Gérando's
Histoire comparée des systèmes de philosophie

[T]he first glance cast on the history of philosophy does not give,
one must admit, all the satisfaction that one could have expected.
A multitude of hypotheses raised in some haphazard way and
swiftly destroyed; a diversity of opinions . . . , sects, even par-
ties, interminable disputes, endlessly recurring misunderstand-
ings, barren speculations, errors upheld and spread through blind
imitation, discoveries slowly made and mixed with false ideas,
reforms heralded in each century but never carried out; a succession of doctrines each overturned by the next . . . human reason
as such in a sad circle of vicissitudes, climbing up during fortunate times, but soon tumbling down again; experience and reason,
common sense and speculation . . . fight constantly and present
each other with reciprocal refutations on every point; idealism
locked in battle with materialism, each in turn snatching away
from the intellect the objects that it believes it knows or the feeling it has of its own dignity and existence; philosophy exalted by
dogmatism to a point where limits are no longer set on its pretensions, then carried by skepticism into the abyss of absolute doubt,
calling out for an unchanging base of support . . . searching for
a sure route toward the truth, but foiled always in its wishes
and hopes; in the end the same questions, which were shared
by the first geniuses of Greece more than twenty centuries ago,
stirred up again today by such voluminous writings devoted to

their discussion: This is the spectacle . . . offered to the eyes of
the observer . . . enough to inspire in shallow minds a profound
despondency.

—Joseph-Marie de Gérando (1804)[1]

While the Kantian revolution in the field of history of philosophy was
unfolding in Germany, another revolution in this field was occurring
in France and in a neighboring corner of Germany. In this and the next
chapter, I discuss the histories of philosophy by Joseph-Marie de Gérando (1772–1842) and Friedrich Schlegel (1772–1829). They conceived and
realized the idea of comparative history of philosophy. De Gérando
authored the *Histoire comparée des systèmes de philosophie, relativement aux*
principes des connaissances humaines (*Comparative History of the Systems*
of Philosophy with Respect to the Principles of Human Knowledge), a three-
volume work published in 1804. It was expanded into four volumes
for the second edition of 1822.[2] Schlegel delivered a cycle of lectures
in 1804–5 on the history of philosophy, titled *Die Entwicklung der Phi-*
losophie in zwölf Büchern (*The Development of Philosophy in Twelve Books*),
which was preserved through auditors' transcriptions.[3] I include de
Gérando and Schlegel in my historiography because, as inventors of the
comparative history of philosophy, they help to disrupt the dominant,
Kantian paradigm at work in many historiographies of philosophy.

Joseph-Marie de Gérando was a professor of moral philosophy
at the Lycée de Paris when he published the *Histoire comparée des sys-*
tèmes de philosophie. He had been appointed to the professorship after
winning a prize from the Institut de France for his work *Des signes et*
de l'art de penser (*On Signs and the Art of Thinking*), 4 vols. (1800). He
won another prize—this time from the Berlin Royal Academy of Sciences—for his essay *De la génération des connoissances humaines* (*On the*
Generation of Human Knowledge) (1802).[4] As the historian of philosophy
for the French state, he presented a *Historical Report on the Progress*
of Philosophy since 1789 and on Its Current State during the Council
of State of February 20, 1808. In the same year in which his *Histoire*
comparée appeared, he became Secretary General of the Ministry of
the Interior, an office that he held for more than six years. In May
of 1805, he accompanied Napoleon I to Milan, where the latter was
crowned King of Italy. De Gérando rose further up the ranks of the
French government. In 1808, he was appointed a Master of Requests
and was sent to Italy to help reorganize Tuscany and the Papal States.
In 1811, he became a Councillor of State and, in March of that year,
an officer in the Légion d'honneur as well as a baron of the empire.

In 1812, he began a term as *intendant* of newly annexed Catalonia. Under the restored Bourbon monarchy, de Gérando continued to serve as a Councillor of State. He held other political offices and teaching positions during his prodigious career.

In the introduction to the *Histoire comparée*, de Gérando rules out the possibility of a general and complete history of philosophy as too vast and too difficult to be hoped for. He believed that such a history would not be interesting to the French public as the utility of it would be unclear. Rather, what de Gérando intended was something more preliminary. He conceived a system of classification (*nomenclatures regulières et simples*) that he hoped would serve as a "general introduction to the entire history of philosophy."[5]

De Gérando distinguished his project from that of the Kantian historians. He would not rely on *a priori* principles of organization, nor would he judge philosophical systems using theoretical criteria. Instead, he would judge them by their *practical* effects in the realms of science, art, and government. His work thus had little in common with the *Traité des systèmes* (1749) by Étienne Bonnot de Condillac. He greatly disagreed with that author, who set out to demonstrate the shortcomings of other philosophical systems on the basis of his abstract principles. He would, in contrast, determine any shortcomings *a posteriori*. The task remained to describe systems of philosophy, but, for de Gérando, this also extended to the "causes" (e.g., "motives") and "effects" of each system.[6]

As to the method, de Gérando stated that his *Histoire comparée* was conceived in accordance with "the experimental method" (*la méthode des experiences*), which, as he pointed out, was the method most neglected by historians of philosophy.[7] This method demands that each system of philosophy be considered without dismissing certain ones outright; that each be judged separately as well as in comparison; and that the causes, circumstances, and effects of the revolutions in philosophy, the division of philosophical schools, and their controversies be studied.[8] The reader is asked to imagine the invaluable treasure of experience and knowledge of almost thirty centuries of errors, disputes, and successes in philosophy.[9] De Gérando recognized, however, that such vast and varied information made a general and comprehensive history of philosophy too difficult and unappealing. He was offering, therefore, what he believed to be a more effective method of study.

It was a remarkable stroke of originality. De Gérando did for the history of philosophy what the naturalists did for the history of nature: He devised a system of classification under which philosophical doctrines could be analyzed (i.e., compared) and sorted into "regular and basic classes."[10] In the *Histoire comparée*, the facts of philosophical history were converted into a kind of natural history, "a geographical map of the doctrines and opinions that constitute the intellectual world."[11]

De Gérando viewed the comparative history of philosophy as an empirical-analytical or observational science not different from natural history. He regarded comparative analysis as taking the place of experimentation and calculation, which, in the case of either natural or philosophical history, was not possible. In another parallel to the study of nature, de Gérando treated each system of philosophy as a complete organism, whose characteristics were inextricably linked, and he regarded generalizations about the history of philosophy as "essentially comparisons and classification of observed facts."[12]

One will recall that, in the late seventeenth century, Daniel Morhof saw himself as realizing Bacon's vision of a universal history of letters that would document the arts and sciences of all epochs and regions of the world; their antiquity, progress, demise, and restoration as well as the circumstances of their invention. This universal history would preserve the knowledge of the rules and methods of cultivation of the arts and sciences and be a record of the divisions of the learned world, their greatest controversies, calumnies, and achievements. This universal history of letters would record the best and most important writers, books, schools, and other institutions of learning that have ever existed. De Gérando, too, saw himself as realizing the idea of inductive or comparative history, which he explicitly attributed to Bacon.[13]

As Bacon had recommended, de Gérando composed a comparative history that established principles of relation, united effects to their causes, and determined the favorable and unfavorable circumstances for the advancement of social knowledge. For de Gérando, it was Bacon who clarified the importance of the history of philosophy. Thus, with respect to his aims, de Gérando falls squarely in the Baconian tradition, whose eighteenth-century anchor was Jacob Brucker.

De Gérando was of the opinion that there is really one fundamental question with which the history of philosophy is concerned. How do we know and how do we know that we know?[14] Brucker had also described the history of philosophy as

> the history of the human understanding, clearly showing
> the extent of its capacity, the causes of its perversion, and
> the means by which it may be recalled from its unprofitable

wanderings, and successfully employed in subserviency
to the happiness of mankind. Whilst it traces the origin
and growth of useful knowledge, it also discovers the
manner in which errors have arisen and been propagated,
and exposes the injury which they have done to science,
literature, and religion.[15]

Like de Gérando, Brucker had conceived the history of philosophy
as "a faithful register of discoveries in the world of science" and "an
important branch of the history of universal erudition."[16]

Early in the first volume of de Gérando's work is a review of
previous histories of philosophy. The French historian of philosophy
singled out Brucker for a long review. He wrote, "Brucker by himself
forms an era in the history of philosophy."[17] Brucker's work is "the
most complete and most extensive that we possess," and the labor
that it must have required "frightens the imagination."[18] Among the
pastor's merits were "a perfectly good faith, a sagacious mind, an
excellent method, an untiring patience, a scrupulous exactitude."[19] De
Gérando praised Brucker also for his research of medieval philosophy.

It was equally important to enumerate the flaws of the *Historia
critica philosophiae*. De Gérando thought that its presentation of barbarian philosophies was "inaccurate," that too much attention was given
to the minor circumstances of the lives of the philosophers, and that the
causes both particular and general of the development of philosophy
were neglected. The principal defect, however, was Brucker's manner of explication, which the French thinker claimed lacked elegance,
variety, and clarity. In addition, it would have been better if the views
of the philosophers had been introduced earlier and the reader given
a choice of different possible interpretations of a doctrine.[20]

While Brucker could be classed among the "compilers" of the
history of philosophy, who restrict themselves to relating the opinions of philosophers without assessing them or utilizing them for
some theoretical or practical end, many historians of philosophy
who have entered the field since Brucker wrote in all-too-theoretical
a manner.[21] Without naming them, de Gérando noted that these more
recent historians, being biased toward particular doctrines, presented
the succession of philosophical opinions as proofs destined to justify
those doctrines.[22] De Gérando was cognizant, therefore, of two distinct
approaches to the history of philosophy prior to his own work.

The *Histoire comparée* is a three-volume work divided into two
parts. The First Part, presenting an "Abridged History of the Principal Systems of Philosophy with Respect to the Principles of Human

Knowledge," occupies the whole first volume and half of the second. The Second Part, titled "Critical Analysis of the Systems of Philosophy on the Generation of Human Knowledge," occupies the remaining half of the second volume and all of the third. The initial chapters are devoted to discussing the design of the *Histoire comparée*, the historiography of philosophy, and the question of the origins of philosophy. These are followed by chapters presenting the facts of the systems of philosophy in the order of their historical chronology.

But what makes the *Histoire comparée* original and unprecedented is its Second Part: a comparative analysis of systems of philosophy. With respect to the principles of human knowledge, systems of philosophy fell into one or another of de Gérando's six asymmetrical classes: rationalism, empiricism, idealism, materialism, dogmatism, and skepticism. De Gérando's analysis of these classes did not follow a linear order of either chronology or logical development. Rather, it was comparable to the procedure of analysis already embraced by contemporary natural historians.

The Second Part begins with the critical analysis of *rational* (or *speculative*) *philosophy*. These systems, which are the oldest in history, present propositions that can be reduced to the principle of identity (also known as the principle of contradiction).[23] Any truth derived from this principle has only a logical, and not a metaphysical, necessity.[24] For de Gérando, history's testimony was overwhelming. The consequences that follow from the principles and methods of rational philosophy have always been the same. These systems have a pronounced and regular preference for *a priori* methods, and in these systems ideas are ranked on a ladder from the general to the particular (or from the abstract to the sensible) with the most universal notions and highest abstractions at the summit. These methods impose a simpler order on human knowledge, but one that is entirely artificial. Only in the perspective of speculative philosophy does it seem necessary. Because speculative principles are expressions of relations between or among the most universal ideas, they must be regarded as original and nonderivative for these relations to have the character of first principles. This results in the hypothesis of innate ideas so essential to speculative philosophy.[25]

If universal principles are anterior to particular truths, if the latter borrow their force from the former, then general notions are necessarily anterior to and independent of those ideas acquired through perception or deduction.[26] It becomes essential then for the speculative philosopher to establish the validity of his system by showing that certain general notions are natural and inherent to the human mind;

that not all our ideas originate from sensory perception.[27] A philosopher who supposes an independent origin for abstract notions will believe that he can proceed from these in establishing a true system of philosophy.[28]

It is a further feature of speculative philosophy that logical relations are mistaken for metaphysical laws. To confound simple logical relations with metaphysical laws is an error almost inevitable in speculative philosophy. Refusing to rank experience with principles of knowledge, the speculative philosopher does not accept the data of experience.[29] For him, knowledge is necessarily anterior to existence and attempts to foretell it or constitute it *a priori*. In spite of everything, all his deductions have only a logical validity. This is to say that the speculative philosopher is restricted to transforming deductions into new combinations of terms. He may believe himself to judge what is, but he knows only what the mind must think. From his confusion arise false ideas of "essence" and "substance," which he assumes is what gives existence to things or determines their manner of existence instead of what they are truly, namely, his mere conceptions.[30]

De Gérando claimed also that speculative philosophy has always resulted in systems of absolute identity. Insofar as speculative maxims are the expression of the principle of identity, insofar as logical formulae are the only means of their transformation, the mind travels in a circle. Since it is impossible to admit any conditions other than those that are already a part of this circularity, in every case one will find the same idea disguised under different expressions. Whatever variety, whatever modifications the mind encounters, it must reject them as inconsequential. This procedure establishes *a priori* the nature of "substance" as the principle of existence, but ultimately finds only necessary existences, that is, eternal and identical substances. This is the end-result of speculative philosophy when pursued to its final consequence. De Gérando found in the historical record four instances when the system of absolute identity appeared: the Eleatic School, Giordano Bruno, Spinoza, and the disciples of Kant. He viewed the Alexandrian Platonists as coming close to a system of absolute identity.[31]

De Gérando held that skepticism and resurgent idealism were other consequences of speculative philosophy.[32] He used Descartes as an example. This speculative philosopher doubted the faculties of sensory perception, but as these are the only means by which the material world is known, his system inevitably leads to the view of idealism.[33] Speculative philosophy has an ill-effect on the sciences because it encourages the mind's dependency on rational formulae, which attach fundamental importance to definitions, and keeps the human mind from moving beyond abstraction.[34]

Furthermore, speculative philosophy has a negative effect on the arts. Speculation can divert the mind from the contemplation of nature, which de Gérando called "the true school of the beaux arts," and from the study of the passions, the true source of eloquence.[35] History showed him that the Eleatics produced "mediocre rhetoricians" (among the Sophists); that neo-Platonic and Arab philosophers (he grouped them together) produced "almost no distinguished writer"; that the Scholastic method "posed obstacles to the restoration of taste"; that the German nation, "among all modern nations the one that has shown more a general penchant for speculative doctrines, is also the one whose literature developed with greater tardiness and difficulty." Again, in the historical record, he could find evidence of speculative philosophy's negative influence on the literary arts.[36]

De Gérando also warned of speculative philosophy's negative effects on morality. He feared that speculative doctrines allowed the mind to prevail over the sentiments. On the basis of speculative doctrines, which are ultimately subjective, one might presume a right to interrogate the moral code. He feared that moral philosophers, in seeking the moral law in certain ideal combinations, could be diverted from the true interests of the moral community. In the delicate application of a moral principle to varying circumstances, speculative doctrines might indiscriminately impose absolute and inflexible maxims, which are so characteristic of *a priori* methods. He recognized a potential for great practical errors and misjudgment in, for example, the speculative doctrines of Plato.[37]

De Gérando wrote that nothing could seem more absurd to ordinary men than *idealism*. He conceded, however, that this philosophy had not yet been refuted.[38] Nearly all ancient and modern philosophers have concluded from both experience and reason that things exist which do not come into the sphere of the senses. But a small number of thinkers deny this. Some of them have gone so far as to limit themselves absolutely to the self, believing that there are no grounds for ascribing any reality to sensory perceptions. This was the case of certain "new sects in Germany" who viewed both sensations and ideas as products of the subject's inner activity. For these thinkers, nothing exists but an intellectual world, which counts as the only reality. "Among the ancients, Pythagoras, Plato, and Plotinus only intimated this doctrine, which Berkeley and Hume among the moderns developed in a brilliant manner. . . ."[39] De Gérando observed that even Leibniz could not avoid a kind of idealism. (This is an observation that he shared with Tiedemann and Buhle.) He noted that Kant, too, sensed in Leibniz the common error of confounding the domain of reason with that of experience.[40]

Leibniz regarded experience as only a series of phenomena or appearances, and so he sought his first truths elsewhere. For him, the mind was the source of all notions. He thought that he could confirm the reality of abstract truths simply through their possibility and existence in God; in the sense that they are perceived by the Eternal Mind and must, therefore, be eternal. The truths of experience were accorded a lesser status by Leibniz, who regarded sensory perceptions as merely phenomena. The title of "substance" as the real existence he conferred solely on the monads, which do not reveal themselves to the senses, but are demonstrable by reason. In connection to Leibniz, de Gérando warned that knowledge came in danger of being reduced to the study of the relations of one's own conceptions instead of the laws of nature.[41]

De Gérando included in the class of idealism the "mixed systems" of those who, after detaching ideas from an immediate relation to external objects, tried to establish some sort of external reality with the aid of long deductions. Leibniz served again as a useful example: He tried to establish the union of mind and matter through his hypothesis of a pre-established harmony between ideas and objects and through his hypothesis of the representative faculty of the intellect, supposed as a kind of mirror of the universe. Thus, Leibniz's philosophy was a modified and restrained kind of idealism.[42] De Gérando added that such "mitigated idealism" also characterized the philosophies of Descartes and Kant.[43]

De Gérando's critique of idealism revolved around the "consequences" of this philosophy. He charged that idealism resulted in "an abyss of paradoxes and uncertainty" between a speculative reason that leads the mind to idealism and a powerful instinct that brings it back to a reality. Characteristic of idealism is a vacillation between the need to trace our perceptions back to externally existent objects and the impossibility of establishing their existence.[44] De Gérando called this "the principal cause of agitation, anxiety [and] vacillation" of the modern philosophical experience.[45]

Uncertainty of whether human knowledge has any reality is another consequence of idealism. For our knowledge to be deemed *real*, a reality must be the source of this knowledge. If knowledge of reality can be obtained through the artifice of deductions, the first *logical* truths of the mind must be taken as *real* truths.[46] If the real existence of external objects is established in this manner, external existence must be placed on the level of basic and immediate knowledge that does not need demonstration. However, if one did not accept a basic and immediate knowledge of external existences, believing rather that the supposed truth of external existences is in fact just an outcome of synthetic combinations performed by the mind, he would fall into "the most absolute idealism."[47] (The idealists of the first kind could find themselves drifting toward absolute idealism as well.) As a further consequence, the absolute idealist will find no refuge other than in a "most complete skepticism," where all reality is removed from our judgments and nothing remains of the material of our knowledge except the identity of ideas.[48] Then, our first ideas having only the value of zero ("$A = A$"), all knowledge would be reduced to a series of equations of the emptiest kind ("nothing = nothing = nothing etc.").[49] According to de Gérando, the absolute idealist cannot escape this circle of nothings, which in all cases does not deserve the title of knowledge.

The history of philosophy shows that distinguished thinkers who have a great talent for combination are led to the most absolute idealism through their method of *a priori* demonstration of the phenomena of existence. As if by necessity, they arrive at that singular hypothesis: that the self creates nature, that the self posits itself freely, or that in this first free act lies the origin of all knowledge.[50] For them, it is inadequate to view the mind as simply the spectator of existence. Rather, the mind is the author of existence. Having destroyed existence, the mind must begin to reconstruct, but when it lacks even the materials, it must straightaway *create*. In this connection, de Gérando pointed to "the new idealists of Germany" who "create entities . . . patently."[51] He refrained from enumerating all the contradictions that arise when the ego is conferred the power to posit itself and other entities. He had shown adequately the ultimate consequences of the principles of idealism.

As a class, *dogmatic philosophy* encompasses more diverse species. De Gérando defined dogmatism as any system of philosophy that steps beyond the natural limit of the human faculties, including the dogmatisms of method and doctrine, "belief," "mystical dogmatism," and "scientific dogmatism."[52]

Mystical dogmatism is included in the analysis because it, too, is concerned with knowledge. In mystical dogmatism, all types of knowledge are placed in the sphere of a superior or invisible intelligence as cause or source of human knowledge.[53] The mystic defines very little. Simply contemplating, he obtains knowledge through immediate intuition. The language of mystical dogmatism is a collection of obscurities. Mystics have a "profound disdain," "almost a sort of horror" of the faculties of sensation and the methods of observation. They liken the experience of the senses to a veil that hides truth. They prefer the immediate intuition of inspiration and ecstasy. They occupy themselves very little with the phenomena of the sensible world and deal rather with ideal conceptions. In their contemplations, they enjoy separating themselves from space and time and crossing into infinite realms. If a mystic offers to explain nature, he claims that his knowledge was obtained through mysterious influences. If he speculates on causes, he arrives at eternal hierarchies.[54]

The mystic favors abstract truths because they consist of very vague terms that are adaptable to any interpretation or deduction. For the mystic, abstract propositions seem to open up communications with the realm of intelligences (not the physical realm). Mystical truths are assumed to be eternal, necessary, and innate and are presented as images of the infinite, as pictures of the essence of things or of their origin. Historically, such images have justified systems of emanation and celestial influences, or they have been personified and turned into supernatural beings or subordinate intelligences that serve as messengers between the Supreme Intelligence and human beings. Finally, since mystical doctrines are completely subjective and require only the exercise of reflection, they lend themselves to habits of silent and solitary meditation. De Gérando gave the examples of Pythagoras, who relied on mathematical truths to support his mysterious doctrines; Plato, whose high regard for abstract notions led him to recommend contemplative practices; the eclectics of Alexandria, who transformed metaphysical principles into many images and eternal hierarchies and genealogies of particular moral and intellectual notions; the theosophers of the fifteenth and sixteenth centuries, who came up with supernatural theories with the aid of some axioms regarding "essences" and "substances"; and Malebranche, who believed he could see all general truths in God.[55]

According to de Gérando, scientific dogmatism has the guise of true science. Scientific dogmatists are interested in discovering causes, but their method is speculation. They are interested foremost in the first cause as the first link in a great chain by which all other causes are explained. The earliest scientific dogmatists created the cosmogonies of the Egyptians and Phoenicians in the attempt to explain the universe through the history of its formation. The origin of things must be explained because without such an explanation all their other explanations would be untenable.[56] Scientific dogmatism has receded in modern times through the critique of Bacon, Descartes, Leibniz, and Newton. The last in this list even restricted proofs exclusively to demonstration. He rejected analogy, resorting rather to analysis, calculus, and experience.[57] Newton continued to employ hypotheses, but these were less arbitrary since they had to be confirmed through demonstration. Thus, his scientific conceptions remained within the realm of phenomena as when he demonstrated universal attraction without claiming to know its nature.[58] A penchant for systematic unity leads the scientific dogmatist to find a single principle that can explain everything and unite all subordinate hypotheses. Such a system, being the product of one mind and not of the agreement of minds, is not susceptible to critique.[59] While the effort to harmonize facts with a ruling idea is good, scientific dogmatism's arbitrary hypotheses, more often than not, distort observations, forcing facts to fit a system.[60]

Comparing scientific dogmatism to mystical dogmatism, de Gérando noted that both turned to speculative philosophy for support. Both engendered controversy and doubt.[61] The history of philosophy demonstrates that the multiplicity of dogmatic systems leads to Pyrrhonism.[62] "Forsaken to hypotheses, philosophy resembles a country delivered to anarchy . . . thinkers despair of the truth as when politicians despair of liberty after long revolutions."[63] As contradictory propositions arise from the same principle, each with equal right, one soon arrives at complete skepticism.

Skepticism (most of the time, de Gérando does not differentiate between Pyrrhonian and Academic skepticisms) is the name of another large class of philosophy, consisting of many different species both ancient and modern. Skepticism confounds all philosophical views into one class, assimilating truths to errors by refuting all "signs" for distinguishing between them. Skepticism annihilates all the laws of reason and principles of method, causing one to despair over reason's feebleness.[64] De Gérando named the skeptics in the history of philosophy: Montaigne, Pierre Charron, La Mothe Le Vayer, Bishop Huet, Pierre Bayle, Joseph Glanville, George Berkeley, and David Hume.[65]

De Gérando claimed earlier that, in the history of philosophy, dogmatism gave rise to skepticism. He now also claimed that skepticism gave rise to new systems of idealism. He saw Bayle in particular as preparing the way for modern idealism by renewing and further developing the arguments of the ancient Eleatics against the existence of matter and by reducing what little certainty remained of sensory experience to a mere modification of the soul. For evidence, de Gérando pointed to Berkeley's idealism, which he viewed as a consequence of the modern trend of skepticism. He pointed also to Hume's philosophy, confirming that skepticism led to idealism.[66] The ultimate consequence of this chain of development, argued de Gérando, was an absolute skepticism that forever destroyed all possible relation between ideas and objects, between ideas and the ego, and rendered uncertain the relation even between ideas themselves. This kind of skepticism destroyed all hope of ever knowing the truth.[67]

The history of philosophy seems to issue a warning. If the spirit of doubt prevails in a country or century, one should guard against the return of dogmatism, but in more aggressive forms. In refusing to accept the simplest truths, one abandons all truths for the most arbitrary assumptions. The history of philosophy presents many such episodes: The two newer Academies dissolved after failing to suppress the dogmatic systems of the Greeks. The Academics fell into disrepute, and this cleared the way for the mystical exaggerations of the Alexandrians. Indeed, the former seemed almost to justify the latter in presenting doubt as an abyss that threatened to engulf the mind. In the fifteenth and sixteenth centuries, skepticism rose up against Scholastic philosophy, but induced inaction. This was followed by "a rebellion of the imagination" in the form of theosophy. As theosophy revived with a new fervor, dogmatic systems proliferated anew. De Gérando was able to recognize the extent to which the doubts of Montaigne were complicit in the errors of Malebranche. Perhaps more than any other time, the eighteenth century favored skepticism, but by the end of that century a mass of rash political and moral systems arose, including the new sects of Illuminism, Mesmerism, and Convulsionism.[68]

In a show of impartiality, de Gérando conceded that Pyrrhonian skepticism was useful in its time; that Pyrrhon and Arcesilas exposed important problems and forced an interrogation of philosophy. In the current era of science, however, skepticism is not so useful. Philosophers have been sufficiently instructed on the dangers of hypotheses and are aware of past errors. The real danger comes from prolonging the uncertainties, which invites the return of dogmatic systems—"just as anarchy invokes despotism."[69]

Empiricism, which de Gérando distinguished from the experimental philosophy, divides into two species.[70] There is an "empiricism of ignorance," where the mind abandons itself to sensory impressions. There is secondly an empiricism based on reflection and analysis, which does not venture beyond knowing particular facts and contingent truths. This latter species rejects all theories as well as inductive and deductive reasoning. It thinks that the idea of a connection between effect and cause is arbitrary. It conceives the mind as completely passive and so reduces all intellectual operations to sensory perception.[71] In practice, however, no empiricist has ever fully adhered to these principles.[72]

Historically, empiricism's contributions to the progress of human knowledge are negligible. The empiricists of antiquity did not produce any innovative or useful ideas, alleged de Gérando. Empiricism did not ever lead to any important discoveries. It was basically "useless to science" and "deadly to morality."[73]

The general descriptions and critiques of rationalism, idealism, dogmatism, skepticism, and empiricism did not exhaust the field of the history of philosophy. One final class of philosophy remained to be analyzed. De Gérando designated *Kantianism* (or *Criticism*) a philosophical class unto itself as it did not fit into any of the other classes. De Gérando understood that Kant's intention was to limit and legitimize claims of knowledge and to resolve the long-standing conflict between dogmatism and skepticism, between rationalism and experience, and between idealism and materialism.[74] Indeed, he thought that Kant was to be commended for recognizing that the certainty and usefulness of knowledge could only be attained through a middle path between dogmatism and skepticism, between rational speculation and empiricism, and between idealism and materialism.[75] De Gérando could not forget to mention that the need for a middle course was a general corollary to his own deliberations on philosophy. In an enlightened era, dogmatism can only be discredited while skepticism must be seen as a passing condition of the mind. Skepticism is, in any case, "too contrary to our nature, too revolting to common sense."[76] After the sciences were perfected through experimentation and after long speculations produced only a succession of failed philosophical systems, the drawbacks of rationalism are now clear. The limitations of empirical philosophy were made evident through the progress of the sciences, which established relations between phenomena, between moral knowledge and natural science, and between physics and mathematics. Finally, the conflict between idealism and materialism exposed the inadequacies of both.

On the Kantians, de Gérando related that they claimed to pose questions anterior to the principles that constitute each of the opposed classes of philosophy and their respective approaches to the problem of human knowledge. Kantians believed that Kant had discovered a route between the opposed approaches; that he had not borrowed from any preexisting school of philosophy; and that his philosophy was not eclecticism, but an independent theory even hostile to eclecticism. Thus, they claimed that Kant had actually invalidated and surpassed all previous philosophies.[77] De Gérando acknowledged that in the history of philosophy there was "no example of a revolution as swift as that which was affected in Germany by the doctrines of Kant . . . it passed suddenly from the profoundest obscurity to the most astounding celebrity."[78] The German public initially found this new species of philosophy repulsive, but, eventually, "one believed himself transported to a world of wonders."[79]

De Gérando saw in Kant's philosophy some positive features: It sets limits on the powers of philosophy. Its goal is to give human knowledge an indisputable foundation. It succeeds in disabusing the mind of many old illusions and precludes newer ones. It exemplifies methodical analysis and classification. Finally, it stirs up hope for a coming golden age of philosophy and of peace among all philosophical sects.[80] De Gérando also saw the flaws: Kant's philosophy flatters the human mind. Readers become too excited at the prospect of new discoveries in philosophy. The obscurity of Kant's system, its "secret charm," attracts those who are fond of mystery. Its difficult proofs are like a long initiation, offering titillation for the intrepid. Contemplative minds are seized with pleasure at the ideal types of pure reason. In this philosophy, Platonic morality is transformed into a monstrous enthusiasm that promulgates its own laws. Those who love singularity find pleasure at Kant's neologisms. The vainest minds are flattered merely by the idea of membership in a privileged sect; of being invested with a supreme power to decide matters of philosophy.[81] De Gérando blamed Kant for the "presumptuous vanity" of his partisans and for their excessive contempt for the doctrines of other philosophers.[82] De Gérando understood well why the Kantians held *Popularphilosophie* in special contempt. Having appointed themselves the legislators of human thought, Kantians were indignant at the *Popularphilosophen*, who dared to assume the same role.[83]

De Gérando rejected the claim that Kant's was unlike any previous system of philosophy, for the exact opposite seemed to be true. Adherents of contrary systems of philosophy became his followers.[84] The *Critique of Pure Reason*, which declares that all knowledge is bound within the limits of experience, attracted proponents of the experimental philosophy. It also attracted proponents of rational philosophy with its claim that all knowledge proceeds *a priori* from the laws of the understanding.[85] Kant repeated Locke's view that there are no innate ideas, but he reiterated with Leibniz that experience results from establishing the connections between phenomena with the aid of inner notions. Kant took from Plato the idea of pure reason and from Aristotle his logic. Kant maintained that "we can know only the simple appearance of things," and this accorded with idealism. He cast doubt on the faculties of the human mind as well as external entities, and this accorded with skepticism.[86]

De Gérando's account of the philosophical developments after Kant did not reflect well on the latter's system. He compared the divisions and debates over Kantian philosophy to those between the Realists and Nominalists of medieval times. The controversies surrounding Kant's philosophy extended themselves into other fields, such as moral and political philosophy, jurisprudence, literature, and matters of taste. De Gérando related that this partisanship reproduced itself in many forms and slid into invective. Universities were infected, and literary gazettes were filled with personal attacks that passed for reviews.[87]

For de Gérando, history is a witness to the fanatics that Kant bore. It is as if Criticism by its very nature inspires mediocre men to high pretensions. It is as if Kantian philosophy exalts the vanity of those who presume to be the arbiters of knowledge. De Gérando thought it remarkable that in defending their system the Kantians relied least of all on the truth of some principle or other, but responded to nearly all objections with the charge that their opponents did not understand them.

Joining irony to stinging critique, de Gérando contended that the only positive outcome of Kant's philosophy was the many successive and unexpected systems that it engendered. These, in turn, occasioned new revolutions, splitting the Kantian school into many sects roiling with their own controversies. Besides orthodox Kantians and "half-Kantians" (who modified Kantianism with elements from Leibniz or Locke), de Gérando identified four main sects, founded by Fichte, Schelling, Bouterweck, and Bardili. (Reinhold was excluded because he did not qualify as a founder of a new sect. He ultimately ceded himself to Fichte though he began as an orthodox Kantian.) De Gérando observed that these four sects, which pure Kantians called "heterodox," came to overshadow the original Kantian school. Heterodox Kantians all agreed that the project of philosophy was still incomplete and Kant's system too indeterminate to be called a system of philosophy.[88]

There is nothing in the historical record, argued de Gérando, to indicate that there was any progress in either scientific knowledge or moral life in the period after Kant. On the contrary, there were "certain unfortunate effects," certain neologisms, dryness of language, partisanship, moral peril, and uncertainty.[89] The stunning contrast between the results and the original hopes of the founder of Criticism has to reflect badly on this philosophy. De Gérando described the situation of philosophy in the aftermath of Kantianism with a political analogy: Philosophy became disgusted with science just as anarchy at times becomes disgusted with liberty. The abuses committed in the name of philosophy did more harm to it than outside attacks against it.[90]

If the history of Kantianism is not enough to condemn it, then perhaps its failure to attain its own lofty goals is. De Gérando considered the claim that Kant successfully refuted idealism: His followers believed that Kant had demonstrated the existence of external objects, but in effect he had demonstrated a thing of nonsense because what he demonstrated was that certain things exist of which we do not know a single property. According to Kant, we know neither the relation to us nor the action on us of the thing-in-itself; neither the relation nor the reciprocal action between things-in-themselves. Any such relation can only be a property or power of things, and not knowing what things are in themselves, we cannot know whether they have in themselves any property or power. By Kant's own admission, his proof of the existence of external objects carries no force or validity because it consists in principles and laws to which he accorded a subjective validity and not an objective validity going beyond the sphere of our ideas and applicable to some external reality.[91] Hence, de Gérando had to deny that Kant succeeded in refuting idealism. De Gérando then invoked the name of Reinhold, who called Kant's system a "transcendental idealism" but also an "empirical realism," and Friedrich Heinrich Jacobi, who said it was in fact a kind of "subjective idealism."[92] Fichte and Schelling viewed Kant's system as a system of idealism in one respect and a "practical realism" in another.[93] On the other hand, there was Bardili, who called the Kantian system a "rational realism."[94] These and other commentators seemed to confirm de Gérando's opinion that a disguised idealism makes up the essence of Kant's philosophy.[95] To say that human knowledge consists of appearances only is to admit that knowledge is futile since there is not even a term of comparison to which the appearances can be related back. In such a system there is no means of examining whether knowledge is true or illusory.[96]

De Gérando next addressed Kant's philosophy in regard to materialism. The materialist outlook affirms the existence of matter and bodies. De Gérando believed that this was not disturbing in itself. Materialism is disturbing in its negative consequences, specifically, the denial of the reality and independence of the mind. He was, therefore, astonished to find that Kant conceded these consequences and even tried to prove them by establishing under the titles of theses and antitheses a series of paradoxes through which he found that the arguments for and against the simplicity and spirituality of the mind have equal force. Kant argued that this simplicity and spirituality could be neither known nor demonstrated; that the self was but an appearance whose reality could not be determined. Kant's thought was in accord with precisely those propositions that made materialism dangerous to morality. By only one circumstance was Kant not a materialist: he did not accept materialism's positive knowledge of the existence of bodies endowed with properties. However, in de Gérando's opinion, this was not a great consolation. Insofar as Kant argued against the reality of the mind, he advanced materialism even while disputing it on the level of external realities. Kant was able to avoid a complete materialism by turning to the "inglorious route" of skepticism—a skepticism in regard to both mind and matter.[97]

The next objection raised by de Gérando had to do with the claim that Kant had refuted skepticism. It was not necessary to come up with new arguments when one could simply refer to the arguments of Kant's greatest critic, Salomon Maimon. He showed that Kant's system, when properly understood, was itself a skepticism concerning both experience and morality. If Maimon is right, Kantianism leads unavoidably to an absolute skepticism.[98] Bouterweck similarly concluded that Kantianism was a "transcendental skepticism," although he could see why Fichte and Schelling described it as a "practical realism."[99]

De Gérando wrapped up his analysis of Kantianism on a conciliatory note. He again acknowledged that Kant had exposed the inadequacies of all previous systems and identified the most essential problems of philosophy, but there was no backing down from his main criticism: Kant failed to achieve what he had set out to do; to find a middle path between perennially opposed systems of philosophy.

The final chapter of the *Histoire comparée* redirects the reader's attention away from the failures of Kantianism to the successes of the philosophies of Bacon and Locke. While Kantianism failed to reconcile the systems of idealism and materialism, the philosophy of experience succeeded in selecting principles from competing systems with which to form its basis. As de Gérando had already shown, rationalism or empiricism is sterile by itself. The former is sterile because it limits itself to ideal recombinations of the principle of identity. The latter's sterility is due to its inability to derive from one fact additional facts. The experimental philosophy unites rationalism and empiricism through the useful employment of reason in observation. The experimental philosophy avoids the excesses of both dogmatism and skepticism by applying doubt to dogmatism and affirmation to skepticism. Unlike rationalism, the experimental philosophy does not require proofs where they are not needed, and this helps to disarm skepticism.[100] The experimental philosophy is not exclusive enough for sectarian spirits, and its principles not mysterious enough for zealots. Its maxims have never been revolutionary. It conforms too well to general reason.[101] To those who believe that the philosophies of Bacon and Locke are to blame for the political upheavals of the end of the eighteenth century, de Gérando would reply that no philosophy could be more innocent of the charge than the experimental philosophy. It could never authorize a rash trial of abstract theories on the people. De Gérando could recommend the experimental philosophy to a state that seeks reforms, but one that also wants to accommodate them to present circumstances as well as to the lessons of the past.[102] Most of all, de Gérando recommended this philosophy because it actually attained the goals of philosophy. It guaranteed morality by ensuring the independence of the mind and by conferring to moral sentiments the status of knowledge. He reminded the reader also of its positive effects on the arts and on taste generally.[103]

In 1804, Napoleon Bonaparte appointed the author of the *Histoire comparée* Secretary General of the Ministry of the Interior.[104] As a minister of the French state, de Gérando was a political moderate who advocated a moderate and prudent philosophy, the key principle of which was to select the best elements from all previous philosophies and to do so with the guidance of independent reason and for the practical benefit of society. He was an eclectic as was the philosophy he advocated.[105] De Gérando claimed as his predecessors Newton, Leibniz, Buddeus, Rudiger, Syrbius, Jean Le Clerc, Hollmann, Brucker, Diderot, and Rousseau—all of whom he identified as eclectics.[106] Kant, too, was an eclectic of a sort, notwithstanding the fact that his philosophy failed to have practical and lasting goodness.[107]

In the comparative analysis of philosophical systems, Kant's system came out badly as did all other idealisms. Comparison also revealed that all modern philosophical systems were eclectic, Kantianism being no exception. Comparative history of philosophy avoided *a priori* schemata, teleology, and conceptual hierarchies. It revealed certain repetitions in the history of thought. These were to be taken as valuable lessons for philosophy in and for the present.

3

India in Friedrich Schlegel's Comparative History of Philosophy

Philosophy is nothing other than *history of philosophy* if one understands history correctly.

—F. Schlegel (undated)[1]

From these investigations it emerges sufficiently that the Indians had real philosophy in both *form* and method and that, at this time, we lack only sufficient documents to be able to incorporate it into the history of philosophy.

—F. Schlegel (1804–5)[2]

Friedrich Schlegel (1772–1829) was a wonderfully erratic personality. His career path led him through literary criticism, university lecturing, journalism, novel writing, Oriental philology, historical studies, and diplomacy. At the time of the French Revolution, his literary values were neo-classical; his politics pro-revolutionary; and his philosophy Fichtean idealism. By his twenty-fifth year, however, he had turned away from both Fichte and neo-classicism. By age thirty-six, he had converted to Roman Catholicism and had become a political conservative. He began work as a diplomat and propagandist for the Austrian government. Between 1797 and 1808, he wandered in and between Germany and France as an impoverished writer and lecturer. Born in Hannover, this son of a superintendent of the Lutheran Church died in Vienna as a member of Catholic Austria's political and intellectual elite. For a long time, he was remembered mainly for being one of

51

the literary theorists of Romanticism, but in 1950 Raymond Schwab christened him the founder of "the Oriental Renaissance."[3] Also, historians of linguistics credit him with propagating Sanskrit studies in Germany. They recount how Schlegel brought attention to the common ancestry of the languages of Europe with Persian and Sanskrit. His work, *Ueber die Sprache und Weisheit der Indier* (*On the Language and Wisdom of the Indians*) of 1808, inspired other Germans to delve into comparative language studies.[4] Schlegel was also the first historian of philosophy to treat Asian philosophical ideas together with European ones in "one basic historical and systematic context."[5] His history of philosophy is the beginning of comparative—in the sense also of cross-cultural—history of philosophy.[6]

Schlegel's career as an Orientalist began after he arrived in Paris in late 1802 or early 1803. He studied Persian with Antoine-Léonard de Chézy (1773–1832), who later became a professor of Oriental languages at the Collège de France. Schlegel studied Sanskrit with help from Alexander Hamilton, the British naval lieutenant and member of the Asiatic Society of Bengal, detained in France after the resumption of war with Great Britain.

In a letter dated May 15, 1803, Friedrich informs his brother, August Wilhelm, that he was learning much from the British officer:

> I have not only made progress in Persian, but have finally reached my great goal, that is, to know Sanskrit. Within four months I will be able to read Shakuntala in the original text, although I may still need the translation as before. It has demanded tremendous effort due to a great complication and a particular method of guessing and labor, since I had to learn the elements without elementary books. Lastly, to my great benefit, it so happened that an Englishman Hamilton, the only one in Europe besides [Charles] Wilkins to know the language and know it fundamentally, came to my aid with advice at the very least.[7]

Schlegel visited the Bibliothèque Nationale for its numerous Persian and some two-hundred Sanskrit manuscripts. In a letter dated August 14, 1803 to August Wilhelm, he wrote that he spent his days copying from Sanskrit manuscripts and lexicons. He worked on Sanskrit three to four hours daily, spent another one or two hours going through his work with Hamilton, and then worked another two or three hours in the evening.[8] Three months later, Friedrich thought

himself competent enough to begin a verse translation of Kālidāsa's
Śakuntalā.[9] A partial translation of the drama, along with his other
translations of Sanskrit texts, was appended to *Ueber die Sprache und
Weisheit der Indier*.

Schlegel spent 1804–8 in Cologne, where he composed and delivered lectures on the history of philosophy to an audience of three
patrons. These lectures were edited and published by C. J. H. Windischmann three decades later.[10] They are included in the *Kritische
Friedrich-Schlegel-Ausgabe* as vols. 12 and 13, bearing the titles *Die Entwicklung der Philosophie in zwölf Büchern, Propädeutik und Logik*, and
Anhang zur Logik. Jean-Jacques Anstett, who edited these volumes,
observed that these philosophy lectures pointed in the direction of
Schegel's conversion to the Catholic Church.[11]

Hans Eichner, Frederick Beiser, and Elizabeth Millán-Zaibert
have argued that Schlegel's thinking took a historical turn in the
years 1796–1808 and that this was, at the same time, a turn away
from the foundationalism of Fichte's philosophy.[12] In his early twen-
ties, Schlegel was an admirer of the French Revolution and Fichte.
Like others enamored with Fichte's philosophy, Schlegel regarded
Fichte as the one who came along to complete Kant's revolution in
philosophy. He believed that Fichte had established the first principle
of philosophy and that an objective aesthetics and ethics, including the principles of republicanism, could now be established.[13] He
admired Fichte also for his strong public support for the French
Revolution.

Schlegel was not a Fichtean for very long. He developed doubts
in the summer of 1796. During a visit with Novalis in July, Schlegel
and his friend shared with each other their doubts about Fichte's
philosophy. On a trip to Jena in August, Schlegel met friends in the
circle of Friedrich Immanuel Niethammer. Manfred Frank suggests
that from this circle Schlegel could have learned skeptical arguments
against Fichte.[14] Schlegel's doubts definitely intensified after meeting
Fichte. In a letter to C. F. Körner, Schlegel complained that Fichte had
too little idea of things that did not directly concern him and that
he was weak in every science *that had an object*. On his side, Fichte
was amused by Schlegel's attempt to win him over for the study of
history. Schlegel was stunned when Fichte told him that he would
rather count peas than study history. At some point in the conversa-
tion, Fichte asked rhetorically, "We are supposed to appropriate the
works of great artists of yore by studying them? . . . Oh, had we a
pure aesthetics first!"[15]

After the meeting, Schlegel decided to write a critique of Fichte's *Wissenschaftslehre*. The surviving fragments of this critique, titled "Geist der Wissenschaftslehre," focused on Fichte's foundationalism.[16] Schlegel had determined that Fichte's first principle of true philosophy—that the self posits itself freely—was a dogmatic assumption. In addition, Fichte's philosophy was too abstract; cut off from human experience. What Fichte lacked but needed was a historical perspective on his own system.[17] On January 30, 1797, Schlegel announced that he had "decisively separated himself from the *Wissenschaftslehre*."[18]

What Fichte could not fathom doing, Schegel would do. The latter was developing a historical perspective not just on Fichte's philosophy, but on all philosophies. A nascent appreciation for the history of philosophy is apparent from a few of Schlegel's philosophical fragments from his early Romantic period (1796–1808). In these fragments, Schlegel inverts the Fichtean valuation of philosophy, while collapsing the distinction between philosophy and history and transvaluating both in their relation to each other. One reads in one of these fragments that Fichte's philosophy is too mathematical and not systematical to the extent that it is not historical.[19] Another fragment states: "As soon as philosophy becomes science, we get history. All systems are historical and *vice versa*. The mathematical method is precisely the anti-systematical."[20] Schlegel went further: "History is nothing but philosophy, and the name can be completely substituted."[21] In other words, it is impossible to do philosophy without doing the history of philosophy.[22]

In his lecture course, *Die Entwicklung der Philosophie in zwölf Büchern*, of 1804–5, Schlegel said more on why it is impossible to do philosophy without having a historical perspective.[23] He provided historical examples: Descartes attempted to abstract his way out of all previous systems in order to create a completely new philosophy, but he failed. Fichte also tried to completely forget all previous thought, but he also failed. They failed because their philosophies were not in fact complete abstractions; they contained reminiscences or refutations of previous systems. In refuting or criticizing a previous system, they attached themselves to it. The whole procedure of foundationalism is flawed, beginning with the assumption that there must be a first principle in philosophy, because any philosophical system supports itself on another philosophical system; because philosophies build a connective chain in which the creation of one philosophical system depends on knowledge of another. All philosophical systems are

linked by history, and to understand any given system, some understanding of the whole chain is required.[24]

Schlegel used the example of Kant: "Kant himself shows that a
critique of philosophical reason cannot succeed without a history of
philosophy, because, as a critique of philosophical reason, his work
is not historical enough, though full of historical relations. . . ."[25]
Kant's philosophy is full of references to the attempts, failures, and
partial successes of past philosophies. Either he appropriated parts
of previous systems or he was responding to previous systems. Notwithstanding this, Kant's approach to philosophy was "not historical enough." Philosophy's past mattered to Kant only insofar as he
could overcome it.[26] Without a historical perspective, Kant could
judge other systems only by the model of his own. His judgments
of other philosophies could be neither historical nor critical, but only
self-referential and dogmatic.[27] Millán-Zaibert makes an important
connection between Schlegel's emphasis on history as essential to
critique and his view of philosophy as being framed by life, as beginning *in media res*.[28]

The First Book of *Die Entwicklung der Philosophie* is titled "Introduction and Historical Characterization of Philosophy According to
Its Successive Development." Interestingly, this introduction begins
with the problem of introducing philosophy.[29] Schlegel embraced a
historical perspective from the outset. He related how, in recent times,
there have been two kinds of introductions to philosophy. An example
of the first kind is Fichte's lectures on the vocation of scholars. It
introduces a person to philosophy in that it conducts him through the
transition from the ordinary perspective of life to the higher, speculative perspective of philosophy. By comparing philosophy to life, it
is the rhetorical option for introducing philosophy. The second kind
of introduction is exemplified by Fichte's short presentation of the
Wissenschaftslehre. It demonstrates the necessity of philosophy for the
sciences; especially a first principle. It establishes one with a definition. This kind of introduction is a comparison between sciences and
philosophy, or a presentation of philosophy's relation to the sciences,
and tends to be encyclopedic.

But if philosophy is to be critical, an introduction to philosophy
ought to be critical as well. The previously mentioned kinds of introductions are, however, of a contrary purpose. One cannot carry out
a comparison of philosophy to life or to the sciences without already
being acquainted with philosophy. The more basic question is, what is
philosophy? Because the answer to this question is disputed, because

the very thing is not fully known, it is presumptuous to argue that all the other sciences should take their first principle from philosophy.[30]

Schlegel then described the third, older kind of introduction, one that was common among the Scholastics: a logic. Usually, it preceded what was regarded as actual philosophy, viz., metaphysics. Logic was regarded as a distinct science. This conception has endured into the most recent times. Kant and Fichte ascribed to this conception, although they greatly restricted its claims. Regardless, the use of a logic to introduce a person to philosophy is no less questionable. Despite philosophers' claims, a logic is not knowledge, but an organon.[31] Logic cannot teach us what truth is or what the fundamental principle of philosophy is. Either would be the concern of philosophy itself; an introduction to philosophy that presents the truth or the fundamental principle of philosophy is not an introduction: it is philosophy itself.[32]

Schlegel continued: A definition of philosophy is no better an introduction if one expects the definition to capture and present the complete concept of philosophy based on a real character description of the object in its entirety. To give such a description in an introduction is impossible. If it were possible, the introduction would be philosophy itself, bringing us back to the problem of introducing philosophy. Schlegel was not opposed, however, to a short, preliminary and superficial definition of philosophy. So, he defined philosophy as knowledge of the inner human being, the causes of nature, and the relation of human being to nature, or, since philosophy is incomplete, the striving after this knowledge.[33]

By beginning with the problem of how to introduce a person to philosophy, Schlegel prepared his auditors to consider seriously his claim that a history of philosophy was the only proper introduction to philosophy. When he called for a history of philosophy, it did not mean an enumeration of philosophical systems in historical succession or a deduction of all possible philosophies or a proof of the necessity of philosophy.[34] None of these passes as history of philosophy.[35] Rather, what he called for was "a critique of all previous philosophies, which at the same time establishes the relation of these philosophies to each other."[36] He sought a characterization and classification of all philosophies or, to borrow from Millán-Zaibert, a "historical taxonomy" that could "free him from the confines of any one system and [put] him in a position to critique the various contributions of other philosophers."[37] Millán-Zaibert articulates the principle behind the method of comparative history of philosophy: "When history is incorporated into the very method of philosophy itself, we can assess a given contribution of a philosopher, not only by classifying her arguments as valid or invalid, sound or unsound, but by comparing the merits of the contribution to other contributions made by other philosophers from different periods."[38] I note that this principle is also what de Gérando claimed to be a major advantage of comparative history of philosophy.[39]

If one compares Schlegel's comparative history of philosophy to de Gérando's, she will find that they share the same form and method, but not the same content. We shall see that Schlegel experienced philosophy as an education and passage out of philosophy whereas de Gérando experienced it as a confirmation of the experimental philosophy as best for state and society.

Schlegel listed five major varieties (*Arten*) of philosophy: empiricism, materialism, skepticism, pantheism, and idealism. (One should note that these are not identical in either kind or number to the classes of philosophy in de Gérando's *Histoire comparée*.) Applying the results of his comparative analyses, he opened with the claim that, of the five varieties, only the fifth (idealism) was truly philosophical. In other words, empiricism, materialism, skepticism, and pantheism are not as philosophical as idealism. In the First Book of *Die Entwicklung der Philosophie,* Schlegel characterizes each of the four inferior classes of philosophy (always in relation to each other) before coming to the class he called "intellectual philosophy," "intellectual dualism," or "idealism."[40] (The reason for the different names will be discussed.) There comes a point in *Die Entwicklung der Philosophie* where Schlegel counts not five, but seven classes of philosophy.[41] I will not dwell equally on each of these classes of philosophy, but, rather, will relate particular points of Schlegel's analysis to illustrate his way of writing the history of philosophy and to access the perspective from which he observed philosophy. As we saw in Chapter 2, de Gérando's comparative history of philosophy reveals its author to be a Lockean, i.e., an eclectic empiricist. In this chapter, we shall see that Schlegel's comparative history of philosophy reveals its author to be a kind of idealist.

Schlegel regarded *empiricism* as the lowest kind of philosophy. Indeed, it can hardly be called philosophy. Rather, it is resignation from philosophy due to the lack of intellectual power to do philosophy. Empiricism sticks to experience, locating truth in sensory impressions; it does not penetrate into the inner nature of matter, on which the materialist's attention is still mainly focused. Empiricism is a complete philosophical standstill or abstention from philosophy in that an empiricist who has any thought must fall into either materialism or skepticism. Empiricists negate the distinction between the sensible and the supersensible by denying knowledge of the latter. This is not a reason, however, that prevents empiricists from going beyond sensory impressions to their source, that is, going from appearances to matter. This is how almost all empiricists are secret materialists. They fear only being recognized as such. Schlegel added that this observation applied especially to his own time.[42]

For Schlegel, empiricism is an oscillation between materialism and skepticism and not a definite variety of philosophy. In this lies its own refutation. It is more powerfully refuted, however, by pantheism. The principle of identity, as an absolute certainty, is pantheism's best proof against empiricism. The empiricist must necessarily concede that $a = a$. This is not a sensible knowledge however; it is a rational knowledge. The empiricist is forced to accept this principle as a higher knowledge, which then refutes and reverses his strict empiricism.[43]

Schlegel held that empiricism arises from extensive decline of the mind. It is resignation from philosophy due to a weakness and inability of human reason to go beyond experience and sensation. It does not have materialism's absolutism, but it is not skepticism either. Empiricism is, therefore, a "middle thing," a variation between materialism and skepticism.[44]

Empiricists, who ground and limit everything to experience, do not recognize such a thing as a science of reason. But if experience were to be abstracted from all rational knowledge, only historical knowledge would remain; so that, for the empiricists, there can be no science (no philosophy) other than history.[45]

Schlegel analyzed skepticism and pantheism in relation to each other and discussed them at some length. Pantheism is the absolute opposite of skepticism since the former is "the most dogmatic of all, most absolute, most evident of philosophical systems."[46] Yet, despite their opposition, there is a path by which pantheism leads easily to skepticism. One could proceed as Zeno did and explain all representations of movement, change, and diversity as empty appearances to such an extent that nothing is true. As long as one denies diversity, there is really nothing that stands in the way of the pantheist's idea of the infinite, but, also, there is nothing that stands in the way of doubting and disputing the unity of the infinite.[47]

Schlegel knew of the several ancient and modern varieties of *skepticism*. He made special mention of one modern variety of skepticism—the one that denies completely the possibility of knowledge of an infinite reality and takes refuge in faith and conviction. Schlegel called this variety "mixed skepticism," because an actual skeptic would accept faith not more—indeed, probably less—than he would knowledge. Schlegel counted six kinds of skeptics: (1) those who come to skepticism from empiricism or atomistic materialism ("the most vulgar" skeptics), (2) those who come to skepticism from dynamic materialism (most prevalent among the ancient Greeks), (3) those who come to it from pantheism, (4) those who come to it from idealism as a passing or (5) fixed condition; and finally (6) "the Jacobian crossing-over from doubt to faith."[48]

Schlegel characterized skepticism: It is related more to polemics than to philosophy. Its greatest strengths are in refuting other philosophical systems, in its effectiveness in polemics. Skepticism focuses on the positive claims or systems of others, disputing them rather than constructing a system of its own. It is not the vulgar skepticism but the higher skepticism that resolves itself, through a critique that extends to all systems of philosophy existent up to the present. "[F]ruitful and real" skepticism is critique. As critique, it should be the first science—or even the science of sciences—since in it lie the principles of all sciences, which must submit themselves to testing and investigation. In a way, Kantian philosophy falls under this variety of skepticism. In comparison to empiricism and materialism, skepticism is superior, for it cannot be refuted by either. Finally, skepticism is more closely related to the "intellectual philosophy" (still to be described) than is either of the other two.[49]

Schlegel described *pantheism*: There is only one pantheism without variety. Its source is pure reason since the principle of identity is its singular foundational principle. Pantheism explains everything straightaway as one and unchanging; it annuls differences as mere appearances. The idea of the infinite is a pure thought that completely excludes concepts of difference, variation, and condition. It entails the thought that finite things are not real. In respect to form and mode of thought, pantheism is on the opposite end from empiricism and materialism. The latter philosophies proceed from multiplicity while pantheism proceeds from the absolute unity of infinite reality. Also, pantheism is opposed to dynamic materialism as the latter accepts not one, but two or three primal principles.[50]

The principle of identity ($a = a$ or $+a$ is not $-a$) is absolutely, infinitely certain, but completely empty. While it may have an infinite intensity of truth, it has no extension whatsoever. Nothing is certain but its unity, which is a negative idea of reality, from which nothing positive can be derived.[51] Pantheism is, therefore, completely content-less and unscientific. A good systematizer, however, can conceal its emptiness with an artificial aggregation of positive ideas and special propositions. Pantheism's first principle can be combined with positive ideas to conceal its inconsequence. The pantheist Spinoza was so certain of the logical consequences of his craftwork that he could hardly wait to bring it to his opponents. In Spinoza's philosophy is "a strong admixture of intellectual philosophy," namely, Descartes'.[52]

In cases of scientifically constructed pantheism, skepticism may not be so opposed to pantheism. In fact, the way to transform pure pantheism into a scientific system is through a negative skepticism, wherein one argues that everything is appearance and deception and (if the concept of highest reality is to be retained) accepts the (negative) idea of the infinite, which throws off even the most spiritual of predicates as limitations on it.[53]

Schlegel contended that a pure pantheist could not build a system, that pantheism was not a system, because a series of pure negations does not make a system. The pure pantheist clings to the first idea—the highest idea that human consciousness is capable of—the idea of divinity. He immerses himself completely in it. Relative to this idea, everything else evaporates before his eyes. The pure pantheist is thoroughly religious, but he has only a negative idea of religion. The religion that has the pantheistic idea as its basis is a negative religion or what some have called mysticism. The negative idea of divinity is, for everyone, easier to grasp, because it has an intense certainty. Scientific and speculative minds have an affinity for it. Lastly, it is historically true that pantheism has appeared more often as religion than as philosophy.[54]

Schlegel claimed that *pure* pantheism never existed in Europe—that it was entirely an Asian phenomenon. According to his account, pantheism emerged in Asia specifically among several Indian sects, including the Indian "penitents" called yogis. These immerse and lose themselves completely in the negative concept of divinity. They strive toward absolute abstraction from everything positive, sensory, and spiritual; toward the complete annihilation of themselves as either sense or intellect. They are, in a way, better pantheists than they are philosophers.[55]

Pure pantheism may have never existed in the West, but a hybrid variety has existed among Christian mystics (Schlegel's example is Simeon Stylites). There have been several Christian mystics who explained divinity as an infinite nothing (due to the negative idea of divinity), to which no predicate or quality can be attached. They named their mode of thought nihilism.[56]

Earlier in these lectures, Schlegel said that there was only one pantheism with no varieties. But his auditors then heard that pantheism's principle could be combined with positive ideas—Spinoza's system being the example. Schlegel contradicted himself more blatantly when he called neo-Platonism an "excellent . . . variety of pantheism"—consisting of a greater admixture. The neo-Platonists sought to unite three different philosophies—those of Pythagoras, Plato, and Aristotle—and so were called syncretists. Schlegel recognized that Plotinus's principle was the same as Spinoza's: Both spirit and matter derive from a higher being, but this being can be thought of as neither spirit nor matter because either predicate is unworthy of Divinity. Like all other Alexandrian systems, neo-Platonism was an admixture, the most logically consequential one, standing in the middle between pure pantheism and idealism.[57]

Schlegel then turned to the variety *intellectual philosophy*. This class is opposed to both empiricism and materialism. If intellectual philosophies do not completely deny the existence of matter, they give matter a secondary, or derived, existence with the argument that matter comes from spirit or that it has reality only in the mind.[58] Prior to Schlegel, "intellectual philosophy" and "ideal[ist] philosophy" were sometimes taken to be synonymous. In Schlegel's classification, idealism is placed within the class intellectual philosophy, which encompasses the two varieties *idealism* and *dualism*: Idealism, as already mentioned, denies the existence of matter, explaining it as mere appearance and deducing it (and everything else) from a spiritual principle. The second variety, dualism, views matter and spirit as original substances or principles, but gives the priority to mind, from which matter is derived. Schlegel added that this dualism is distinct from "materialistic, intellectual dualism" without explaining what the latter is.[59]

Intellectual philosophies are antithetical to skepticisms since the former attempt to explain the relation of spirit to matter and prove this relation in the universe by providing a dogmatic construct of the universe that pretends to show either that matter comes from spirit or that the appearance of matter arises from spirit or that matter is subordinate to and ordered by spirit.[60] The opposition between intellectual philosophies and the philosophies of the other classes is not absolute. There is a side to intellectual philosophies that is not necessarily in conflict with other systems. Higher empiricism as *Lebensphilosophie*, dynamic materialism, higher skepticism, or pantheism-turned-into-realism is compatible and often combined with intellectual philosophy. Precisely because intellectual philosophy can assimilate the philosophies of all other varieties; because it is the most universal, most inclusive, and richest of all philosophies, contradictions are prone to arise in it and, hence, a new *skepsis*. From Schlegel's historical perspective, the greatest, most remarkable systems have been those of intellectual philosophy. This class is outstanding for delivering what philosophy wants: a system. It is a far more capable philosophy in this regard than pantheism and all other varieties.[61] Morally and aesthetically, none of the other philosophical classes can be praised for ideas higher and more beautiful than those of intellectual philosophy.[62]

For Schlegel, the greatest example of intellectual philosophy is Plato's. This philosopher set consciousness higher than being, mind above body, in order to induce an idea of the divine as the most perfect, most unlimited, all-encompassing intelligence; as the highest, most perfect understanding that brings forth primal images, from which it builds all things. There is, however, a latent materialism in this philosophy, for in it the world and all things are created by the most perfect intelligence from an originally existing material. Herein lies the imperfection of this system and, actually, of most systems of intellectual philosophy. They contain the seeds of their own degeneration into intellectual dualism. These systems fall short of their original intention, which is to give primacy to mind (over body). Failing to achieve unity of principle, this idealism degenerates into dualism, in which two originary principles are acknowledged and mind is regarded as conditioned by matter and even subordinate to it (matter is seen as the first and older of the two). To the extent that matter sets limits on the divine, the former is superior to the latter.[63]

Reason begins its swing from intellectual dualism to materialism as it comes to realize that intelligence is unthinkable without matter. It is not active without matter. Without an object, it cannot even be passive; it simply cannot be. Thus, there must be something beyond the intelligence, something other than itself. Here is the root of the error that assumes the primacy of matter.[64] This is how the highest systems, the intellectual philosophies, are inherently flawed.

The highest goal that philosophy can set for itself is to know God, but even intellectual philosophy misses this goal. It is a goal that cannot be reached by asserting that the intellect is the highest spirit; by claiming that its nature is divine. Only God creates whereas the intellect can only represent. This is why intellectual philosophy can never explain *creatio ex nihilo*. Intellectual philosophy is, in the end, the best approximation of God's nature of which man is capable.

Schlegel believed that intellectual philosophy could not have been solely the work of man, for intellectual philosophies seem to draw on a higher perspective, on a supernatural source. Schlegel suggested obliquely that intellectual philosophies derive from divine revelation.[65]

Idealism is Schlegel's name for the modern variety of intellectual philosophy. It is related to intellectual dualism as much as are the ancient varieties of intellectual philosophy. Intellectual dualism starts out from excessive reverence for the intellect, the idea, or the world of intelligibles as infinite and sublime, while idealism starts out from contempt for the body and sensory perceptions, regarding the latter as appearances. Schlegel identified two historical circumstances that contributed to modern idealism: The first was developments in modern physics that showed sensory representations to be subjective and illusory (they did not reveal the objective character of things). The second was the influence of Christianity and its general contempt for sensation. Berkeley, to take an example, became an idealist out of mere religiosity. There are also the examples of Malebranche and Leibniz, who constructed idealist systems under the influence of the Church Fathers.[66]

Both ancient and modern varieties of intellectual philosophy agree on the primacy of intellect. In this essential respect, dualistic and idealistic philosophers do not differ from each another. Idealists deny the existence of the external world or explain it as mere appearance while dualists do not, but both accept the existence of an intelligible world (i.e., ideas).[67]

The characterization of idealism reached the point where Schlegel analyzed what he regarded as its major flaw. This is the failure of idealist systems to adequately explain appearances. In Berkeley's idealism, an appearance has the status of an illusion without purpose or rule. To the extent that his system is an idealism, Leibniz resorted to a completely arbitrary hypothesis to explain appearances. Kant and Fichte tried to reduce appearances to the laws of the human understanding, but invited the question, what guarantees the truth of these laws? What is *it* that determines the laws of the understanding? Fichte's efforts notwithstanding, it could not be the understanding that determines these laws, because the understanding is what these laws condition. To determine these laws, one can only go beyond the self; one can only assume the existence of a not-self. It may not be true after all that the external world is empty appearance.

Schlegel brought out other arguments against the idealist's thesis of empty appearances: The not-self cannot be so empty as to contain no being at all or have no basis whatsoever in being, because appearances, as either images or words, are still meaningful; they still speak to the understanding.[68] Furthermore, one who maintains that the external world is empty appearance cannot also maintain the existence of infinite reality, which is a thesis still affirmed by all idealists. "A diverse and well-designed empty appearance would be a whole world of nothing. But how can an empty world of nothing exist beside the divinity of infinite reality?" asked Schlegel. "How can *empty appearance* exist in an *infinite reality*?"[69] His queries never satisfied, the idealist is easily conducted to pantheism or skepticism.[70]

After summarizing the three component characteristics of modern idealism (the dissolution ["empty appearance"] of real bodies, the arbitrary determination/delimitation of the self, and the principle of activity in cognition), Schlegel turned to the problem of the origins of philosophy. On this question, he was as critical as ever. He stated that the question could refer to, actually, two questions. The first concerns the mere possibility of philosophy. The second concerns the historical origin of philosophy. The first is the more speculative question: What is the origin of philosophy? Is the origin divine or human? If philosophy's origin is human, from which human faculty did it arise and how did it develop? Is philosophy possible as a science? The second question asks: How is a system of philosophy related to others or how did it arise from other systems? This question seeks to trace, if possible, the successive developments of philosophy back to an original source.[71] The second question can facilitate the answer to the first question or, at least, clarify the way in which one could come closer to answering the more speculative question.[72] For a variation on the second question, one could ask "whether one ought to begin absolutely with Greek philosophy—not go[ing] back farther in order to derive it from earlier, Oriental philosophy—whether Oriental philosophy is even to be admitted into the history of philosophy."[73] This question breaks down into two particular questions: (1) Is Greek philosophy related to Oriental philosophy? Is it part of Oriental philosophy? Does the former derive completely from the latter? (2) Can Oriental philosophy be incorporated into the history of philosophy? Are there adequate documents for a historical-critical investigation of its spirit, emergence, development, coherency, form, and method? Schlegel told his auditors that answers to these questions have been both affirmative and negative and that those who have answered negatively were correct to maintain that history should be based on reliable documents only and never on unreliable tradition. He recommended, however, that competent accounts and excerpts by those who had access to the sources be regarded as reliable as authentic original works. But he conceded that neither kind of documents actually existed for Oriental philosophy. There have been excerpts of

Egyptian, Phoenician, Chaldean, and magi philosophemes since the time of the Alexandrians, but these were so obscure and mixed up with Greek ideas or so obviously falsified that no historical use could be made of them. Schlegel, thus, fully acknowledged that adequate documentation of Oriental philosophy was lacking.[74]

On whether Greek philosophy derives from Oriental philosophy, the deniers have said that the origin of Greek philosophy must be explained through itself, because the most ancient of Greek ideas exhibit such originality that there is no reason to derive them from an earlier, foreign source. They have said of the ancient Ionian physicists that their doctrines have the stamp of autonomy and originality; that there is nothing similar in Oriental philosophy so far as is known; and that, rather, there is a great difference in fundamental ideas between Oriental and Ionian philosophies.[75]

But the case is quite different with Pythagoras and Plato. In either philosopher's thought, there are doctrines that do not serve as first principles, although they are the most significant of his philosophemes. These philosophemes definitely contradict the dominant mode of Greek thought, including Greek religious and moral ideas, and were completely unknown to the Greeks or were rejected by them, while the same philosophemes were accepted universally among several Oriental nations.[76] Plato's doctrine of Ideas and reminiscence, which seemed so strange and paradoxical to the moderns as well as to the Greeks, is a dominant Indian doctrine. Evidence of this can be found not only in the scholarly books of the Indians, but also in their popular plays. A singular idiosyncrasy or paradox, such as what is peculiar in Plato's thought, could derive from a doctrine or religious belief held universally by the Egyptians and Indians if that doctrine does not cohere with the rest of Greek thought and if the philosopher, whose idiosyncrasy it was, knew the Oriental doctrine.[77]

Schlegel believed that it could definitely be established that Plato's doctrine of transmigration was taken from the Egyptians. Whether the latter had gotten it from the Indians is not yet established. This doctrine is so completely interwoven with the rest of the body of opinions and ideas of the Indians and so characteristic of the Indian mode of thought that no ancient Indian writer fails to mention the transmigration of the soul. The origins of Greek philosophy can be explained through itself in the case of Ionian physical philosophy, but the same cannot be said for either Pythagorean or Platonic philosophy.[78]

In Schlegel's opinion, they who deny that the ancient Oriental nations had philosophy go too far. They sometimes concede that the

Orientals had representations of divinity and possessed knowledge of the nature of things, but they deny that this knowledge had a philosophical form; that their ideas were assembled or executed scientifically and systematically. They argue that the knowledge in Oriental texts is mere folk belief. They ignore what ancient Greek and Roman sources say about Oriental philosophy and claim that, in any case, it is completely inaccessible; that nothing can be decided either for or against Oriental philosophy.[79]

Schlegel recounted what the deniers of Oriental philosophy have said about A. H. Anquetil du Perron's translation of the *Zend-Avesta*.[80] Anquetil du Perron believed that he had transmitted to the West the writings of Zoroaster, but others charged that this text was attributed falsely to the legendary Persian sage; that it contained no real Persian tradition; that it was not a reliable document of ancient Persian or Indian philosophy or that it had simply no relation to the latter. Schlegel agreed that the attribution to Zoroaster did not have the slightest probability. He then presented the counterarguments: These mostly liturgical, mystical-religious texts for priestly use do contain ideas that are closely related to philosophical ideas; so much so that they betray definite principles and philosophical systematicity. The priestly caste, who were in possession of all knowledge, could have performed both scientific and religious recitation of these philosophical ideas.[81]

Schlegel recounted that a number of translations of Indian texts appeared in the years following the publication of Anquetil du Perron's translation. These had a religious and poetic form, but also a philosophical content. Furthermore, translations of Indian texts that were neither poetic nor scriptural were already available in Europe. They demonstrated fully that the Indians had philosophy "even *in respect to form*."[82]

Schlegel gave as an example the Sanskrit text *Bhagavadgītā*. A "preeminent, philosophical document," the *Bhagavadgītā* is actually an episode in the Indian epic *Mahābhārata*.[83] According to Schlegel, while the early chapters are poetical, the rest of the *Bhagavadgītā* is more scientific. Though the language is versified, it is simple and almost no different from prose. The *Bhagavadgītā* is more strictly philosophical in form than *De rerum natura* by Lucretius, who is given a place within the history of philosophy. The *Bhagavadgītā* presents the Vedānta philosophy. Vedānta meant *finis scientiae, finis vedae*, where *veda* means science or knowledge, and is considered to be the source of all knowledge. Vedānta is the philosophy related to the scriptures of the dominant faith among the Indians. Thus, Vedānta is the orthodox philosophy of the Indians or, equally, a philosophical commentary on the Indian religion. Schlegel contended that, in its essential principles, Vedānta is consonant with Platonic philosophy to an extraordinary degree.[84]

Having said his rejoinders to the deniers of Oriental philosophy, Schlegel listed off four schools of Indian philosophy without further ado: "Vedanta" (already mentioned), "Sankhya" (which Sir William Jones regarded as having a great similarity to Pythagorean philosophy), "Nyagya" (which Jones compared to Aristotelian logic), and "Mimansa" (moral philosophy).[85] Schlegel concluded his discussion of Oriental philosophy with the following words: "From these investigations it emerges sufficiently that the Indians had real philosophy in both *form* and method and that, at this time, we lack only sufficient documents to be able to incorporate it into the history of philosophy."[86]

In arguing that the Indians had real philosophy in respect to both form and method, Schlegel opposed himself to the nascent opinion among some historians of philosophy that the Orientals did not know philosophy. This opinion, which was elaborately defended starting in the 1780s, is the subject of the next chapter.

The Exclusion of Africa and Asia from the History of Philosophy

The Formation of the Kantian Position

> The valorization of difference may operate in two ways: either by *self-racialization*, the affirmation of proper racial identity and (secondarily) of one's own superiority, or by *other-racialization*, the affirmation of racial difference centered on the inferiority or malfeasance of the Other. Whereas other-racialization is finalized by the relation of *domination*, itself reinforced by those of oppression and exploitation—a logic of interest and profit—self-racialization is finalized by the relation of *exclusion* that, by a paradoxical logical procedure, ends in the extermination of the "other" agency, that is, by the destruction of the differential relation as such.
>
> —Pierre-André Taguieff[1]

At the end of the eighteenth century, the question of whether philosophy has Greek or Oriental origins became a matter of renewed debate. The last time the question was so earnestly debated may have been in ancient times. Alluding to an existing debate over the origins of philosophy, Diogenes Laertius states his position in the opening lines of *Lives and Opinions of Eminent Philosophers*: Philosophy could not have arisen among the barbarians because they had no word or concept of it. Philosophy was an invention of the Greeks.[2]

In recounting philosophy's origins, early modern historians of philosophy remained within the frame of Biblical history. In the many works of history of philosophy from the sixteenth, seventeenth, and

eighteenth centuries, Adam, Moses, the Jews, or the Egyptians figure
as the first philosophers. Besides Diogenes's text, which was available
in several Latin and vernacular editions, extremely few early modern historians of philosophy regarded the Greeks as the first philosophers. If they did so, they were invariably following Diogenes, who
recounted a twofold Greek origin of philosophy:

> [Philosophy] started with Anaximander on the one hand,
> with Pythagoras on the other. The former was a pupil of
> Thales, Pythagoras was taught by Pherecydes. The one
> school was called Ionian, because Thales, a Milesian and
> therefore an Ionian, instructed Anaximander; the other
> school was called Italian from Pythagoras, who worked
> for the most part in Italy.[3]

This passage occurs in Diogenes's prologue, which is followed by
the first chapter: on the life and opinions of Thales. Diogenes's claim,
however, is much grander: "These authors [of contrary views] forget
that the achievements which they attribute to the barbarians belong
to the Greeks, with whom not merely philosophy but the human race
itself began."[4] Whether Diogenes means here that the barbarians are
un-Greek or that they are not human is not clear from the passage.
None of Diogenes's early modern imitators who adopted his position
claimed that the Greeks were the first humans. Furthermore, none
of them were troubled by the stories of various Greek philosophers
traveling to and studying in Egypt as they simply repeated them.[5]

The opinion of most early modern historians of philosophy
(including the ones who imitated Diogenes) was that philosophy
emerged first in the Orient. Giovanni Tortelli's *De orthographia*, which
was published and republished at least seven times during the second half of the fifteenth century and possibly the first post-medieval
work of history of philosophy modeled on *Lives and Opinions*, begins
with Zoroaster.[6] Johann Jacob Fries's *Bibliotheca philosophorum classicorum authorum chronologica* (Zurich, 1592) begins with the confusion of
languages after the destruction of Babel.[7] In the *Historiae philosophicae
libri VII* (1655) by Georg Horn, not Thales but Adam is designated the
first philosopher.[8] The first chapter of *The history of philosophy: containing the lives, opinions, actions and discourses of the philosophers of every
sect* (1655–62), which draws much of its material from Isaac Casaubon's Latin edition of *Lives and Opinions*, is devoted to Thales, "who
first introduced Natural and Mathematical Learning into *Greece*."[9]

Its author, Thomas Stanley, noted that some ancients were confused about Thales, who they believed was born in Phoenicia. He was born, rather, in the city of Miletus in southern Ionia and was of Phoenician descent.[10] Stanley recounted further that Thales traveled to Crete, Asia (Phoenicia), and Egypt, where he conferred with the priests and astronomers of Memphis. "Thus having studied Philosophy in *Egypt*, he returned to *Miletus*, and transported that vast Stock of Learning which he had there collected, into his own Country."[11] There are two elements in this account of Thales that can be seen repeatedly in early modern histories of philosophy: (1) the first philosopher of Greece as Oriental or cross-over figure and (2) the African (e.g., Egyptian) or Asian origin of Greek knowledge.

In Stanley's *History of Philosophy*, Oriental philosophies are covered at the end (the last six parts deal with Chaldean, Persian, and Sabean philosophies). This does not mean that Stanley disputed the status or priority of Oriental philosophy; for he states, "Philosophy is generally acknowledged even by the most learned of the Grecians themselves, to have had its Original in the East. None of the Eastern Nations, for Antiquity of Learning, stood in competition with the Chaldeans and Ægyptians." Citing Cicero, he designated the Chaldeans "the most ancient of Teachers."[12]

In the seventeenth century, overwhelmingly common were histories of philosophy that began with the Orientals. *De philosophia et philosophorum sectis* (1657) by Gerardus Joannes Vossius surveys the philosophies of the ancient Asians (Chaldeans, Jews, Persians, Indians, Phoenicians, and Phrygians) and Africans (Egyptians, Ethiopians, and Libyans) before turning to the philosophies of the ancient Europeans (Thracians, Druids, and Greeks).[13] Thomas Burnet's two-volume *Archaeologiae philosophicae sive doctrina antiqua de rerum originibus* (republished several times since the first edition of 1692) starts with Noah.[14] The Cartesian philosopher Abraham de Grau begins his history of philosophy with Moses, but names Thales *primus sapiens*.[15] In *Système de philosophie: contenant la logique, métaphysique, physique & morale* (Lyon, 1691), Pierre Sylvain Régis states that the first philosophers were Greeks.[16] (Régis, too, was a Cartesian.) At the turn of the eighteenth century, Johann Franz Budde (Buddeus), a theologian and *polyhistor* at the University of Halle, held that Adam was the first philosopher.[17] In his 1716 thesis submitted to the University of Wittenberg, Polycarp Leyser argued that the Indians (and not the Hebrews) were the progenitors of all "erudition."[18] Lorenz Reinhard's *Compendium historiae philosophiae* (Leipzig, 1725) and Friedrich Gentzken's *Historia philosophiae* (Hamburg, 1724) begin with "barbaric philosophy."[19] From the *Historiae philosophiae synopsis sive De origine et progressu philosophiae* (Naples, 1728) by Giambattista Capasso et al., one learns that Adam was the first sage and that philosophy spread from the Hebrews to the other nations.[20]

In the mid-eighteenth century, Samuel Formey published a history of philosophy in which Adam figures as the first philosopher. The author comments that Adam must have been a bad philosopher to have been overcome by Eve.[21] In 1742, Johann Ernst Schubert surveyed the philosophies of the Chaldeans, Persians, Phoenicians, Arabs, Jews, Indians, Chinese, Egyptians, Ethiopians, Druids or Celts, Scythians, early Romans, and Etruscans before he surveyed the philosophies of the Greeks.[22] The other history of philosophy appearing in that year, Brucker's *Historia critica philosophiae*, also begins with the philosophical ideas of the barbarians, namely, Hebrews, Chaldeans, Persians, Indians, ancient Arabs, Phoenicians, Egyptians, Ethiopians, Celts, Etruscans and Romans, Scythians, Thracians, and Getes (Figure 1).[23] It is not until his Part II that Greek philosophy comes up. Brucker even treated Malabar, Chinese, Japanese, and Canadian (Native American) philosophies in an appended volume published in 1767.[24] Regarding philosophy's origins, Brucker made a careful distinction: The barbarians had philosophy, but the Greeks (beginning with the Ionians Thales and Anaximander) had "the correct manner of philosophizing." The Egyptians happened to arrive at their knowledge through custom and chance.[25]

In the 1780s, Friedrich Victor Lebrecht Plessing published four separate works, all arguing that a system of Egyptian knowledge was at the root of all Greek philosophies.[26] Plessing and other Egyptomaniacs assumed that Jewish, Greek, and Egyptian philosophies were built on surviving remnants of a more ancient system, which they did not necessarily distinguish from divine revelation. They regarded this ancient theology (*prisca theologia* or *prisca sapientia*) to be as old as, and related to, the Mosaic revelation.[27] Renaissance philosophers supposed that this ancient knowledge was somewhat better preserved in the Greek texts of Hermes Trismegistus, reputed to be an Egyptian high priest. The Florentines Marsilio Ficino and Giovanni Pico della Mirandolla compiled Hermes's texts into a *Corpus Hermeticum*.[28] Even after 1614, the year in which French classicist Isaac Casaubon disclosed that the *Corpus Hermeticum* was not as ancient as believed, historians of philosophy did not modify their account of the Egyptians in the development of philosophy.[29]

The belief that scientific knowledge first arose in Egypt or Asia persisted into the late eighteenth century. Johann August Eberhard's

HISTORIA PHILOSOPHIÆ

A N T E D I L U V I A N Æ

P O S T D I L U V I A N Æ, & quidem

BARBARICÆ, inter gentes

Orientis, Hebræorum
Chaldæorum
Perfarum
Indorum
Arabum
Phœnicum.

Meridiei, Ægyptiorum
Æthiopum.

Occidentis, Celtarum f. Gallorum
Britannorum
Germanorum & Septentrionalium verfus oc-
cidentem habitantium
Romanorum veterum.

Septentrionis, five Hyperboreorum
Scytharum
Thracum, Getarum, &c.

GRÆCÆ, quæ fuit vel
Mythologica
Politica
Artificialis; quæ per duos quafi ramos propagata, eft
fectarum ortarum vel

a Thalete, Jonicorum
Socraticorum genuinorum
Cyrenaicorum
Eliacorum
Megaricorum, f. Erifticorum
Academicorum, & quidem
Academiæ primæ
mediæ
novæ f.
quartæ
quintæ
Ariftotelicorum
Cynicorum
Stoicorum,

a Pythagora, Pythagoricorum, f. Italicorum
Eleaticorum
Heracliteorum
Epicureorum
Pyrrhoniorum, f. Scepticorum.

Hift. phil. Tom. I.

F

Ut

Figure 1. Table of contents of the first volume of Jacob Brucker's *Historia critica philosophiae* (1742–4).

Allgemeine Geschichte der Philosophie (Halle, 1788) is an example.[30] Eberhard's general history of philosophy is organized into three major periods. The first period spans from the origins of philosophy to 500 AD. The second spans from 500 to 1500, and the third from 1500 to Eberhard's present. The first division further divides into three segments: the first covering "non-Greek peoples," namely, the Hebrews, Chaldeans, Persians, Arabs, Egyptians, Indians, Chinese, Phoenicians, Scythians, Getes, and Celts; the second covering the Greeks; and the third Romans. This is the order in which Eberhard presented the early history of philosophy in lectures at the University of Halle.

During the second half of the eighteenth century, a major alternative to the belief in an Egyptian origin of scientific civilization was the belief in an Indian one. John Zephaniah Holwell, a former governor of British Bengal, claimed that the mythology and cosmology of the Egyptians, Greeks, and Romans were adopted from Indian Brahmins and that the Hindu scriptures complete the Biblical revelation.[31] Alexander Dow, a colonel in the army of the East India Company and translator of Muhammad Qāsim Firishtah's *History of Hindostan*, wrote that the Hindus were a nation older than all others and that India was the source of all human "wisdom." Dow's English translation, prefaced with a "Dissertation Concerning the Customs, Manners, Language, Religion and Philosophy of the Hindoos," was translated into French by 1769 and German by 1772–4.[32] Dow's French translator affirmed that the Persians, Egyptians, Greeks, and perhaps also the Chinese had inherited their philosophies from the Hindus.

As early as 1756, in *Essai sur les moeurs et l'esprit des nations*, Voltaire entertained the hypothesis that the first human beings assembled into tribes on the banks of the Ganges River. He called India the cradle of all the arts.[33] After reading a French manuscript titled *Ezourvedam* in 1760, Voltaire became convinced that India rather than China had been the site of the world's oldest civilization and, formerly, the most pristine religion, which he believed was a kind of deism. This French text of a supposed Veda was printed in 1778 and was translated into German in the following year. Three years later, Pierre Sonnerat declared it a forgery.[34]

In 1761, under the immediate impression of the *Ezourvedam*, Voltaire added a section to his *Essai sur les moeurs* in which India is described as the most ancient civilization, on which all others depended.[35] Voltaire wrote to the Marquis du Deffand: "we owe [to the Indians] our numbers, our backgammon, our chess, our first principles of geometry, and the fables which have become our own."[36] Voltaire wrote to Frederick II of Prussia: "our holy Christian religion is solely based upon the ancient religion of Brahma."[37] A felicitous geography such as India's had to produce in men an abhorrence for killing and a feeling of universal charity.[38]

Voltaire was not a disinterested student of Indian civilization. He utilized information about the history, religion, and wisdom of the Indians for his attacks against Christian dogmas and the Catholic Church. He relished the thesis that the Indians have historical priority to the peoples of the Bible. Voltaire presented Brahmanism as prefiguring the corruption of religion by priest and pope. The ancient Brahmins knew an uncorrupted monotheistic religion, but they let it degenerate into superstition, polytheism, and vapid ritualism for their self-gain.[39]

In 1775, Voltaire wrote in open letters addressed to Jean-Sylvain Bailly that astronomy, astrology, and the theory of metempsychosis had spread from India to the West. In his replies, Bailly argued that the Persians, Chinese, and Indians had to be descended from a common ancestral people and that the barbarous Greeks were taught by the Brahmins.[40] Bailly and a colleague, Guillaume Le Gentil, promoted the view that Indian astronomy was original and most ancient.[41] In "Remarks on the astronomy of the brahmins," which John Playfair read before the Royal Academy of Edinburgh on March 2, 1789, the mathematician maintained that Indian astronomy was the most ancient; not derivable from the astronomy of either the Greeks, Arabs, Persians, or Tartars.[42]

Dow's and Holwell's views were repeated many more times by others during the eighteenth century. In an account of his *Travels in Europe, Asia, and Africa*, which was available in three separate editions, William MacIntosh repeated the claim that India was the "mother of science and art."[43] French botanist Pierre Sonnerat, who published an account of his journeys to the East Indies from 1744 to 1781, further circulated the stories of Indian wisdom. He reported of similarities between the mythology and religious doctrines of the Indians and those of other Asian nations, explaining that India was the birthplace of all nations, their religions, and laws. Sonnerat's *Voyage aux Indes Orientales et à la Chine* was available in several German editions.[44] Christian Wilhelm Dohm recounts similar stories in *Geschichte der Engländer und Franzosen im östlichen Indien* (1776). This work was brought out within a year of the publication of Dohm's translation of Edward Ives's travel account.[45] "[T]he World does not now contain Annals of more indisputable Antiquity than those delivered down by the ancient Bramins," declares Nathaniel Brassey Halhed in *A code of Gentoo laws*, his translation of the Persian text of the *Vivadārṇavasetu*.[46]

Belief in the Asian origin of the human species was perpetuated by Johann Gottfried Herder. He proffered the thesis that the written languages of the West went back to Oriental prototypes; more specifically, that Greek grammar was descended from Oriental antecedents.[47] Herder makes similar claims in *Ideen zur Philosophie der Geschichte der Menschheit* (1784–91).[48] His earlier work, *Auch eine Philosophie der Geschichte zur Bildung der Menschheit* (1774), contains more of the same concerning human origins.[49] One of Herder's friends was Friedrich Majer, a mythologist who claimed to have discovered "original monotheism" in ancient Indian sources.[50] Majer's unfinished *Allgemeines Mythologisches Lexikon* (1803–4) contains the thesis that both the priests of Egypt and the sages of Greece inherited their wisdom from the Indians.[51]

Not every Indomaniac located the ultimate origin of scientific civilization in India. William Jones did not regard India as the ultimate source, but as an offshoot. He conjectured that Pythagoras as well as Plato and the sages of India derived their sublime theories from a third, earlier source.[52] Jones wrote in a letter to Lord Monboddo (James Burnett) that, even after a cursory study of the philosophy of the Brahmins, one could identify Platonic doctrines in the Brahmin school of Vedānta.[53] He detected the influence of Indian logic on Greek logic, and, as already mentioned, he was the first to announce an apparent kinship among Greek, Latin, Germanic, Celtic, Persian, and Sanskrit languages.[54] Jones's friend and associate N. B. Halhed still preferred to think that the ideas of Pythagoras, Mani, and Thales had an Indian source.[55] Scholarly papers by Jones and other members of the Asiatic Society of Bengal were published in the Society's journal, *Asiatic Researches*. The first three volumes (1788–90) were translated into German (1795–6) and French (1802 and 1805).[56]

That philosophy's origins are Greek was, in the eighteenth century, the opinion of an extreme minority of historians. This opinion was most elaborately expounded by Christoph Meiners (1747–1810), professor of philosophy (his title was *ordentlicher Lehrer der Weltweisheit*) at the University of Göttingen, member of the Göttingen Royal Society of Sciences, and author of at least forty-four monographs (including several multivolume works) and one hundred and eighty journal articles on psychology, aesthetics, the histories of science, philosophy, and universities, and the natural history of ancient and modern peoples (early anthropology or ethnology).[57] Britta Rupp-Eisenreich attributes to him a significant role in shaping anthropology in Germany and France.[58] Meiners published a two-volume history of ancient Greek and Roman sciences that by the nineteenth century reached a Europe-wide readership through a French translation prepared by J. C. Laveaux.[59] Meiners is included in Johann Gustav Droysen's account of the "Göttingen Historical School," which Droysen credits with developing *Weltgeschichte, Universalgeschichte*, and the natural history of mankind. Meiners was a contributor to the Enlightenment science of man, "the central science of the time," "the royal science of the second half of the century."[60] It is also significant that Meiners was a professor at Göttingen.[61] According to John Zammito, Meiners laid out a theory of knowledge in *Revision der Philosophie* (1772) that served as a kind of manifesto for the Göttingen School.[62]

Meiners was an anthropological writer of some status among the educated and bureaucratic elites of late eighteenth-century Germany. Though other anthropological writers strongly disagreed with his views and may have ridiculed him in private, in public they praised him for his vast learning and paid him deference. As a university professor and privy councillor (*Hofrat*), Meiners enjoyed the esteem and support of the Hanoverian regime. Susanne Zantop makes the case that in the context of certain eighteenth-century intellectual trends, cultural attitudes, and political developments, Meiners could have been an academic writer who had a significant following. He was esteemed enough to be asked by Tsar Alexander to lead the reorganization of the Russian university system. He subsequently became an honorary professor of the University of Moscow.[63]

Among Meiners's numerous works is a one-volume history of philosophy, *Grundriss der Geschichte der Weltweisheit* (1786; 2nd ed. 1789).[64] It is the only work by Meiners of the history of philosophy genre. What Meiners argues concerning Oriental philosophy in this work is consistent with his account of the rise of scientific civilization in *Geschichte des Ursprungs, Fortgangs und Verfalls der Wissenschaften in Griechenland und Rom* (1781) and with his overall vision of human nature in *Grundriss der Geschichte der Menschheit* (1785; 2nd ed. 1793).[65] Reading these works in conjunction will yield the ultimate explanation as to why Meiners excluded Africa and Asia from the history of philosophy.

With alarmist rhetoric that opens his preface, Meiners censures the "unhistorical enthusiasm" spreading to "certain secret schools among us" (in Germany?) of attributing "the most groundless ideas and systems" to "the raw or little-cultured [*wenig gebildeten*] peoples of the oldest antiquity." He characterizes this "unhistorical enthusiasm" as an "illness of the mind," "the effect of the demise of all genuine scholarship and critique" suffered by the French ("our neighbors beyond the Rhine") as much as by the ancient Greeks and Romans.[66] With *Geschichte des Ursprungs, Fortgangs und Verfalls der Wissenschaften in Griechenland und Rom*, published five years earlier, Meiners had begun his campaign against the very old opinion that colonists from Asia and Africa transmitted their sciences and arts to the uncivilized, aboriginal inhabitants of Greece. In that work, Meiners asserts that this is improbable and even contrary to history.[67] From his study of classical sources, he deduced that these foreigners were more like "refugees" than settlers, driven out of their home country by the fear of punishment for crimes they had committed or by powerful opponents, and that they did not have time enough to prepare themselves for the long years required to found new cities in Europe or to bring along every kind of knowledge and useful article necessary for a civilized existence.[68] According to Meiners, these refugees encountered in Greece "men who had an invincible hatred of foreigners," who frequently attacked and robbed them, and who could not be driven out of their lands or become accustomed to the lifestyle of the newcomers. Even after the foreigners were well established in Greece and developed advanced weapons, they remained surrounded by numerous undeterred tribes who fought against them. It did not help these settlers to have maintained no contact with their countries of origin, for they "were plundered and carried off as much as others by their former countrymen." Egyptian and Phoenician settlers, not being able to subdue the Greeks, "handed down little or nothing of cultivating knowledge and skills, except for their gods and rituals of worship, the beginnings of agriculture, and a completely useless script, and a certain number of words."[69] Meiners was claiming that, despite Egyptian and Phoenician settlements, the native Greeks did not acquire the elements of civilization from either Oriental nation. This was the Göttingen professor's elaborate reply to those who believed what classical sources state: that colonists from Egypt and Phoenicia founded civilization in Greece.

Let us turn to Meiners's *Grundriss der Geschichte der Weltweisheit*. Following the scholarly convention, this *Outline of the History of Worldly Wisdom* begins with short sections on the Chaldeans, Phoenicians, Egyptians, Arabs, Ethiopians, Persians, Hindus, Chinese, and Celts. However, every one of these sections was actually an occasion for Meiners to argue that the peoples of Africa and Asia never developed philosophy. Meiners defended his claim in several ways:

It is very difficult to judge the intellectual achievements of the Chaldeans, and of the Orientals in general, because of defective documents, adulterated traditions, entrenched prejudices of secretive sects, and the teachings of priests.[70] No ancient Greek writer ever attributed his nation's sciences to the barbarians. (On its surface, this statement is false.) In fact, several Greeks attest to the infantile or mediocre quality of Oriental knowledge.[71] The "delusion" of an Oriental origin of science was spread by the historians of Alexander the Great and by non-Greek writers who used Greek knowledge in attempts to elevate the status of their nation vis-à-vis the Greeks. Ultimately, neither the form of government nor the religion nor the architectural works of the Chaldeans give reasons to assume that the arts and sciences flourished on the ancient banks of the Euphrates and Tigris.[72]

Meiners did concede some things to the Phoenicians: Their contributions to civilization were not insignificant, but their achievements do not warrant counting them "among the enlightened peoples."[73] (He gave no further explanation.) The fragments of Sanchuniathon, which are often consulted for information on Phoenician doctrines and sagas, were probably forged. Likewise, the Phoenician account of Creation could have been a priestly forgery. Some have wanted to ascribe to the Phoenicians a genuine concept of God, but the persistent custom of human sacrifice among them and the Carthaginians does not speak in favor of this.[74]

Meiners held a relatively higher opinion of the Egyptians: "Among all the peoples of the ancient world, none other can claim with greater justice renown for originality and early civilization than the Egyptians."[75] Their monuments surpass those of all other Asian and African nations in boldness and durability, "but in respect to true beauty and scale" they fall behind the Greek.[76] The climate, their form of government, and religion prevented the growth of the arts and sciences. The late and drawn-out development of Greek science indicates that the Greeks had never borrowed the elements of science from the Egyptians. "[The study of] history and geography, natural history, medicine, and mathematics of the Egyptian priests remained in a perennial childhood before their enlightenment [Aufklärung] through the Greeks."[77] According to Martin Bernal, playing-down the role of Phoenicians and Egyptians in the founding of Greek civilization was central to the strategy of scholars, starting in the late eighteenth century, who re-imagined an exclusively Greek pedigree for European civilization in conformity with their assumptions about European racial superiority.[78]

When sources gave conflicting accounts of the civilization of the barbarians, Meiners indulged his prejudice. In regard to the Ethiopians, he chose to follow Herodotus and Strabo and not Diodorus Siculus. The reports of the first two are that the Ethiopians were a barbaric people who had adopted a few of their customs from the Egyptians and not much else.[79] (Diodorus, on the other hand, reports that Egypt was a colony of the Ethiopians.) Meiners opted to follow Herodotus regarding the Persians. That Greek historian states that they were a barbarous nomadic nation as late as the era of Cyrus II. Meiners also dismissed the ancient opinion that the monuments at Persepolis were older than the first Persian conquests. He doubted both ancient and modern accounts of Zoroaster, stating that the Persian sage was overrated.[80] He acknowledged that modern Parsis were unanimously attributed with the worship of the true God, but so far as he could tell, the evidence "[bore] out no exact proof."[81]

When Meiners doubted certain ancient authors and not others, the choice can only be described as arbitrary. For instance, he did not deem as credible the reports of Nearchus and Onesicritus (in the company of Alexander the Great), Megasthenes (the envoy of Seleucus Nicator to Chandragupta's court at Pataliputra in 302–291 BCE), Apollonius, and Palladius.[82] These ancient writers testify to the existence of philosophy in India. As for the similarities between various Brahmin and Greek schools of philosophy, Meiners had an explanation:

> It is most probable that the Hindus were students of the Greeks. This becomes probable not only through the many thousands of Greeks settling in Hindustan after Alexander, through the Greek kings who ruled for a long period over part of Hindustan, through the Greek language which persisted in this country for several centuries; but also through the many other undeniable traces of Greek and Christian knowledge left over among the Hindus.[83]

Philosophy was transmitted to India by Greek settlers. Meiners was not open to the reverse possibility: that philosophy was transmitted to Greece from India.

Meiners then questioned the credibility of the reports on the civilization of the Chinese. He contended that the antiquity of Chinese religion was exaggerated and that the reports of the Jesuits were embellished in order to reflect favorably on the Chinese, who were a superstitious and polytheistic people.[84] The Jesuits had claimed that they had discovered monotheism in the sacred scriptures of the Chinese. Meiners did not think that these sacred scriptures were actually sacred because they deal only with a few moral principles. He was not surprised that certain Chinese writers expressed clear concepts of

God, world, and soul. This could easily be explained by the influx into the country of Brahmins, fakirs, Christians, and Arabs as recently as the ninth century.[85]

Where did philosophy first arise if not in the East? Adopting the position of Diogenes Laertius, Meiners claimed that philosophy first arose in the Greek cities on the western edge of Asia (Ionia). Conditions in this region promoted material prosperity, which in turn nourished the first flowering of art and science.[86]

Historiographers of philosophy have known about Meiners's *Grundriss der Geschichte der Weltweisheit*, but they seem to have missed *Grundriss der Geschichte der Menschheit* and other anthropological writings by Meiners. Previous historiographers of philosophy have not mentioned that Meiners's account of the historical origin of philosophy is completely consistent with his racist anthropological views. The *Grundriss der Geschichte der Menschheit* (*Outline of the History of Mankind*), which introduced university and *Gymnasium* students to Meiners's anthropology, begins by laying out in a synoptic fashion the results of his researches into the natural history of mankind. In the opening pages, the author presents the human species as two large divisions: "the Tartar, or Caucasian" and "the Mongolian." Under the second division are listed the Chinese, Tibetans, Kalmucks, Samoyeds, lower-caste Hindus, and the blacks of New Guinea, New Holland (Australia), and Africa. The peoples of this division Meiners describes categorically as "weaker in body and mind" and "more depraved and vicious" than those of the Caucasian division. Under the Caucasian division, two races (*Racen*) are distinguished: Celtic and Slavic.[87] Under the Celtic race are listed Greeks, Germans, Italians, Gauls, Spaniards, Britons, Irishmen, and Scandinavians. Meiners did not provide any specific names of Slavic peoples. In Meiners's classification, the Celtic race possesses intellectual and moral qualities superior to those of the Slavic race. (Apparently, his anthropological studies did not turn him into a cultural or moral relativist.) In the second edition of *Grundriss der Geschichte der Menschheit*, published in 1793, the names Caucasian and Mongolian are replaced with "the white, or light-colored, and beautiful" and "the dark-colored and ugly."[88] This change was probably an attempt to redress the confusion and criticism arising from the initial naming of his two large divisions. Meiners now also introduced a third white race. The Egyptians, Jews, Arabs, Persians, and upper-caste Hindus were brought together under an "Oriental" (white) race. In 1793, Meiners still maintained for the Celtic peoples the distinction of being the white race with the greatest intellectual and moral qualities.[89] "All these white peoples have several common characteristics, yet the Slavic and Near-Eastern peoples agree with each other more than with the Germanic and other Celtic nations."[90]

From reading only a portion of Meiners's corpus, it becomes clear that innate differences between the races explained for him literally everything about the course of human affairs, beginning with the way in which human groups were dispersed over the earth and the ancestry and kinship between nations. Racial differences explained why the "great law-givers, sages, and heroes" were white and why Mongolian peoples never developed sciences. If some dark-and-ugly nations did exhibit some scientific activity, this could have come about only through their interaction with Whites. In any case, history showed Meiners that the arts and sciences tended to degenerate in the hands of dark-and-ugly nations. Finally, racial differences explained why Europeans have almost always dominated all other peoples of the earth and why political rights have existed among Whites, while "the most horrible despotism slams its unshakeable throne upon the majority of peoples of the earth." For Meiners, the laws and political constitutions of European nations and the European Enlightenment itself were direct evidence of the superior intellectual and moral faculties innate to their race.[91]

Fortunately for our historical investigation, Meiners left behind works of both ethnology and history of philosophy. They show us how racism and Eurocentric history of philosophy go hand in hand. Tiedemann and Tennemann, the only other eighteenth-century historians of philosophy to exclude Africa and Asia, did not publish ethnological works and never in print discussed the differences between human races, but in their histories of philosophy they deploy a set of racist anthropological tropes that Meiners had formulated for his works of history of philosophy and history of science.

The second eighteenth-century historian of philosophy to exclude Africa and Asia was Dieterich Tiedemann (1748–1803).[92] It is not a trivial fact that Tiedemann was a childhood friend of Meiners's. Born less than one year apart, they were students at the same *Gymnasium* in Bremen and then at the Georg-August University in Göttingen. According to biographical dictionaries, it was through Meiners's influence that Tiedemann gave up the study of theology to devote himself fully to philosophy.[93] While Meiners stayed on at Göttingen, becoming a professor in 1772, Tiedemann accepted a position as tutor in the household of Baron Budberg in Livonia. His return to Göttingen five years later, in 1774, was facilitated by Meiners. Tiedemann completed his education under the classicist Christian Gottlob Heyne and, in 1776, became a professor of classical languages at the Collegium Carolinum in Kassel. In 1786, along with most of the Collegium professors, he was transferred to the University of Marburg, where he was promoted to the rank of *professor ordinarius* of philosophy and also named Privy Councillor.

In the years 1791–7, Tiedemann brought out a six-volume work of history of philosophy: *Geist der spekulativen Philosophie von Thales bis Sokrates*.[94] In the foreword, the author concedes that historians of philosophy are "all unanimous" that philosophy came from the oldest nations of Africa and Asia.[95] He, on the other hand, would exclude the Orientals because their opinions, though touching on philosophical themes, are not backed up with reasons, are not based on concepts and experience, and so do not qualify as philosophy. (One recalls that a similar analysis of Oriental philosophies was offered by Jacob Brucker, but he did not derive from it a reason to exclude the Orientals from the history of philosophy.) Tiedemann also rejected philosophy that was created through the poetic muse or supported with reputations, revelation, or tradition.[96] He urged that these kinds of opinions be barred from the history of philosophy.[97] So far as he could tell, the doctrines of the Chaldeans, Persians, Indians, and Egyptians "contain mere poetry of times still half-brutish" or are based on religious representations.[98] Tiedemann declares, "We have no right to speak of the philosophy of these peoples, nor do we have the right to include such doctrines in the history of philosophy."[99]

Johann Gottlieb Buhle, a professor of philosophy at Göttingen and a Kantian, seemed more open to the possibility that the oldest philosophical ideas derive from the religions of the oldest nations. His *Lehrbuch der Geschichte der Philosophie und einer kritischen Literatur derselben* (1796–1804) follows the convention of giving brief summaries of the philosophical ideas of the barbarian peoples (Egyptians, Jews, Phoenicians, Chaldeans, Persians, Indians, Chinese, Celts, and Scandinavians).[100] Buhle added several caveats, however: Historical certainty is not possible. Myths are not reliable for discovering which people was the first civilizers or whether a people could even evolve from a brutish condition to a civilized one. Even if it were discovered who the first civilizers were, it would still leave open the question of whether philosophy was native to that people.[101]

Such difficulties, however, did not stop Buhle from weighing the reasons for an Indian origin of philosophy against those for an Egyptian origin. Based on historical records available to him, his assessment was that the Egyptians were one of the oldest nations, and, according to the majority of ancient and modern scholars, they were the people from whom all culture, religion, and philosophy spread.[102]

To those who asked from whom the Egyptians were descended or to whom they were culturally indebted, Buhle replied that the question could not be answered to one's complete satisfaction. There were divergent views: One recent scholar, relying on the reports of Diodorus Siculus, claimed that the Egyptians were a colony of the Ethiopians, but this claim was sharply contested by Buhle's colleague, Meiners. More recently, the Ethiopian thesis was strongly defended by Arnold Hermann Heeren, another colleague at Göttingen.[103]

In an early section, "On the Philosophy of the Hindustanis," Buhle proceeds cautiously, stating that the obscurity of ancient Indian history and the dearth of solid historical facts make it impossible to decide whether the western Asian nations received their religion and philosophy from the Indians or the reverse. He ventured to say, however, that the latter possibility was more likely. His reasoning was that Indian religion and philosophy, at least from the time of Alexander's conquest, consisted of no original cult and no original system of philosophy, but appeared rather as a fabric woven together from the religions and philosophies of other peoples, which later came to appear as original. Buhle knew that India, since very early times, was a country visited by foreigners for trade or settlement. Therefore, it seemed to him more likely that civilization spread from Egypt to India.[104]

Buhle then described a similar situation between Greek and Indian philosophies. He was aware that elements of various Greek philosophies were espoused by opposing Brahmin schools. Some Brahmins taught that the world was created from atoms. Other Brahmins attributed the world with two eternally opposed principles. Yet other Brahmins claimed that the highest intelligence, the perfect and divine Being, was the source and creator of all things or that a divine world-soul subsisted throughout nature from which the souls of men and animals arose and to which their souls returned. Some Brahmins claimed that the world was eternal, while others claimed that the world would be destroyed in time.[105] Buhle's explanation was one already formulated by Meiners: The mixed-up doctrines of the most celebrated Greek philosophical schools were disseminated in India by Greeks after Alexander's conquest and by Romans and Arabs thereafter.[106] I regard Buhle as a borderline case of the exclusion of Africa and Asia from the history of philosophy.

Tennemann, the third historian of philosophy of the eighteenth century (after Tiedemann) to exclude Africa and Asia, tried to get around the debate by simply asserting the Greek origin of philosophy. The first volume of his *Geschichte der Philosophie* (1798–1819) begins right away with the Greeks, but without mentioning that doing so is controversial. The first line of the first chapter reads: "The Greek nation is singular in history. . . ." This is followed by some arguments for Greek originality. The author then states, "The physical and political constitution of Greece, the spirit and character, the education and activity of the inhabitants [brought] together so many important advantages for the development and cultivation of the human mind, which one will not easily come across in other countries of the time."[107] Greek philosophy meets the requirement that philosophy be independent of political interests.[108] This requirement is set by Kant himself in his lectures on logic from the early 1770s: "This much is certain: Before *philosophia* had utterly and completely separated itself from the power of the government and from the authority of the clergy in a nation, no philosophy could really be produced."[109] While not denying the philosophical spirit in other nations, Tennemann singled out the Greeks for developing it independently.[110] Philosophy developed in Greece "without the admixture of foreign elements" and was transmitted to all subsequent civilized peoples.[111] Tennemann did not make reference to an ongoing debate, but from these statements it is evident that he had to address the question of philosophy's origins at least in order to make a strong statement against the theory of Oriental beginnings.

Like Meiners, Tiedemann, and Tennemann, de Gérando excluded Africa and Asia from the history of philosophy. Of the twenty-nine general histories of philosophy produced in Germany after Brucker, de Gérando recommended the histories by Tiedemann, Buhle, Meiners, Tennemann, Eberhard, Bardili, Gurlitt, Fülleborn, and Garve. He recommended also the notes accompanying Ernst Platner's *Philosophische Aphorismen*, the learned dissertations by Christian Heyne, the published proceedings of the Göttingen Society and Berlin Academy of Sciences, and Michael Hissmann's *Magazin für die Philosophie und ihre Geschichte*.[112] Informed by some of the newest German works on the history of philosophy, de Gérando argues in his *Histoire comparée* that "the collections of opinions of the ancient sages of Asia, Phoenicia, and Egypt" do not belong in the history of philosophy because they do not form an ensemble of connected parts, "because they appear to rest on an instinct of belief rather than on a critical analysis," and "because it [the instinct of belief] carries no trace of discipline and methods." Most importantly, "they appear to be entirely foreign to that *first philosophy* that we defined in the introduction to this work; to that philosophy which alone can give to human opinions a legitimate sanction, by subordinating them to the fundamental principles that constitute the prerogatives and rights of reason."[113] De Gérando then expounded a Greek beginning for philosophy:

> It was among the Greeks, and around the time of their prosperity and glory, that philosophy, by a first and brilliant revolution, first started to take on a systematic form, to reform the ideas theretofore fragmentary and incoherent into a reasoned theory, founded on immutable principles, explained by the rules of logic, and guaranteed by reflections made on the faculties of the human mind. From that moment we see the whole history of philosophy divide itself into five great periods, of which the beginning is signaled by a change almost total in the heart of ideas, by the appearance of extraordinary men, by the founding of new schools, by great political circumstances, and finally what matters greatly to be noted here, by a variation no less perceptible in the systems relative to the *first philosophy*, that is to say, to the principles of human knowledge.[114]

Another early nineteenth-century participant in the debate was Friedrich August Carus (1770–1807), a philosopher at the University of Leipzig.[115] In his *Ideen zur Geschichte der Philosophie* (1809), Carus weighs the arguments for the exclusion of non-Greek peoples from the history of philosophy against the arguments for retaining them.[116] He enumerated the arguments of his peers: The ideas of non-Greek peoples are not genuinely philosophical or are a later, Hellenized product. Conditions were not favorable to philosophy (hot climate, despotism, etc.). Available philosophical sources are fragmentary, exhibit "leaps of fantasy," lack coherency with Greek philosophy or lack coherency altogether. Historical ties between Greek and non-Greek philosophies are indeterminate. The travel accounts of ancient Greeks tend to be poeticized and, thus, are suspect. Historical sources are scant. Philosophical sources are either nonexistent, very deficient, or extremely obscure. Most of these documents are still awaiting critical clarification.[117]

Carus then enumerated the reasons that spoke loudly against a complete exclusion of the non-Greek peoples. Firstly, the activity of reason is never completely dormant. If one were so strict about the philosophical integrity of the products of reason, then the history of philosophy may not even begin with Thales; for his thought was not systematic. It is not so impossible to imagine some relation between the so-called barbaric and Greek philosophies. Both Greeks and barbarians have their origins in the same early period of human history. Both raised themselves above the state of immaturity (i.e., they became civilized). There is also the concrete geographical and chronological connection between Greek philosophy and Asia Minor. Even if the Greeks poeticized their voyages, should we regard their accounts as nothing? Could later authors have lied or deluded themselves about the ties between Egypt and Hindustan? Even the most rigorous critique still leaves intact the commonalities between the Ionians in the time of Anaxagoras and the Persians. Even if it were true that Hellenic systems have nothing in common with Oriental philosophy, this would not be true of the systems of the Alexandrian philosophers, Church Fathers, and Arabs. Carus was inclined even to argue that Europe's philosophical heritage was half-Oriental and half-Greek. He was referring to the transmission of Greek philosophy to modern Europeans by way of the Oriental world, which was similar to what happened with Christianity. He could also point to the Oriental and mystical qualities of neo-Platonism.[118]

Concerning philosophy's origins, Carus did not think that the question was so important. It suffices to know something about the social order, religion, and morality of the Orientals, which could yield information about "philosophical culture" before Thales. An alternative is to begin one's history of philosophy with the era of Alexander the Great, when the Orientals allegedly became acquainted with Greek ideas.[119] Nevertheless, Carus invoked the law of continuity, according to which no gaps in nature exist: Some mention of whatever preceded Greek philosophy is necessary.[120]

Still excluded are America and the greater part of Africa. The peoples of those parts remain "shrouded in darkness."[121] Carus excluded Egypt as well because there was no evidence of "metaphysical philosophy" among the Egyptians. Indians and Persians, however, met Carus's qualifications, but in their case philosophy was religion or the first philosophical systems sprang from their religion.[122] Carus also noted the similarity between Brahmin and Greek schools and, like Meiners and Buhle, explained it as resulting from the diffusion of Greek thought in India in the period after Alexander the Great.[123]

In discussing the Greeks, Carus was as unequivocal as Tennemann regarding this nation's "incredible originality."[124] The Greeks were blessed, he declared. They show intelligence in every branch of science. Under the early and favorable conditions of a mild climate, prosperity, and the enriching confluence of several peoples; with the qualities of freedom, independence, and a good political constitution, the Greeks paved the way for "true and genuine philosophy."[125] Carus did not outright reject the claim that the Greeks had acquired some of the substance of their culture from the Egyptians, but he did not have to. He just had to question the significance of this. He asked rhetorically, is there any people that received no contribution to its culture from another people? Obviously, no. For Carus, this still did not diminish the "creative genius" that set the Greeks apart from all other peoples.[126] "They, the sublime nation, gave back to the Asian and African the meager knowledge that was received from them but with prolific increase. They remained the only nation that developed itself and then showed itself to be more humanized and delicate than all others."[127] In the history of the history of philosophy, this may be the first formulation of the trope of Greek "creative genius" or creative transformation. Instead of denying African and Asian influences on Greek culture, Carus asserted that whatever cultural elements the Greeks got from foreign peoples, through their innate capacities and creative activity, the Greeks developed and transformed them into real culture, for which they must take the credit. We shall see this trope again in Tennemann's *Grundriss der Geschichte der Philosophie* and in Hegel's lectures.[128]

But what did Greek creative genius mean in practical terms for the history of philosophy? Carus recommended that non-European philosophy (*aussereuropäische Philosophie*) be included, but separated from the historical development of Greek philosophy.[129] Here, Carus struck the perfect compromise, reflecting his perfect ambivalence, between total exclusion and unqualified inclusion. Carus's compromise is important because in it Tennemann and Hegel would find their solution.

Tennemann was still several years away from completing the eleventh volume of his *Geschichte der Philosophie*, when he published a one-volume epitome, *Grundriss der Geschichte der Philosophie* (1812).[130] In the second edition (1816) of the *Grundriss*, Tennemann answers criticisms of his approach to the history of philosophy, including the criticism that he began his history with the Greeks instead of the Orientals. Tennemann defended his work, stating that the reasons given by Carus and Carl Bachmann in favor of Oriental philosophy did not prove that Oriental philosophy constituted an inseparable part of the history of philosophy.[131] He did not deny that the study of Oriental philosophemes was of serious interest.[132] However, the scholarly interest in the Orient Tennemann wanted to clearly distinguish from the interest of the history of philosophy proper. Notwithstanding these points, he would present for the first time a brief overview of the philosophemes and religious ideas of those preeminent Oriental peoples who had a connection to the Greeks—namely, the Indians, Tibetans, Chinese, Egyptians, Chaldeans, Persians, Hebrews, and Phoenicians. Even the archaic Greeks were included in the group of philosophemic peoples. The short paragraphs, constituting the "brief overview," conclude the formal "Introduction" to the *Grundriss der Geschichte der Philosophie*, which is followed by the actual history of philosophy in three parts or periods, with Part One covering Greek philosophy. Tennemann still insisted, therefore, that the history of philosophy begins with the Greeks. The argument that this people was uniquely original he already used in 1798, but he now also argued that while all peoples have the same capacity to turn philosophy into a science, not all peoples have done so and, thus, not all peoples can claim a place in the history of philosophy.[133] Though it is true that the Greeks were dependent on others for some of the material and stimulus for their philosophy, they proceeded independently in their philosophical training.[134]

Tennemann contrasted the Greeks to the Orientals: In age and culture, the Orientals may have preceded the Greeks, but they never reached the same grade as the Greeks. Their wisdom has the character of divine revelation or was formed out of *Phantasie*. The character of their thought being mytho-symbolic, reason is not the basis of their beliefs, speculative views, and assumptions. Oriental thoughts regarding God, world, and mankind, which are not to be denied, were not intended as and did not result in philosophy. Tennemann cited climate, despotism, and the caste system as conditions opposed to the free development of the mind.[135] Then, as if he had not exhausted the issue, Tennemann added the following paragraph:

> Therefore, the beginning of the history is with the Greeks and in the period when a higher grade of reason developed out of the culture of fantasy and understanding; a period in which they strove after clarity of concepts and structures of knowledge and began to seek principles. This happened from the time of Thales.[136]

Like other proponents of the Greek origin of philosophy, Tennemann had to explain away persistent stories of Egyptian, Phoenician, and Phrygian colonies in early, uncivilized Greece. The Kantian philosopher did not have to deny that colonists brought "some ideas and perspectives from Asia." He just had to question how much of this foreign material was taken up by the Greeks. Doubts about the influence of Egyptian and Asian colonies in Greece were as good as positive arguments for the exclusion of Egypt and Asia from the history of philosophy.

"This much is agreed upon," asserted Tennemann, "that the Greek nation, through its spirit and character, possessed not just a peculiar ability for learning, but also a high grade of intellectual power," which enabled them to transform foreign inventions and ideas into something peculiarly their own.[137] This is the now familiar trope of Greek "creative genius," which Carus introduced into the historiography of philosophy and to which Hegel would resort in his lectures on the history of philosophy. By incorporating Carus's trope of the Greek transformation of foreign ideas, Tennemann bolstered his arguments supporting the Greek beginning of philosophy.

Tennemann argued that it was Greek thought that was passed down to the Romans and modern Europeans. The successive stages or periods of this passing-down constitute the history of philosophy.[138] It so happens that the philosophers in this line of transmission are all Celtic (white). If an Oriental nation had science, it could only have come into possession of it by appropriating the scientific learning of the Greeks or another white nation. These implicit and explicit arguments could have been taken right out of Meiners's publications, specifically the *Geschichte des Ursprungs, Fortgangs und Verfalls der Wissenschaften in Griechenland und Rom* and the *Grundriss der Geschichte der Weltweisheit*.[139] The component arguments concerning the geography, climate, material prosperity, and political culture of Greece that make up the claim of the Greek invention of science were conceived earlier in the Enlightenment, but Meiners was the one who brought them together in the form in which one finds them in Tennemann's *Grundriss der Geschichte der Philosophie*.

In Chapter 1, I showed that Tennemann's approach to the history of philosophy conforms to Kantian principles that determined the organization and content of that history. I now pose the question, does the exclusion of Africa and Asia from the history of philosophy—the determination that philosophy is European—specifically conform to Kant's thought? The answer is most definitely yes if we refer to Kant's own statements. "No people on earth began to philosophize earlier than the Greeks, since no people thought through concepts, but instead all thought through images. They first began to study rules *in abstracto*. . . . The Greeks were the founders of mathematics, who demonstrated it from first grounds and elements. They are the core [*Kern*] of the human race and its benefactors."[140] Here, in this passage from Kant's logic lectures from the early 1780s, the Greeks may be understood as "the core of the human race and its benefactors" in the sense that they founded science.[141] Kant states that they were the founders of mathematics, which is one of the two kinds of rational cognition recognized by Kant. The second kind is philosophy.[142]

Later in these logic lectures, one encounters the claim that the Greeks were the first to discover mathematical demonstrations:

> The Greeks are the first to have discovered demonstrations. No people knew what it was to demonstrate before this emerged among the Greeks. It is said that the Greeks learned their wisdom from the Egyptians. But the Egyptians are children compared to the Greeks. They did have various cognitions, but not sciences. The Greeks first enlightened the human understanding. . . . No people knows what demonstrations are except those who have learned it from the Greeks. All those who did not learn it from them hold it to be folderol, and yet demonstrations are the sure step that extended insight made into mathematics.[143]

In this passage, Kant identifies mathematical demonstrations—of the kind the Egyptians do not exhibit—with scientific knowledge. He also contradicts the view that the Greeks learned science from the Egyptians, characterizing the latter as "children" in respect to science, and he claims that "[t]he Greeks first enlightened the human understanding." Let us recall that Meiners wrote in his *Grundriss der Geschichte der Weltweisheit* that Egyptian sciences remained in a childhood state before their "enlightenment" through the Greeks.[144]

Logik: ein Handbuch zu Vorlesungen (1800), a logic manual prepared by Gottlob Benjamin Jäsche based on Kant's lectures, contains a rare sketch of the history of philosophy as Kant must have told it.[145] Regarding the beginning of philosophy, Kant states:

> From [a foregoing] determination of the distinction between common and speculative use of reason we can now pass judgment on the question, with which people we must date the beginning of philosophy. Among all peoples, then, the *Greeks* first began to philosophize. For they first attempted to cultivate cognitions of reason, not with images as the guiding thread, but *in abstracto*, while other peoples always sought to make concepts understandable only *through images in concreto*. Even today there are peoples, like the Chinese and some Indians, who admittedly

deal with things that are derived merely from reason, like God, the immortality of the soul, etc., but who nonetheless do not seek to investigate the nature of these things in accordance with concepts and rules *in abstracto*. They make no separation here between the use of the understanding *in concreto* and that *in abstracto*. Among the *Persians* and the *Arabs* there is admittedly some speculative use of reason, but the rules for this they borrowed from Aristotle, hence from the Greeks. In *Zoroaster's Zend-Avesta* we find not the slightest trace of philosophy. The same holds also for the prized *Egyptian* wisdom, which in comparison with Greek philosophy was mere child's play.

As in philosophy, so too in regard to mathematics, the Greeks were the first to cultivate this part of the cognition of reason in accordance with a speculative, scientific method, by demonstrating every theorem from elements.[146]

Neither Chinese nor Indians, neither Persians nor Arabs had either philosophy or mathematics (unless they borrowed it from the Greeks). Neither the *Zend-Avesta* nor Egyptian wisdom ("mere child's play") is philosophy. As speculative or rational cognition, philosophy began with the Greeks.

Although Kant recognized that there was some question as to "[w]hen and *where* the philosophical spirit first arose among the Greeks," he did not refrain from pronouncing that "[t]he first to introduce the speculative use of reason, and the one from whom we derive the first steps of the human understanding toward scientific culture, is *Thales*, the founder of the *Ionian* sect. He bore the surname *physicist*, although he was also a mathematician, just as in general *mathematics* has always preceded philosophy."[147] Starting in the early 1780s, students heard Kant defend the thesis of the Greek invention of not just philosophy, but of science in general.

In recent years, several important essays have appeared on the topic of Kant's racism.[148] Two scholars in particular, Robert Bernasconi and Mark Larrimore, have done much to raise awareness (not seen since 1950) of Kant's ideas of race and stimulate debate on whether and how Kant, the racist, can be reconciled with Kant, the moral universalist and anti-imperialist. Bernasconi and Larrimore have revealed a major European philosopher who, over the whole length of his teaching career, returned regularly to the problem of human diversity and inequality and sought to make positive sense of human affairs with a theory and anthropology of race.

Was Kant a racial thinker? According to Bernasconi, he was a founding theorist of race.[149] Was Kant a racist? A first-time reader of "Observations on the Feeling of the Beautiful and Sublime" (1764) may well be shocked and disturbed by Kant's racial stereotypes and racist remarks.[150] These include a passage where Kant, invoking David Hume, claims that not a single negro has ever been found who accomplished something great in art or science or showed any other praiseworthy quality.[151] A couple of pages later, he states that someone black from head to toe is proof that what he said was stupid.[152]

Is Kant's philosophy racist? Bernasconi and Larrimore argue that Kant's anthropology certainly is and his philosophy of history probably is. Starting in the 1770s and until his retirement in 1796, Kant formulated and defended a (pseudo-)scientific concept of race. He published three essays on race: "Of the Different Races of Human Beings" (1775; republished in 1777), "Determination of the Concept of a Human Race" (1785), and "On the Use of Teleological Principles in Philosophy" (1788).[153] The Kantian theory of race was consolidated and passed down to the nineteenth century through the vehicle of Christoph G. Girtanner's book, *Ueber das kantische Prinzip für die Naturgeschichte* (1796).[154] In "Of the Different Races of Human Beings," Kant identifies four distinct races: "the race of the Whites, 2) the Negro race, 3) the Hunnish (Mongolian or Kalmuck) race, and 4) the Hindu or Hindustani race."[155] In "Determination of the Concept of a Human Race," Kant again divides humanity into four races, but he now identifies them exclusively by skin color, referring to the race "of the Whites, the yellow Indian, the Negro and the copper-red American."[156] In using skin color as the prime marker of race, Kant would make a lasting contribution to the science of race. Eight years later, Meiners would rename his "Caucasian" and "Mongolian" divisions "white" and "dark."

Bernasconi argues that Kant made a crucial contribution to the modern science of race. With his concept of race, he was able to secure the unity of humanity as a natural genus while still accounting for permanent differentiations within the species. Bernasconi sums up the Kantian definition of race: "Races are deviations within this genus which maintain themselves over protracted generations, even when displaced geographically, and which produce hybrids or mulattoes, that exhibit the characteristics of both races when they interbreed with other deviations or races."[157] Thus, Kant was able to explain, as no one before him could, why racial characteristics were permanent. He did so with a theory that seeds or germs (*Keime*) in the original human beings developed to produce skin color and other characteristics under specific climatic conditions. Once the seeds had developed, the human characteristics were not subject to further change.[158]

Kant was a powerful thinker of race, who was not incapable of adopting the racial and racist ideas of others. I argue that a kind of racist feedback-loop existed between Kant and Meiners. Frank W. P. Dougherty has already noted that Meiners incorporated Kant's definition of race into the second edition of *Grundriss der Geschichte der Menschheit* and even included an explicit reference to Kant's 1785 essay.[159] Kant shared more than a few racial-anthropological descriptions and opinions with Meiners. Because Meiners published overwhelmingly more in empirical anthropology than Kant, it is more likely that the latter got his racial descriptions from the former. In Kant's anthropology lectures, the name Meiners does not appear. This is not surprising given that Meiners was a strident critic of Kant's Critical Philosophy and a rival in anthropology.

Kant's description of the races, like Meiners's, entails a hierarchy of worth. Like Meiners in his article "Ueber die Bevölkerung von America" (1788), Kant in his anthropology lectures described the native Americans as uneducable, emotionally and sexually unexcitable, barely fertile, weak, and lazy.[160] Like Meiners in "Ueber die Natur der Afrikanischen Neger" (1790), Kant described Blacks as being trainable for servitude, but not capable of self-governance and moral independence.[161] Meiners's claim of a Greek origin of scientific civilization and his characterization of Oriental knowledge are consonant with Kant's statements that the Greeks founded mathematics and philosophy and that the Hindu/Indian/yellow race never achieved an abstract concept and that their moral precepts are not based on principles. Kant said in lecture, "All Oriental peoples are not in the position to establish through concepts a single property of morality or law. Rather, all their morals are based on appearances."[162] To be completely clear, that yellow peoples are "not in a position" means that they lack the capacity for science. Only white peoples have the capacity for abstract concepts. Also, the Whites are said to be the ones who brought about all the revolutions in human history. Hindus, Americans, and Negroes have never been agents of human history. The white race is the only one marked by historical progress.[163]

Again, Kant taught that the Hindu race did not develop philosophy because they did not have that capacity. In his anthropology lectures, Kant explicitly attributes this lack *not* to the form of government or customs of the Asians, but to their descent (*Abstammung*).[164] Montesquieu had famously argued that the form of government or customs of a people determined its character. Kant taught his students that it was the other way around. It is race that determines the form of government and customs.[165] I submit that it was Meiners who presented the full version of this argument in his article "Ueber die Ursachen des Despotismus" (1788).[166] There, he argues that "the weaknesses, lack of feeling, and limitation of mind" of Mongolian peoples have led to their complete subjugation by their lords.[167] "A similar weakness, lack of feeling, and idiocy," to which Meiners adds "cowardice," in Negroes and Americans were the causes of their easy submission to arbitrary domination.[168] "Therefore, the freedom or slavery of peoples has existed in all parts of the earth and in all the eras like the inner worth and unworth of the same, and never was a nation oppressed by a despot without deserving this destiny and having forged its own chains."[169] The claim that despotism prevented philosophy's development in the Orient is not a "cultural" analysis. Already in Tennemann, it is a claim about the yellow race.[170]

Kant's views on race can also be found in his *Reflexionen*.[171] In *Reflexion 1520*, Kant affirms the white ancestry of Europeans: "Our (ancient) human history goes back with reliability only to the race of the Whites. Egyptians. Persians. Thracians. Greeks. Celts. Scythians. (not Indians, Negroes.)"[172] Here, Kant denies that the ancestry of the Whites goes back to the "Indians" or "Negroes" (non-white races of the Old World). Here also, he uses "Celtic stock" and "Germanic blood" as terms equivalent to "the race of the Whites."[173] Kant's use of the racial name Celtic is startling because it is a usage that was idiosyncratic to Meiners.

According to Larrimore's analysis of *Reflexion 1520*, Kant excludes the non-white races from human history because they made no contribution to it. They made no contribution "because they did not have it in them to do so."[174] That non-white nations are excluded from the history of philosophy would be in perfect conformity with Kant's thought because, as it was so much already alleged, they made no contribution to it, not having it in them to do so.

Tennemann's exclusion of Africa and Asia from the history of philosophy is grounded in the racial anthropology that Kant and Meiners developed in the last quarter of the eighteenth century. I would emphasize that Kant did not provide an alternative to Meiners's racism. Instead, Kant and Meiners were a tag-team, working in tandem to shape a modern scientific discourse of race. Kant is as responsible as Meiners for the exclusion of Africa and Asia from the history of philosophy and for rising Eurocentrism in the discipline.

5

Systematic Inclusion of Africa and Asia under Absolute Idealism

Friedrich Ast's and Thaddä Anselm Rixner's Histories of Philosophy

> The life of philosophy is a harmonious one, and hence the history of philosophy must be a harmonious one. That is, it must reveal how all the forms of philosophy emerged from one Being, from philosophy itself; how each developed in its particularity, how one life flowed out of itself into multiplicity, and finally how the forms, as external life, resolved themselves and flowed back into the unity, from which they first arose.
>
> —Friedrich Ast (1807)[1]

As I showed in Chapter 1, Kantian thinkers strictly delimited the domain of philosophy, separating it from the domain of history. According to Reinhold, philosophy is a scientific knowledge that is independent of experience. According to Grohmann, philosophy is knowledge of a kind that is neither empirical nor temporal. The philosophers that I discuss in this chapter without exception adhered to Kantian distinctions between philosophy and history. F. W. J. von Schelling (1775–1854), Friedrich August Carus (1770–1807), and G. W. F. Hegel (1770–1831) were not Kantians in any strict sense, but in their approach to the history of philosophy they proceeded from Kantian principles.[2] I begin this chapter by exposing important continuities between the Kantians and the new idealists with respect to history of philosophy writing. I then describe the histories of philosophy of two of these new idealists, Georg Anton Friedrich Ast (1778–1841) and Thaddä (or Thaddeus) Anselm Rixner (1766–1838). They constructed their histories of philosophy such that philosophy begins in the Orient (with India as the precise beginning point) and completes its first cycle or period entirely in the Orient before the second cycle begins in Greece. That the Orient is included in Ast's and Rixner's histories demonstrates that *a priori* construction does not in principle entail the exclusion of the Orient.

In an essay titled "Abhandlung über die Frage, ob eine Philosophie der Geschichte möglich sei," published in the 1798 volume of *Philosophisches Journal*, edited by Niethammer and Fichte, Schelling argues that the concept of philosophical history is self-contradictory.[3] Taking his concepts from Kantianism, he defined history as a knowledge of particulars not reducible to general laws, while he likened philosophy to mathematics in method and goal as *a priori* knowledge.[4] Christian Weiss, a lecturer of philosophy at the University of Leipzig, expressed the same ideas more succinctly: "History may not become philosophy, and philosophy may not become history," for history concerns itself with the mutable, while "true philosophy knows no mutation" and is as "permanent as the laws of nature and reason."[5] This is precisely the basis on which Schelling bestowed upon philosophy the status of science, which he denied to history.

It was as if, for Schelling, the disparity between history and philosophy, as two modes of knowledge, was too great. This barred the possibility of their synthesis, for not just a contradiction, but, indeed, a deadly theoretical conflict exists between them; one in which the success of the one would be the extermination of the other. Schelling wrote,

> [T]he more the boundaries of our knowledge widen, the narrower the boundaries of *history* become (hence . . . the sphere of one's historical knowledge stands in inverse relation to the sphere of his actual knowledge. . . .) For if we were to fulfill our entire task and realize the Absolute, then for each individual as well as for the whole of the race there would be no other law than the law of our perfected nature; consequently, all history would end.[6]

History as knowledge could become so trivial as to become extinct.[7]

By 1801, Hegel had formed some views on philosophy's relation to its own history.[8] Any philosophical system can be studied as history, but to what end? Philosophy, the expression of "the living Spirit," will not reveal itself to an alien spirit, namely, history's.[9] Hegel compared history's interest in knowing past opinions to the collecting of mummies. History is indifferent to the truth.[10] Carus, too, affirmed the distinctions drawn by the Kantians between history as "knowledge derived from material accidentally given" and philosophy as "knowledge of the self-acting mind . . . of its universal, necessary and unconditioned action."[11]

That the concept of *history of philosophy* may hold an inherent contradiction did not preclude a theory of history of philosophy. In the same 1798 article, Schelling states, "The system . . . that is to serve as the focal point of a history of philosophy must itself be capable of development." This development cannot be historical, but must be *logical*, since "development" refers to the "organizing spirit [that] must rule in this system" and, one assumes also, in the history of philosophy for which this system is to be the focal point. "[A]ll progress in philosophy is also only a progress through development."[12] I point out that Schelling's theory accords fully with Kantian principles of historical writing.

The Kantian requirement of a universally valid concept of philosophy is affirmed by Carus in *Ideen zur Geschichte der Philosophie*. He called for a "normative idea" (*Norm-Idee*) of philosophy, to be used as the standard by which to determine the merit of each philosophical project, a standard that would also give coherency to the history of philosophy.[13] Friedrich Ast, a classical philologist at the Bavarian university in Landshut, argued that, without this theoretical approach to the history of philosophy (and history in general), the *facta* were in danger of being inadequately or erroneously organized.[14] The right approach would be to present the *facta* as so many revelations of the (Platonic) Ideas while recognizing in the *facta* a higher reality, of which history is the temporal copy. The historian is at once a philosopher, presenting "the life of the Ideas" as historical reality.[15]

Carus conceptualized the history of philosophy as development as well as demonstration of "the changes of the immutable in accordance with necessary natural laws."[16] Thaddä Anselm Rixner, who taught philosophy at the Lyceum in Amberg, agreed that the schema of history, especially the history of philosophy, was to be determined by retrieving the "law" that articulates itself in the accidents of philosophy. The accidents are to be ordered in accordance with this law. The lawful nature of the history of philosophy makes it possible to rationally derive the present from the past and the future from past and present. If experience generates the material of history (*facta*), then speculation discovers the law of necessity. Like the orthodox Kantians, Rixner demanded that the history of philosophy be given an ideal treatment, that systems of philosophy no longer be arranged according to nation or chronology. Rixner condemned as "entertainment of scholarly impertinence" those histories of philosophy that presented one philosophical system after another as so many accidents or particulars.[17] He explicitly required *a priori* schematization to come before the historical study of philosophy; so that all systems could be grasped in relation to "the total organism of the world in its universal, rational aspect."[18] The philosophical historian, according to Carus, is one who can detect and represent "reason's instinct toward freedom," which is behind the progress of philosophy.[19]

Carus and Rixner were as contemptuous as the orthodox Kantians were of the older histories of philosophy that presented "a litany of only the missteps of reason," "a gallery of incoherent opinions having no relation to the truth," and the "so many common, vacuous school compendia offering an arbitrary aggregate of philosophical systems and doctrines."[20] Huet, Adelung, and Meiners are mentioned as three examples of historians who presented reason in a humiliating light. Carus charged that their motive was to elevate the status of revelation.[21] He worried about the effect on students of these histories, which offer merely a mass of opinions. He worried that the multiplicity of divergent and mutually contradictory opinions of past philosophers would create skeptics.[22] It was imperative for the historian of philosophy to resolve the seeming contradictions in philosophy's history.

In *Grundriss einer Geschichte der Philosophie* (1807), Ast differentiates between philosophy's eternal essence and philosophy's forms. The contradictions between the universal and the particular disappear, he argued, as soon as one realizes that the historical forms of philosophy are copies of philosophy's eternal essence. In its unfolding into particular forms and elements, philosophy reveals its infinite bounty, proving also that it is living and real. Ast, who had studied at Jena when Friedrich Schlegel, Fichte, and Schelling lectured there, hoped to demonstrate through his history of philosophy that the multiplicity of divergent systems stood in a relation of identity to one, eternal essence of philosophy. He would show that this multiplicity is actually a unity without denying that the empirical life of philosophy is still real. Indeed, without its empirical life, philosophy would be as good as "dead," that is, merely formal. Ast would have it both ways: Philosophy's reality is *both* universal *and* particular. Philosophy reveals itself through particular philosophies. Ast posited a complete harmony between the eternal and the temporal, the one and the many; between the infinite and the finite.[23] Rixner conceptualized philosophy in a similar way. He referred to the two "sides" or "elements" of philosophy: the inner, ideal element ("soul") and the outer, real element ("body") of philosophy.[24]

Ast equated historical systems of philosophy to "incarnations" of the Spirit, to "visible radii of the invisible." "All systems, ideas, and opinions are revelations of one Spirit."[25] Rixner explained philosophical doctrines as so many different outward rays (*Strahlen*) of one and the same universal science of reason (*Vernunft-Erkenntnis*).[26] Only one philosophy exists throughout civilizations and eras. Philosophy's task is the same in all eras and cultural settings: "to view the many as one, to restore itself [philosophy] and all things in God."[27]

Carus, Ast, and Rixner turned to organic metaphors to explain historical processes, including the development of philosophy. Carus compared the mind's "directedness toward the eternal truth" to the directedness in the organic products of nature.[28] Rixner endeavored to portray the life of Spirit as "a self-grounded and self-enclosed organism," striving to know itself.[29] Both philosophy and history were analogized to the life of nature:

> Just as external life, as a whole, emerges and vanishes, so do the forms of life change in uninterrupted movement. Each particular form has its particular life, its own birth, growth and dissolution. . . . Unity, opposition, and unity . . . are the elements or periods of universal as well as particular life. Philosophy can know the nature of things only through these elements. History can present its temporal life only through these periods.[30]

Philosophy, history, nature—Ast conceptualized each and all as "a gradually opening and closing, eternally emerging, self-revealing circle."[31]

The opening chapters in both Ast's *Grundriss* and Rixner's *Handbuch* present the author's theory of the history of philosophy. It gives the reader an orientation to the history of philosophy as four parts or periods: the first being that of *Urphilosophie*, or *Orientalismus*; the second "realism," which characterizes the tendencies of Greek philosophy; the third "idealism," the general term characterizing the philosophy of the Middle Ages; the fourth modern philosophy, or the period of the "interpenetration of idealism and realism."[32]

For Ast, these four periods complete the history of philosophy and correspond to the four periods that complete human history. Every historical period is thus a philosophical period; there is no historical period that is not a philosophical period. The history of philosophy may be viewed as "an element" of the history of mankind, its four periods being characterized as follows: The first is "undivided unity," life in its original state. The second, emerging out of the original unity, is the "external life" of "free development and civil society." This is the period of the Greco-Roman world. Life's withdrawal from external existence into the inner spirit characterizes the third (Christian) period. The fourth (modern) period sees the harmonious development (*Bildung*) of the external and internal elements into one, freely developed life.[33] This fourth period, Ast wrote further, is the period of the mind's striving to unite realism and idealism, but, at another level, is "the re-awakening of the Oriental perspective."[34]

Rixner also divided human history into four great periods and characterized them much in the same terms: The first period is that of undivided unity before human self-reflection. It is the period of the first humans, the first ancestors, the "golden age of innocence," of "Asiatic primeval religion," from which virtually everything arises, including realistic polytheism, idealistic monotheism, and even the Christian doctrine of the Trinity (the "transfiguration into a higher unity of polytheism and monotheism"). In this first period, myth and poetry, fantasy and reason are born. This is the period of the "All-Is-One" in philosophy.[35] Here, the primary and immediate object of philosophical inquiry is pure Being, the universe, or nature.[36] To the second period belongs the emergence of life's "external element" or "real element" from life's undeveloped unity. This is the period of the Greco-Roman world, of plastic religion, of the worship of gods and heroes, and of epic poetry.[37] In the third period, Spirit turns away from externals and inward, from observation of nature toward meditation on the self. In this period, the "ideal element" prevails over the "real element" as in the religion, dogmatics, mysticism, and asceticism of medieval Christianity. Here, poetry is lyric, while philosophy is scholastic and theosophical. The fourth period is the unification of external and internal life into a beautiful and harmonious whole. It is the "second golden age," which still awaits the perfection of science and art. The religion of this present period is the explication of Christianity as both revelation and rational religion, as what is divinely confirmed through history, while this period's poetry is the product of the interpenetration of objectivity and subjectivity, of plasticity and allegory.[38] Philosophy in this period is once again the philosophy of the All-Is-One, but now as a developed science of reason in the course of its self-apprehension, through which the opposition of the two (real and ideal) elements of philosophy is resolved.[39] Modern philosophy is the realization of the original (Oriental) unity of being and thought, of the real and the ideal. The modern period brings such oppositions into the harmonious unity of one philosophy, which is neither realism nor idealism, but *both*.[40]

Philosophy's development from Oriental to modern periods Ast and Rixner schematized or visualized as a circle. They designated Indian philosophy as the primeval philosophy out of which all systems of philosophy flow. Ast wrote, "The primeval philosophy [*Urphilosophie*] is the seed of all philosophy—the ideas of the Orient are thus the primeval ideas [*Urideen*] of all philosophy. . . . Everything flows out of the Orient as the land of primeval mankind."[41] But the Orient is the source of not just philosophy. It is actually "the center from which religion, art, and science flowed and spread throughout all spaces and periods of mankind."[42] Ast called Christian and Greek cultures "the seedling[s] of Oriental culture," for the ideas of Christianity as much as the ideas of Greek paganism can be traced back to the Orient. "The highest and purest ideas of Pythagoras, Plato and others agree with Oriental philosophy in a manner most worthy of wonder; so that it often seems as if they are but copies of those primeval ideas that arose in the Orient."[43] All philosophy can be traced back to the "cradle" of the human race, which Rixner identified as India.[44]

Ast and Rixner would not have disputed Tiedemann, Tennemann, or de Gérando that the philosophy of the Orientals is not distinct from their religion. Indeed, in the Oriental world, poetry as well as philosophy are "completely engulfed in religion"; both "rejoice in one life under the magic of religion."[45] The primeval thoughts of man are but his immediate sensory impressions of the universe. He does not think himself separate from this universe. All his thoughts relate to the infinite, the idea of the divine, manifesting itself in infinite forms, but remaining throughout the one, unchanging Being. Primitive man relates spatial and temporal infinity to the nature of a higher spirit that manifests itself in the universe through infinite powers or "elements." Thus, Oriental man views Creation as the self-manifestation of God and every transformation of the universe as a new incarnation of Him. God is regarded as the basis and goal of all things, the source of all truth and goodness, while evil (the temporal or finite) is conceived as divergence from God.

"Unity, opposition, and unity . . . are the elements or periods of universal as well as particular life."[46] "Unity, opposition, and unity" is also Ast's *a priori* schema of the history of philosophy. In the beginning, philosophy is a unity, but then splits into the opposition of "realism" (Greco-Roman philosophy) and "idealism" (Christian philosophy) only to be reunited as "ideal-realism" (modern philosophy).[47]

The circle of unity, opposition, and unity holds also on the level of particular periods of philosophy. For instance, within the first period of history, out of Indian philosophy (or unity) emerges the realism of the western Asians (Chaldeans and Persians) in opposition to the idealism of the Tibetans.[48] Chaldean-Persian realism transforms into Egyptian materialism, while Tibetan idealism transforms into Chinese moral philosophy.[49] It is the "real element" in *Orientalismus* that develops into the Chaldean worship of the stars (Sabianism), Persian worship of fire, and Egyptian worship of plants and animals. From this last development arises the "cheerful" Greco-Roman worship of gods and heroes. It is the ideal element in *Orientalismus* that develops into the Tibetan religion of tranquility and immersion in God (through a more intellectual or genuinely metaphysical view of things) and its later product, "Chinese rationalism." (Rixner considered Christianity to be the final development of the ideal element of *Orientalismus*.[50]) The splitting of *Orientalismus* into religion, on the one hand, and natural philosophy, on the other, ultimately results in the mysticism of the East and the nature worship of the West. Within the Eastern sphere, the cycle progresses with the development of Tibetan and Japanese mysticism on the one side and Chinese ethics ("with all religious motivations completely removed") on the other.[51] The development of the real element of primeval philosophy arrives at the poetic or symbolic forms of nature worship that are devoid of meaning.[52] According to Rixner, the Persian worship of fire, the Chaldean veneration of the stars, the Egyptian worship of plants and animals, and the Scandinavian Edda can all be traced back to "the original poetic and religious view of nature" of the Indians.[53]

As sources on India Ast listed Palladius's *De Gentibus Indiae et Brachmanibus*, Sebastian Gottfried Stark's *Specimen sapientiae Indorum veterum* (Berlin, 1693), Dow's "Dissertation," the *Ezourvedam*, Halhed's *A Code of Gentoo Laws*, Wilkins's *Bhaguat-Geeta*, the *Bagavadam*, and works by Anquetil du Perron, P. Paulino a Sto. Bartholomaeo, and Friedrich Majer. Ast also cited the *Asiatick Researches* and a more recent work by Jonas Hallenberg, *Die geheime Lehre der alten Orientaler und Juden* (1805). By the time that Rixner sat down to compose his *Handbuch* (1822–3), additional sources were available, including essays on Indian philosophy by Henry Thomas Colebrooke, reports on and preliminary translations of the Vedas, and Joseph Görres's article in the *Heidelberger Jahrbuch der Litteratur* (Vol. IV, Book 5: 74ff.) arguing for the authenticity of the *Oupnek'hat*.[54] These sources were used for evidence of the very high antiquity of Indian philosophy and of the derivative character of Egyptian, Phoenician, and Hebrew culture; for Ast, they confirmed that the majority of the philosophical ideas of the western Asian nations were passed down from older nations.[55] Ast even supposed that the Egyptian people migrated out of Asia.

According to Ast, religion in Egypt began as "astrological and symbolic" religion, but sank to "calendar religion" and animal worship. The materialistic outlook of the Egyptians seemed to explain their great architectural feats and their embalming of the bodies of their dead. Ast did not dispute that Egypt was the motherland of European arts and sciences, but he added that in a strict sense the "far Orient" was their ultimate origin. The transmigration and immortality of the soul and male and female (good and evil) principles were beliefs that the Egyptians held in common with all other Oriental peoples, notwithstanding that these appear to have been reshaped in relation to Egypt's geographical setting.[56]

Ast and Rixner recounted the development of Greek philosophy out of Greek religion. Ast discerned that the fundamental ideas circulating among almost all Greek philosophical schools were originally religious doctrines. He saw in the "esoteric, Orphic-mythical" religion of early Greece the source of both "exoteric, popular religion" and Greek philosophy. The esoteric doctrines persisted in the Greek mysteries and in the philosophical ideas and principles of Pythagoras, Plato, and others up until and including the neo-Platonists.[57] A similar account is given by Rixner: From esoteric, Orphic religion emerged both Greek philosophy and the "exoteric, popular religion."[58]

However, in regard to its ultimate origins, Greek culture is Oriental, Ast and Rixner maintained. Stated more concretely, Greek culture developed from the "real element" of *Orientalismus*. It is, indeed, "the decisive predominance of the real." Ast even called Greek myth a "mere copy" of earlier Indian myth. Due to the plastic culture of the Greeks, their myths are shorn of almost all musical and mystical qualities. Indian myth turns to plasticity so as to present the Idea in sensory form. An Indian deity is not bound to the idea of that deity, which is really an "intimation of a higher, spirit-life." In Greek myth, by contrast, it is as if the form of the divine is mistaken for the essence of the religion.[59] Like Ast, Rixner regarded the plastic and aesthetic polytheism of the Greco-Roman world as the highest transfiguration (*Verklärung*) of the real element of Orientalism.[60]

Yet, more emphatic statements were necessary to dispel all doubts about the origins of Greek culture. Ast wrote, "That the Greeks received their culture [*Bildung*] from the Orient partly through Oriental peoples who migrated to Hellas and partly through contact with the Egyptians, Phoenicians, and others is a fact."[61] Even without the support of historical accounts, the agreement of Greek *Urideen* with Oriental religion and philosophy leads one to conclude that these ideas either came from the Orient or were "formed through the Orient." Among the oldest doctrines of ancient peoples are the ideas of the birth of all things out of water or from a cosmogonic egg. For Ast, it was clear that such ideas existed before the Greeks, who were awakened to "a higher, intellectual life . . . through these ideas."[62] One could historically establish the Oriental origins of Greek culture and of the Greek people themselves. Ast related that there were two ways through which civilization reached Greece. One was through the north, probably via the Caucasus and Thrace. The other was through the south; with the emigration of Egyptians, Phoenicians, and Lydians. He cited the stories of Cecrops (the Egyptian who arrived in Attica around 1550 BCE), Danaus (the Egyptian who settled in Argos around 1500), and Cadmus (a Phoenician who arrived in Boeotia also around 1500). There is also the legend of Pelops's crossing from Asia Minor to Greece some time before 1300 BCE.[63] In a footnote, Ast clarified that, though these figures were mythical, there was some historical truth to them because the oldest names in Greek legends, which came to identify whole peoples, were originally names of actual historical persons.[64]

Rixner, too, argued that the Greeks had to thank the Orientals for their religion and philosophy. He, too, pointed to the agreement between Oriental ideas and the dogmas of the oldest Greek mysteries. He cited the legends of Cecrops, Danaus, Cadmus, and their colonies. He stated for emphasis that the first two were Egyptians while the third was a Phoenician—"hence, all together Orientals."[65] "Oriental light" penetrated northern Greece even before the Egyptians and Phoenicians.[66] Thus, one must distinguish two cultures in Greece: an earlier culture—"perhaps originating directly from India"—of frank mysticism, which endures in Doric culture, and the later, Ionian culture with tendencies toward external imagery and sensory development.[67]

The beginnings of Greek thought were Pelasgian, Oriental, and mystical, but, through the Phoenicians and Egyptians, it changed into realism, i.e., polytheistic popular religion. In a development that has an Egyptian parallel, the Hellenes over time lost the original simplicity of the knowledge and worship of God, descending into realistic polytheism.[68] The "Hellenic tendency" further developed into Ionic philosophy, while the old, Pelasgian "simplicity" and "inwardness" developed into Doric (or Italic) philosophy. In Doric southern Italy, the first idealist philosopher among the Greeks, Pythagoras, was born.[69]

The figure of a circle helped Ast to conceptualize the history of Greek philosophy. The first epoch of Greek philosophy as the unity of philosophy and religion is succeeded by the epoch of the separation of real and ideal elements. "Actual philosophy," or philosophy separated from religion, emerges with the realist natural philosophy of the Ionians (Thales, Anaximander, Anaximenes, Diogenes of Apollonia, Heraclitus, Anaxagoras, and Archelaus). The philosophy of Anaxagoras (born around 500 BCE in Clazomenae), which Ast regarded as "neither realism nor idealism" but something "floating between both," completes this second epoch of Greek philosophy.[70] In Anaxagoras's philosophy Ast recognized the dissolution of earlier autonomous realism and the transition to Greek idealism.

For Ast, this in-between stage of realism's transition to idealism is the story of Spirit's ascension from the study of nature to the study of the self. While the realist understands objective being in physical terms, the idealist understands it in terms of how he represents it to himself. The idealism of the Italic philosophers (Pythagoras, Alcman, Hippasus, Archytas, Philolaus, Eudoxus, Xenophanes of Colophon, Parmenides, Zeno, and Melissus of Samos) occupies the third epoch of Greek philosophy.[71] Ast saw in Zeno's system Italic philosophy's devolution into dialectics and sophistical disputation and further into a frank sophism through the work of Gorgias.[72] In the dualistic system of Empedocles (flourished in Agrigentum around 460 BCE), Ast recognized a stage of Pythagorean philosophy that came closer to realism.[73] The trend progresses through the atomism of Leucippus and Democritus, at which point the spirit of Pythagoreanism "complete[s] its life cycle."[74] That moment is not simply a reversion to realism, but is Spirit's reconciling of the ideal with the real.

The opposed elements of Ionic and Italic philosophies are harmoniously united, constituting Attic philosophy, in the fourth epoch of Greek philosophy.[75] Whereas Ionic philosophy rests on sensory perception and Italic philosophy (e.g., Pythagoreanism) on reason, Attic philosophy rests on the union of Ionic and Italic ideas. While Ionic philosophy is physical and Italic philosophy contemplative, Attic philosophy is speculative and ethical. From knowing the nature of things and the self, the Attic philosopher comes to know their essence, including the divine essence. Having come into this knowledge, he resolves to live according to its truth.[76] Attic philosophy unites experience with conceptual knowledge, theoretical perspectives with the observation of nature. Previous conceptual oppositions are resolved in Attic philosophy in accordance with rational principles.[77] The development of Atticism can be conceptualized as a cycle with three stages or manifestations: (1) dialectics, or sophism; (2) the philosophies of Socrates and Plato ("the apogee of Greek philosophy," "the pinnacle of not just Attic, but of all Hellenic wisdom"); and (3) the philosophy of Aristotle.[78] The Greek period of philosophy concludes with Epicurus (341–271 BCE), whose philosophy is "a harbinger and prelude to the decay of classical antiquity, on whose ruins a new era of mankind, namely, the Oriental-Christian one was to blossom."[79] (See Figure 2.)

The closing of the second period of philosophy is, of course, the opening of the third. The spirit of the Christian Middle Ages is that of idealism. As in the case of Greek philosophy, medieval philosophy unfolds into an opposition between real and ideal elements, viz., mysticism and dialectics. Both are harmoniously united in the earliest Christian philosophies—for example, the philosophy of the mystical-Aristotelian Augustine. Christianity is the object and goal of the medieval philosophers. Dialectics and mysticism are not distinct epochs in, but simultaneous elements of, medieval philosophy. Dialectics is the outer (objective) element; mysticism the inner (subjective) one.[80]

The opposition (and harmony) between dialectics and mysticism, between "freedom and constraint," exists not just in the philosophy, but in the total life of the Middle Ages. On the one hand, there is the high ideality and profound mysticism of the Orient, and,

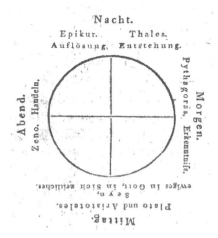

Figure 2. Diagram of the epochs of Greek philosophy in Thaddä Anselm Rixner's *Handbuch der Geschichte der Philosophie* (1822–3).

on the other, there is the sensible and free European life as seen in Greek philosophy, especially Aristotle's dialectics, and in "the heroic, northern spirit of chivalry."[81] Ast identified the source of medieval philosophy as Church neo-Platonism, a combination of Platonic and Aristotelian doctrines and Christian religious ideas. If this Christianized Platonism is the mystical element of the "theological philosophy or philosophical theology" of the Middle Ages, then Aristotelianism is the logical and dialectical element.[82] Not since the Oriental period was philosophy so inextricably linked to religion.[83]

Concrete historical circumstances attend philosophy's transition from medieval to modern. They are the decline of Scholasticism and mysticism, the rise of free cities and the third estate, the development of vernaculars for literary and scientific discourse, the rediscovery of classical authors, and the curtailment of ecclesiastical control over education. For Ast and Rixner, these historical contingencies did not diminish the lawfulness and necessity of philosophy's development. In accordance with the laws of development, oppositions arise in time as Spirit develops from unconditioned unity to plurality. Every opposition, however, already strives toward unity or harmony—this, too, is in accord with the lawful development of Spirit. Realism and idealism, the two moments of philosophical history, flow out of the primeval philosophy only to regain their unity in a "higher" stage.[84] The modern period is the moment of philosophy's return to unity. Ast and Rixner divided modern philosophy into three epochs (real, ideal, and ideal-real).

In the first epoch arise the systems of Bacon, Descartes, Spinoza, the British empiricists, and the French materialists. In the second epoch, the systems of Leibniz, Berkeley, Kant, and Fichte. In the third, the systems of Schelling and his disciples. In the first epoch, the two opposing tendencies are Baconian (observation of nature, "realism of the understanding") and Cartesian (speculation, "realism of reason").[85] One sees in Descartes' system defects that are general to modern reflective philosophy—above all, the unresolved dualism of being and thought.[86] In England, the "empiricism" of Bacon, Hobbes (an empiricist?), and others becomes so well established that it repels Cartesianism and Spinozism. In that country, an empirical materialism forms in opposition to the speculative rationalism of Spinoza, but passes into a merely practical point of view before it finally destroys itself in the skepticism of Locke, Shaftesbury, and Hume.[87]

In England and France, empiricism sinks to materialism and "naturalism," but in Germany the Spirit rises up to oppose realism and empiricism. The second epoch of modern philosophy is inaugurated by Leibniz, who is named by Rixner as the "father of modern idealism" and the founder of (modern) German philosophy. In this epoch comes a wave of battles between the "common human understanding" and speculation.[88] John Locke is the champion of the claims of common human understanding and experience, while Berkeley and Leibniz, who oppose Descartes, Locke, and Spinoza, are champions of the ideas of speculative reason.

The systems of Kant and Fichte close the second epoch of modern philosophy and prepare the ground for the next. Kant's philosophy is the starting point of a new epoch of idealism. His philosophy is more a potential system than a perfected one as it does not have its own particular character, being neither purely dogmatic nor purely idealist; neither purely empirical nor purely speculative. Ast's comments are reminiscent of de Gérando's; the latter philosopher remarked that Kant's philosophy seemed to oscillate between opposing elements of philosophy.[89] Ast's schema took him even further: He conceptualized the transcendental-idealist stage as consisting of three substages (Kant, Jacobi, and Fichte) analogous to the three-stage cycle of modern-idealist philosophy (Leibnizian, Berkeleyan, and Kantian idealisms).[90] One should try to imagine three circles within a circle and circles mirroring circles. (See Figure 3.)

Rixner offered an account of Kant's contribution that diverged somewhat from Ast's account: Kant marks the beginning of the most recent reform and even perfection of philosophy. Kant's philosophy is a "universal Protestantism" against all previous philosophical pretensions and transgressions. Kant was critical, but he was not constructive, revealing a mind more negating than affirming. His philosophy is a negative system in the sense that it dwells merely on formal-logical and abstract categories without constructing a positive system of knowledge. It breaks down the untenable and one-sided dogmatics of earlier philosophy, but does not offer a new or better system. Kant's system is not an edifice of positive doctrine, but a "general, negative Protestantism," which was still epoch-making as it successfully disrupted the shallow proofs of dogmatic systems and induced the rebirth and perfection of philosophy.[91]

The philosophy of Schelling marks the beginning of the third epoch of modern philosophy. This philosopher transformed the subjectivism of transcendental idealism, whose "highest blossom" was the Fichtean system, into the philosophy of absolute reason. Schelling accomplished this by joining idealism to Spinoza's rational realism, a path pointed to already by Lessing, Herder, Friedrich Schlegel, and Wilhelm Traugott Krug.[92] Transcendental idealism tried in vain to unite the realms of being and thought by attempting to bind subject and object in the forms of consciousness (Kant) or subjectively in feeling (Jacobi) or in the free ego (Fichte). Proceeding from the transcendental philosophy, Schelling led the subject back to its original, unconditioned identity on the model of Spinoza's system. He decided that there was no "real" in itself, but only a real determined through ideality.[93] For Rixner, Schelling's system is the completion of philosophy as a self-apprehending, absolute science that unifies previously separate forms (idealism and realism) through the identification of being and thought.[94]

In the 1822–3 edition of Rixner's *Handbuch*, Schelling's *Identitätssystem* is presented as the final and consummate system of philosophy, the capstone to the history of philosophy. In Ast's *Grundriss* of 1825, however, the *Identitätssystem* is presented merely as the most recent system with its own shortcomings. Ast's account of Schelling's philosophy includes this critique: Modeled after Spinoza's system and incorporating the ideas of Plato, Schelling's idealism proceeds from the infinite and absolute—unlike transcendental idealism, which negates the infinite and proceeds from finite subjectivity. The unity achieved by Schelling is but a negative principle.[95] What had been the problem of previous systems of idealism remained the problem of Schelling's system. Like previous idealisms, it grounds the eternal unity of all life in realism and conceives this unity as the indifference of the subjective and objective realms. This kind of unity is not a pure and absolute principle in itself, but a negative one, being conditioned by the sublation (*Aufhebung*) of oppositions. However, oppositions are supposed to arise insofar as opposition is a condition of life, but the *Identitätssystem* denies life along with the oppositions that constitute it. This system abstracts from reality as much as transcendental idealism and is thus merely formal in the sense that abstract reason conceives things as *real*, but in terms of the unconditioned, formal law of unity (or identity). Moreover, the *Identitätssystem* is one-sided, being predominantly speculative and theoretical. Its speculation is still abstraction from the real life of things. It equates the universe with the Absolute and, further still, with the divine. Schelling's system falls into pantheism no less than Spinozism.[96] Being merely rational speculation, Schelling's system does not account for living things and leaves unresolved the real opposition between the finitude of individuality and the infinity of the divine. The project of philosophy remains incomplete. The history of philosophy, true to its concept, is a cycle.

This chapter has shown that Ast's and Rixner's histories of philosophy combine an *a priori* schema with an Asian (specifically, Indian) point of origin (Figure 3). The next chapter will show that Hegel employed a similar *a priori* schema, but combined it with a Greek point of origin. Schemata, as we shall see, can simply be modified.

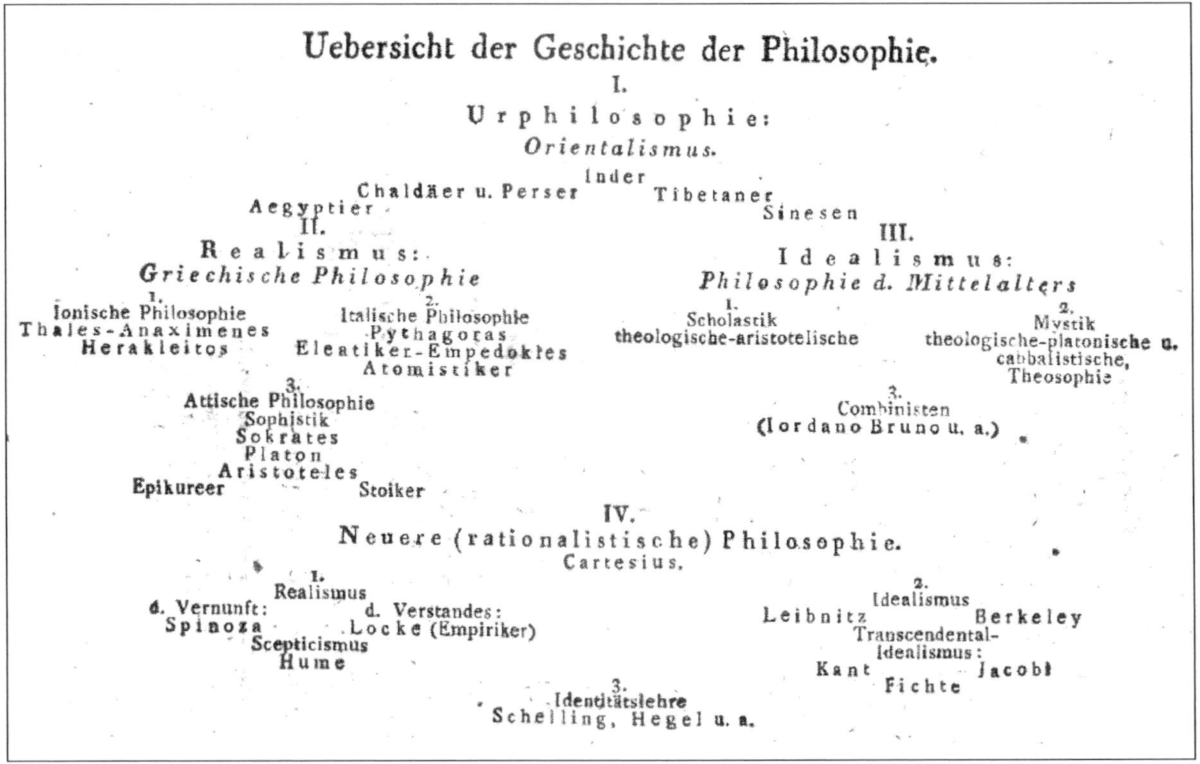

Figure 3. "Overview of the history of philosophy" in Friedrich Ast's *Grundriss der Geschichte der Philosophie* (1825).

6

Absolute Idealism Reverts to the Kantian Position

Hegel's Exclusion of Africa and Asia

History, especially the history of philosophy, is the history of the Spirit, the Spirit of the world, as it apprehends itself. It is not the subjective, but the universal Spirit.

—Hegel (1819)[1]

What this history presents to us is the succession of noble minds, the gallery of heroes of thinking reason, who are through the power of this reason immersed in the essence of things, nature, and mind, in the nature of God; and who have acquired for us the highest treasure, the treasure of the knowledge of reason.

—Hegel (1820)[2]

For us, real philosophy begins in Greece.

—Hegel (1829/30)[3]

In the early decades of the nineteenth century, some German Orientalists saw in their translation projects the opportunity to expand the literary canon.[4] For some of them, the writing of history of philosophy presented an opportunity to expand the philosophical canon. Writing the history of philosophy presented Tennemann and Hegel with opportunities as well, but to a contrary end. They (re)wrote the history of philosophy so as to shift their audience's orientation away from Asia (to sever Germans completely from their Asian roots was not possible) and confer on them the sense of an exclusively Greek and Roman heritage. Hegel's affinities are well known. In the winter semester of 1825/26, he said to his students, "When we speak of Greece, every educated man, especially we Germans feel at home."[5] This statement was more prescriptive than descriptive since, in Hegel's time, Germans' ideas of their roots were divergent and competing.

Where does Hegel, the historian of philosophy, fit within the schools of history of philosophy? In fundamental respects, Hegel is of the same school with Ast and Rixner as all three imposed similar *a priori* schemata—identical in many details—onto the historical data of philosophy. That Hegel agreed more with the disciples of Schelling than with the Kantians is not surprising, but it is definitely surprising that, on the question of Oriental philosophy, Hegel sided with Tennemann. In his lectures on the history of philosophy at the University of Berlin, Hegel presented the Kantian position as his own: Philosophy did not occur in Asia, where political freedom is absent. Philosophy arose only with the historical dawning of self-consciousness. Philosophy first arose in Greece.

The previous chapters give the historical background against which Hegel's statements on Oriental philosophy can be analyzed. We shall see that his statements track very closely to Tennemann's. Indeed, just like Tennemann, Hegel was eventually compelled to give an extended account of Oriental philosophy (whereas in his earlier history of philosophy courses he dispensed with the Orient swiftly). It should be noted that he gave this account even while he explicitly denied the Orientals a place in the history of philosophy: "The first is Oriental philosophy, but it does not enter into the body of the whole presentation; it is only something preliminary, of which we speak in order to account for why we do not occupy ourselves with it further and what relation it has to thought, to true philosophy."[6] In Chapter 4, I argued that the exclusion of Egypt and Asia from the history of philosophy was justified with anthropological arguments taken from Christoph Meiners. I argued that these justifications are racist in an unambiguously modern sense and that they are consistent with the view that philosophy was developed by Whites through the intellectual capacities innate to their race. This chapter will show that Hegel used these same justifications for excluding Egypt and Asia from the history of philosophy. This fact alone compels a probe of

Hegel's thought for racism. How did Hegel comprehend human diversity? Did he have any concrete views of race? If so, what were they?

These questions deserve scholarly attention, but few historians and even fewer philosophers have given them their due. The four exceptions are Darrel Moellendorf, Karlheinz Barck, Robert Bernasconi, and Michael H. Hoffheimer; they have pursued the question of racism in Hegel's thought. In "Racism and Rationality in Hegel's Philosophy of Subjective Spirit" (1992), Moellendorf argues that the notorious Eurocentrism of Hegel's philosophy of history, with its negative portrayal and judgment of native Americans and Africans, seems to have a basis in Hegel's race theory as laid bare in his *Philosophy of Subjective Spirit*.[7] Moellendorf argues further that the *Philosophy of Subjective Spirit* provides a tacit justification for the enslavement of Africans.[8] Even more intriguing is his conclusion that Hegel's racism does not necessarily follow from his philosophical account of Spirit and that the source of his racism must be sought elsewhere.[9] Whereas Moellendorf locates this source in "the general ideology of the nineteenth century," I locate it in the racial anthropology of the late eighteenth century.[10]

In a 1998 essay, Bernasconi investigates Hegel's use of published travel accounts and his representations of Africans in his lectures on the philosophy of history.[11] He found that Hegel distorted the information in these sources "with systematic intent" so as to portray African peoples as "barbaric, cannibalistic, preoccupied with fetishes, without history," without culture, and "without any consciousness of freedom."[12] Hegel seems to excuse the enslavement of Africans by Europeans with the claim that it is a state better than the one in which Africans enslaved by Africans find themselves. One can also infer from his *Philosophy of History* and *Philosophy of Right* that Hegel regarded European colonization of Africa as civilizing, legitimate, and beneficial to the Africans.[13] From another of Bernasconi's articles, "With What Must the Philosophy of World History Begin? On the Racial Basis of Hegel's Eurocentrism" (2000), one learns that Hegel excluded Africa and Siberia from history, relegated China and India to "pre-history," was ambivalent about Egypt, and oddly designated Persia as the beginning of real history. He differentiated Europeans into nations, but did not think it necessary to do so in the case of Africans and Asians.[14] These and other particulars of Hegel's account of world history suggested to Bernasconi that that account was organized along the lines of a racial taxonomy.

More recently, Michael H. Hoffheimer has argued that a racial hierarchy structures not only Hegel's philosophy of history, but also his philosophy of religion.[15] Hegel's explanation for the demise of the native American population under European colonialism, which centers itself on racial characteristics, "can be read as ambivalent rationalizations for European colonial genocide."[16] This is the thesis that Karlheinz Barck advanced two decades ago in his article "Amerika in Hegels Geschichtsphilosophie."[17] Hoffheimer states that Hegel's attitude toward contemporary slavery was "studiedly ambiguous."[18] Hegel's account of African humanity, which involves a race-based explanation for the supposed tendency of Africans to fall into slavery, could be and were read as justifications for slavery. Long passages of Hegel's descriptions of Africans were read aloud in debate by L. Q. C. Lamar in 1860, a Mississippi congressman who defended slavery in the House of Representatives.[19]

The present chapter extends the investigation of racism in Hegel's thought to his lectures on the history of philosophy. This will reveal that in composing these lectures Hegel used Meiners's and Tennemann's strategies and arguments for excluding Africa and Asia from the history of philosophy. We know from Johannes Hoffmeister that Hegel was a reader of Meiners's publications since the time he was a *Gymnasium* student.[20] "As a young man Hegel had already shown an interest in those authors who were among the first to deny that the Greek philosophers had learned extensively from the Egyptians and the Persians."[21] Among those authors was Meiners. Hegel's review of previous works of history of philosophy shows that he knew Tennemann's work. However, the greater evidence of a racial structure to Hegel's history of philosophy is found in the manuscripts and students' transcriptions of his lectures.

Hegel lectured on logic, metaphysics, and the history of philosophy more regularly than on other subjects. Nine times between 1805 and 1831 he held a lecture course on the history of philosophy (1805/6, 1816/17, 1817/18, 1819, 1820/21, 1823/24, 1825/26, 1827/28, and 1829/30). During his tenure at Berlin (1819–31), he lectured every second year on the subject. He began a lecture course on the history of philosophy in November of 1831, but succumbed to cholera before finishing his introductory remarks.[22] Manuscripts and student transcriptions of his lectures at Berlin indicate that he was becoming increasingly engaged with Asian thought.[23] In the first of these Berlin courses (1819), a few paragraphs in the Introduction are the sum total of his remarks on "Oriental philosophy." By the winter semester of 1825/26, Hegel had added a much longer section on Asian thought, which was placed between the Introduction and Part One of his history of philosophy. This is significant because what was, in 1819, a brief excursus on Oriental philosophy became, in 1825/26, a longer section on the same, though still separate from the actual history of philosophy.[24] In an important dissertation on *Orientalism, Classicism, and the Birth of Western Civilization in Hegel's Berlin Lecture Courses of the 1820's*, Stuart Jay Harten suggests that major changes made in the mid-1820s to Hegel's account of Indian civilization were induced by religious controversies.[25]

The placement of Oriental philosophy toward the end of the Introduction in Hegel's history of philosophy lectures perfectly replicates the placement of the same in Tennemann's *Grundriss der Geschichte der Philosophie* (Figure 4).[26] In the latter work, a "short overview of the religious and philosophical perspectives of the Oriental peoples" occupies the last section of the Introduction (see Figure 5). In both Tennemann's and Hegel's histories of philosophy, the Introduction concludes before Part One of the history of philosophy begins. The effect of this is that the Orient is literally not part of the history of philosophy.

Early in his Introduction, Hegel addresses "the most common objection to the study of philosophy": that there is not one philosophy, but many and that it is not possible to decide which is the true philosophy because of the multiplicity of systems and criteria of truth. Hegel said of this "supposed non-partisan sobriety" that it was "completely unsound."[27] While acknowledging that there have been many different philosophical systems in history, he reaffirmed that truth is singular. For him, this was an "insuperable feeling or belief" and "instinct of reason."[28] If only one philosophy can be true, must all the rest be errors? Does the history of philosophy present a litany of the missteps of reason? As in the case of Reinhold, Carus, and Rixner, Hegel's exasperation at historians who presented not the history of philosophy, but "a gallery of opinions," is palpable. There is nothing more useless and tedious than a succession of mere opinions, for "[a]n opinion is a subjective representation, an arbitrary thought, a figment." By virtue of the concept of philosophy, "there are no philosophical opinions." Philosophy is, by Hegel's definition, the "objective science of truth, science of its necessity, of apprehending knowledge—not opining or the spinning out of opinions."[29] It is not a succession of opinions or errors, but a "succession of rational events" and should be presented as such.[30] "The succession of the systems of philosophy in history is the very same as the succession of the logical determinations in the development of the Idea."[31] If one were to abstract the fundamen-

Wilhelm Gottlieb Tennemann's

D. u. ordentl. Prof. der Philos. zu Marburg

G r u n d r i s s

d e r

Geschichte der Philosophie

f ü r

den akademischen Unterricht.

D r i t t e

vermehrte und verbesserte Auflage

herausgegeben

v o n

A m a d e u s W e n d t

D. und ordentl. Prof. der Philosophie zu Leipzig.

L e i p z i g,

bey Joh. Ambrosius Barth.

1 8 2 0.

Figure 4. Title page of Wilhelm Tennemann's *Grundriss der Geschichte der Philosophie* (1820).

Inhaltsübersicht.

Figure 5. First page of the table of contents of Tennemann's *Grundriss der Geschichte der Philosophie* (1820).

tal concept of the systems of philosophy appearing in history; if one were to strip it of the empirical shells, he would get the stages of the development of philosophy according to logical necessity.[32] Hegel was more explicit in 1829/30: "The course of the science of logic and of the history of philosophy must be, in and for itself, the same. . . . In the major moments, in the junctions, the progress of logic and of history must be one. Thus, the progress of logic is a voucher for the progress of the history of philosophy and *vice versa*."[33]

In conceptualizing both history and philosophy, Hegel resorted to the figure of the circle and so had something else in common with the Schellingians. Ast had described the history of philosophy as "a gradually opening and closing, eternally emerging, self-revealing circle."[34] Hegel schematized the history of philosophy with circles: "[A] development is always a movement through many developments. The whole of philosophical development is a series of developments turning back within themselves."[35] In a circle, each development is to be viewed as both an end and a new beginning ("the last stage . . . is the first stage of another").[36] Hegel could as well have been describing Ast's schema of the history of philosophy (see Figure 3). Circles also structure the branches as well as the whole of Hegel's philosophical system. Paragraph 15 in the *Enzyklopädie der philosophischen Wissenschaften im Grundrisse* (1830) states:

> Each of the parts of philosophy is a philosophical whole, a circle that closes upon itself; but in each of them the philosophical Idea is in a particular determinacy or element. Every single circle also breaks through the restriction of its elements as well, precisely because it is inwardly [the] totality, and it grounds a further sphere. The whole presents itself therefore as a circle of circles, each of which is a necessary moment, so that the system of its peculiar elements constitutes the whole Idea—which equally appears in each single one of them.[37]

In his handbook of the history of philosophy, Rixner refers to the "two elements" of philosophy—the ideal and the real (Rixner: "soul" and "body"). In a similar sense, Hegel spoke of philosophy's inner nature and outer "expression" or "appearance."[38] Also like Rixner and Ast, Hegel described the history of philosophy as a succession of appearances (Ast: "incarnations" or "rays"; Rixner: "copies") that presents, however, "one idea in its totality and all its parts," "one vitality."[39] All three Absolute Idealists referred to "unity" and "opposition" as the two ruling principles (the two "elements," "periods," or "components") of the development of philosophy.[40] But Hegel was alone in determining that the "two parts" (*zwei Teile*) are what underlie Greek and Germanic philosophies respectively.[41]

It is more or less obvious what the referent of "Greek philosophy" is, but what is Hegel's idiosyncratic term "Germanic philosophy" a reference to? Hegel's other name for "Germanic philosophy" is "modern European philosophy," referring to the philosophies whose authors are members of the Germanic nations in the modern period.[42] Who are the Germanic peoples? For an answer, I turn to the 1819–20 edition of the *Allgemeine deutsche Real-Encyclopädie für die gebildeten Stände* (in the twentieth century, renamed *Der Grosse Brockhaus* and then *Brockhaus Enzyklopädie*). According to the article "Germanien und Germanen" in the *Real-Encyclopädie*, the Germans are the people who inhabit the lands bounded by the Rhine, Danube, Vistula, and the northern seas, but also Denmark, Norway, Sweden, Finland, Livonia, and Prussia. The physical appearance, customs, and language of the inhabitants of this part of Europe indicate a common origin.[43] The referent of *germanische Völker* in Hegel's lectures is not the same as that of the *Real-Encyclopädie's Germanen*. According to Hegel, the Germanic peoples are the Allemanni, Suebi, and Franks who, starting in the sixth century, settled in the lands of Spain, Portugal, and France; the Angles, Saxons, and Normans who settled in Britain; the Ostrogoths and Langobards of Italy ("whose origin is the Scandinavian coasts") and the Franks who later subjugated them; the Goths who migrated out of Scandinavia to both eastern and western Roman empires; the Normans who came to occupy Lower Italy; and, finally, the "pure" and "free," i.e., *unmixed* Germanic peoples ("Allemanni, Thuringians, Bavarii, Saxons, etc.").[44] Hegel separated the "Slavic nations" (among which he listed Hungarians, Magyars, Russians, Albanians, Alanians, and Bulgarians) as *other*; as not coming into the domain of history ("This Slavic section does not come into the domain of history just as the Eastern does not, which is turned so inwardly into itself even in the most modern times."[45]) What is the basis of Hegel's distinction between Slavic and Germanic peoples? Whatever be the basis, it should go to explain the identity between Spaniards and Britons, Frenchmen and Germans, and Italians and Scandinavians.

One thing is already clear. The basis of Slavic difference is not language. In Hegel's lectures, the difference between Slavic and Germanic languages does not come up at all. What does come up, however, is that the Slavic peoples are "Asiatic."[46] The Slavic peoples of the northeast of Europe ("mainly Russia and Poland") inhabit "northern plains of an idiosyncratic kind" that have a "connection to Asia." "They first entered lately into the succession of historical states and constantly maintained the connection to Asia."[47]

Already, Hegel's ethnological conceptions are strongly reminiscent of Meiners's. This is because, for one thing, Hegel shares with Meiners an account of world history in which the racial unity among Germans, Spaniards, Frenchmen, Italians, Britons, and Scandinavians is assumed. Whereas the description of Germans in the *Real-Encyclopädie* implies an ethnic identity distinct from that of the French, Spanish, Anglo-Saxon, or Dutch people, Hegel's term *germanische Völker* unites all the peoples of Western Europe not so much on the basis of shared cultural traits as on shared racial descent.[48] Meiners had given to Western Europeans the racial name "Celtic" (the name "Germanic" he used secondarily) partly to separate out Slavic peoples. Meiners held that "the Slavic and Near-Eastern peoples agree[d] with each other more than with the Germanic and other Celtic nations."[49] Or as Kant used to say in lecture, "Slavonic is still Asiatic."[50] I submit that "Germanic" is Hegel's racial name for Western Europeans.

Moellendorf, Bernasconi, and Hoffheimer have argued that concrete conceptions of race inform Hegel's philosophy of history. The remainder of this chapter will show that concrete conceptions of race inform Hegel's history of philosophy as well. I begin, however, by situating Hegel's writing of the history of philosophy in relation to contemporaneous trends in historiography. I will compare Hegel's historiography to Ast's and Rixner's on the one hand and to Tennemann's on the other. My comparisons will reveal that, as a historian of philosophy, Hegel stands much closer to Tennemann than his disparagement of the latter's work may lead one to believe.[51]

Ast and Rixner used the terms "realism" and "idealism" to name the two basic types of philosophical systems that they saw in history. In their accounts, philosophy's separating and uniting occur over the great cycle of human history, but separating and uniting occur also at the level of specific epochs of philosophy. The modern era is the time of philosophy's return to unity, epitomized by the "ideal-realism" of Schelling. Hegel's thought on this does not differ essentially from Ast's and Rixner's, for he claimed that the goal of modern philosophy was "to reconcile this opposition, to apprehend the reconciliation in its highest extreme, to grasp the most abstract, greatest splitting of being and thought."[52] Like Ast and Rixner, Hegel resorted to organic metaphors. He described both philosophy *and* its history, considered separately or together, as "an organic system, a totality that contains in itself a wealth of stages and moments."[53] He used the analogy of

seed and tree (it comes up in his other courses as well) to describe
the movement of philosophy: The seed contains in itself an entire tree.
Nothing arises from the seed that is not already in it. This seed is as
simple as a point when viewed under a microscope. Yet, this simple
point is pregnant with all the qualities of the tree.[54] Philosophy stands
in a relation of identity to its own development just as the seed does
to the tree. The seed and the tree are two and yet one. Similarly, philosophy and history are two and yet one. Like the seed, philosophy
develops without a change to its essential nature.[55]

Like Ast and Rixner, Hegel saw a necessary correlation between
philosophical history and general history.[56] A form or stage of the
Idea arises in the consciousness of a particular nation at a particular
time. Conversely, a particular nation expresses a particular form of the
Idea, which is also the shape of its worldview. Then—it may be centuries later—a higher stage of the Idea is expressed through a different
nation.[57] A determinate form of philosophy corresponds to a determinate people with a particular social order and form of government,
morality, communal life, capacities, customs, arts, sciences, religion,
and so forth. A determinate stage of the Idea can also correspond to
a time not of growth but of decline. The rise of a new state upon the
ruins of a previous one is but the birth and development of a higher
principle. What one nation does not achieve the next one may. The
World-Spirit has not only time enough; it has "whole generations,"
"nations enough to expend."[58] Every philosophy belongs to its era
just as every individual is a son of his era and people.[59] Paradoxically,
however, philosophy is said to have arisen with the Greek stage of
religious, scientific, artistic, and political development.[60]

In the *Ideen zur Geschichte der Philosophie*, Carus states, "[T]he
first philosopher had to have been a citizen. . . . A sphere of political
freedom is presumed."[61] In the *Grundriss der Geschichte der Philosophie*,
Tennemann explains the absence of philosophy in Asia from the side
of political and social anthropology: Political conditions in Asia, i.e.,
despotism and the caste system, prevented the free development of
the mind.[62] Hegel said in his lectures that philosophy first arose when
civic freedom first blossomed.[63] What was specifically missing before
that historical moment was "that stage of self-consciousness where
man knows absolutely that he is free."[64] Hegel made reference to the
Hindus and the Egyptians. In their world, the individual does not
determine who he is. Rather, he is determined by his birth. Some
have compared European hereditary nobility to Indian caste, but the
comparison must be rejected, for birth is so decisive in the Orient that
personal freedom has no role. Faced with the Oriental God or mon-

arch as the representation of the "universal, absolute Substance," the individual can only be conceived as devoid of personal freedom.[65] The animal worship of the Indians and Egyptians and the moral precepts of all Orientals were cited as further evidence of the worthlessness of the individual.[66]

Such anthropological views were the full extent of Hegel's effort, in the lectures of 1819, 1820/21, and 1823/24, to justify the exclusion of Egypt and Asia from the history of philosophy. By 1825/26, however, Hegel's treatment of Oriental thought had changed significantly. For the first time, Hegel presented an analysis of Indian and Chinese thought. He still excluded Jewish and Muslim thought. The reason that he gave was simply that the Jews and Muslims had adopted the philosophies of the Alexandrians, Persians, Indians, and other Orientals.[67] Hegel still barred the Egyptians from the history of philosophy as he had done in 1819.[68] He had had terse words for Chinese thought, but, in 1825/26, he gave it, along with Hindu thought, a relatively intricate treatment (though still confined to the Introduction). Hegel even addressed some basic points of Persian thought, although he did so in the section dealing with India. But what is most significant about the 1825/26 lectures is the addition of an anthropological excursus on "the Oriental character"[69]:

In the Orient, the subject, the individual, "I for myself" is not a person, but a negative determination relative to the objective sphere, the supersensible or hypersensible "Substance."[70] When the individual has a negative status in relation to Substance as true Being, the highest he can aspire to is "eternal beatitude" as a state of immersion in the Substance, as a lapse of consciousness and difference between him and Substance—in a word, annihilation. In the aspiration to beatitude, individuality is a negative condition. It is an injustice, a finitude. The individual as a nonsubstantial is an accident, worthless and devoid of rights. The individual will is likewise nonsubstantial and arbitrary, determined by nature (or by birth as in the caste system). The absence of self-consciousness is the "fundamental condition of the Oriental character."[71]

Hegel did not deny noble and sublime aspects of Oriental subjectivity as one can find in Hindu texts, but he argued that the noble-mindedness of the Oriental, his sense of independence was actually an effect of his arbitrariness—the arbitrariness of the Oriental character.[72] The noble-mindedness that accompanies rights and morality, respected by all and valid for all, is something other. The noble-mindedness of the Oriental is merely an accident of his particular character and not morality or law. It happens to be, however, the cause of the "consummate independence" of Oriental subjectivity, which lacks permanence and determinateness.[73] Objectivity or lawfulness does not pertain here. Whereas in the West we find justice and morality, in the East we find only the natural order—"no conscience, no ethics." In the natural order, however, the highest noble-mindedness is of the same level as "blind arbitrariness."[74]

In the 1825/26 introductory remarks, Hegel divulges that he has been studying Oriental thought. He mentions the enduring fame of Indian learning. But concrete findings of more recent times, he says rather vaguely, confirm the "general character" (that is, Hegel's general characterization) of Oriental man. This information was to be taken as confirmation that "actual philosophy" first arose in the Occident, where subjectivity is substantial and not debased; where the Absolute is grasped objectively; where the individual is no longer a slave or, in other ways, a dependent doomed to annihilation.[75]

Ast and Rixner as well as Tennemann had observed that Oriental philosophy was indistinguishable from Oriental religion. While Ast and Rixner did not use the nondistinction of Oriental philosophy from Oriental religion as a reason to exclude the Orient from the history of philosophy, Tennemann used it as such a reason. My question is, is this a philosophical reason? Is this not a technical or trivial reason?

If there is more to Tennemann's reason, it may be this: Oriental philosophy falls in the domain of the Orientalists or ethnologists; the history of philosophy does not. Only philosophers are in a position to write the history of philosophy. For Ast and Rixner, who traced Greek philosophy back to Oriental and religious roots, the nondistinction between philosophical and religious thought could never be a reason to exclude the Orient, especially since in their view the earliest epoch of Greek philosophy was one in which philosophy and religion were not distinguishable.[76] In Hegel's history of philosophy, philosophy's autonomy from religion is made into a key distinction that sets apart the European from the Oriental. Roman, Greek, or Christian philosophy is distinguishable from Roman, Greek, or Christian religion; Oriental philosophemes (Tennemann) are not distinguishable from Oriental religious representations. When Hegel argued that Oriental philosophy was actually the religious representations of the Orientals and that there was no philosophy in the East (distinct from religion), he was using Tennemann's justification for excluding the Orient from the history of philosophy.[77] Hegel's use of the distinction between philosophy and religion to more narrowly delimit philosophy landed him in perplexity after 1827, when he acknowledged the existence of Indian philosophy autonomous from Indian religion.[78] "This distinction was always going to be especially difficult to sustain when it came to a discussion of the beginnings of philosophy, because the concept of philosophy itself, like conceptuality itself, was a product of the history of philosophy."[79]

The East is not the West because the East lacks what is essentially Western: the "principle of individual freedom," which is dominant in the "Greek element" and even more so in the "Germanic element."[80] Hegel offered a quaint comparison to illustrate: The Greek gods appear more individualized, more like persons, while the Oriental gods are not so individualized. Oriental representations have a general character. They bear more the element of universality, a quality normally prevalent in philosophical reflection. It may seem that Oriental representations are individualized in their form (the examples of Brahma, Vishnu, and Shiva), but, actually, their individuality is superficial.[81]

Orientalists should not presume to have the authority to pronounce on philosophy or its history. Hegel, who could not be called a Sanskritist or Indianist because he knew no Indian languages, pronounced on Indian religion. In Hegel's lectures on the history of philosophy, the account of Oriental philosophy turns out to be in part an account of Oriental religion:

In all religions, what is most important is "Being-in-and-for-itself" or the one eternal God. In Oriental religion, this Being is understood as universal Substance. The Indians represent Brahma as the "outright non-sensible," the "highest being," "l'être supreme."[82] With the Oriental view of divine nature, only one kind of relationship is possible between the individual and God. It is the kind of relationship in which the individual has value only through identification with Substance. It is precisely through this identification, however, that individual consciousness is extinguished. That is, the individual ceases to be a subject for himself. When the Hindu gathers himself in thought, his concentration falls upon "non-consciousness" (Bewußtlosigkeit). "[T]he moment of this pure concentration is Brahma—then I am Brahma."[83] In contrast, Greek or Germanic subjectivity is that in which the subject, knowing himself to be free, seeks to preserve himself. In Oriental thought, however, Substance is the only existent, and from this the nonexistence of rights, individual consciousness, and will is a direct consequence.

In the Oriental perspective, if consciousness arrives at a determinate concept, this would be a state of separation from Substance. On the other side, unification with Substance means the destruction of all particularity. This accords with the excessive sublimity of Oriental religion. If there are reflections, if there is an enumeration of particulars, if there is a logic, it is merely superficial, "completely external," "highly pitiful, empty, pedantic, mindless"; "like the old Wolffian logic."[84]

An acute analysis of Oriental consciousness was not enough. The exclusion of Egypt and Asia from the history of philosophy had to be defended also rhetorically by knocking down old opinions about the antiquity and sophistication of Oriental knowledge.[85] One had to undermine the reputations of the great civilizations of the East. This was, of course, not a new endeavor in the historiography of philosophy. Hegel suggested that Chinese civilization was not as old or advanced as had been thought. He was aware of the great fame of Confucius, of his "good, competent moral teachings," but he told his students not to expect profound philosophical insights from the Chinese sage. Europeans really had nothing to gain from Confucius's teachings. Cicero's *De officiis* was a better alternative ("perhaps better for us than all the works of Confucius"). Hegel related what (nameless) "competent judges" had concluded about Confucius: that his reputation would have been better preserved *had he not been translated*. A book of sermons is better than the "completely ordinary" and "circuitous" ethics of Confucius. Hegel was able to concede, however, that the Chinese had "abstract thoughts of pure categories" as evident in the text "Yi-Jing." The thought displayed in this book remains, however, on the level of "abstract understanding."[86] Hegel expressed doubts about Chinese civilization in general: "[T]hey have a great reputation for learning, but this reputation, as well as the great length of their history etc., has been much reduced through better knowledge."[87] He also doubted claims made about Indian antiquity: "Recently their astronomical works have been studied, and here one sees that their great antiquity actually is not chronological in our sense. Nothing can be more convoluted than the chronology of the Indians. . . . They speak of many epochs, of their immensely long line of kings, of an enormous tally of names, but all is vague. . . ."[88]

There comes a point in these lectures where Hegel concedes that European religion came from the Orient ("from Syria, which is only one stride away from Greece"), but this seems not to disrupt his claim that "all [European] science and art originated directly from Greece" and "indirectly, through the Romans," who were "the models and teachers of the Europeans."[89] As evident in these lectures, the question of the origin of philosophy is a version of the question of the origin of (European) civilization. Like Meiners and Tennemann, Hegel designated Greece as that origin.

As European identity was dependent on the question of Greek origins, it was important for Hegel to address the latter. He agreed that the search for Greek origins did lead one to the Orient. At the same time, he argued that it was not necessary to look beyond Greece itself for the complete developmental cycle of Greek science and art. Moreover, whatever the Greeks received from the Orientals, they "reshaped," "reformed," "rebirthed."[90] This trope Hegel did not have to invent as he could have easily found it in the 1825, 1820, or 1816 edition of Tennemann's *Grundriss* or in Carus's *Ideen* (1809). Hegel trafficked in other graecophilic clichés as when he called the Greeks the bridge from savagery to civilization and the inventors of history.[91]

Hegel divided Greek philosophy into three epochs corresponding to the three moments of Spirit's development. The first epoch spans the period from Thales to Aristotle. The second epoch is occupied by Greek philosophy under Roman domination. The third is occupied by neo-Platonism and ends with the fifth-century philosopher Proclus. In Hegel's schema just as in Ast's and Rixner's, the first products of philosophy are the most general: "Philosophy begins with the absolute in general," with "what is simple": "the Infinite, Being, Water, etc." Upon such a universal foundation arises the stage at which the universal is apprehended as "determining itself, as active thought, the universal as acting . . . the *nous* of Anaxagoras and . . . Socrates."[92] The stage of the sophists, Socrates, and the Socratics brings forth the principle of subjectivity. In Plato and Aristotle, subjectivity attains complete formation as "objective thought."[93] By this stage, however, unity of thought gives way to the opposition of thought and being. The determination of thought and being (or thought from being) in this second epoch of Greek philosophy corresponds to the principles of Stoicism and Epicureanism. These two systems are attended by a third system, skepticism, "which recognizes neither the principle of thought nor the principle of being and admits no truth."[94] In Hegel's schema, Alexandrian philosophy (encompassing both neo-Aristotelianism and neo-Platonism) is "the consummation of Greek philosophy," the system that "absorb[s] all earlier forms of philosophy into itself," the system with which "the history of Greek philosophy ends."[95] I note that Hegel's periodization of Greek philosophy cuts out what, in the Schellingians' histories of philosophy, is the first epoch of Greek philosophy—the epoch of "esoteric, Orphic religion," when philosophy and religion are one.[96]

Hegel advanced a tripartite division of the history of philosophy. (So did Tennemann.) Under this tripartition, the Middle Ages is the period in which the realm of ideality is argued as *the* reality. A similar account of philosophy during the Middle Ages is given by Ast and Rixner. Hegel is alone, however, in calling it a transitional period "of historical more than philosophical significance," for in this period "thought is in the service of the Church" and philosophy is merely "formal."[97] Let us recall that on a similar basis Hegel excluded the Orient.[98] Free thought was absent from Europe during the Middle Ages just as it was absent from the ancient Orient, but, for Hegel, this did not entail the exclusion of medieval Europe from the history of philosophy. Medieval Europe is included in the history of philosophy even though, according to Hegel, free thought reemerges at the beginning of the sixteenth century (through the revival of the ancient Greek systems).[99] Hegel identified the Protestant Reformation of the sixteenth century with Spirit's "returning-to-itself," with Spirit's regaining of freedom at a time when external authority is replaced by individual consciousness.[100]

Hegel marked the beginning of modern philosophy with Descartes. Slightly before him come Francis Bacon and Jacob Böhme, who epitomize the two opposing tendencies in modern philosophy. Through Descartes and Spinoza, thought and being become more determinate. In the latter's system, thought and being are united as absolute Substance while the subjective aspect is denied. The principle of subjectivity is reasserted by Leibniz. His metaphysics is developed further by Wolff. At the same time, the practical and moral sciences and the observational sciences are developed through Locke. Skepticism then ensues. The last epoch of philosophy is the one inaugurated by Kant. He establishes "the absolute form of the Idea," the consequences of which Fichte pursues, but only from the side of subjectivity. Even after Fichte, the need to unite the content (absolute Substance) with the absolute form remains. This unification Schelling achieves. All previous philosophies are contained and transfigured in Schelling's system, which is the final system in Hegel's account of the history of philosophy.[101]

What I have argued in this chapter is that Hegel's history of philosophy, like Meiners's and Tennemann's, is actually the history of the philosophical deeds of white Man. The Greek and Germanic peoples who exclusively populate Hegel's history of philosophy correspond racially to the Celtic peoples in Meiners's natural history of mankind. From ancient to modern times, from Thales to Schelling, from Miletus to Berlin, the agents of philosophy are Whites. Hegel's history of philosophy bears a dialectical unity, it also bears a racial unity.

Hegel's history of philosophy is the consolidation, four decades later, of the "radical modification" of the history of philosophy.[102] His work can be regarded as the capstone to the onto I logic I al reorganization of the history of philosophy. Historical systems of philosophy are seen as occupying and representing stages of thought with each system being a "particular mode of presentation of a moment of the Idea," "a necessary point of passage of the Idea."[103] Accordingly, the historical systems of philosophy are each and all stages in the development of one system.[104]

It is in a very particular sense, therefore, that any past system is "refuted" since the "fundamental idea" persists in and through the systems of philosophy appearing in history.[105] No philosophical principle is abandoned if its essence is sublated in what supersedes it.[106] Earlier philosophies—e.g., the Platonic, Aristotelian, and neo-Platonic—are still "living," although they no longer have their previous forms. They are sublated as moments of a progression that continues on to higher developments.[107] Thought's development is a "deepening," a process of "cohesion," a becoming "stronger," "more intensive," "richer."[108] Hegel denied the possibility of a "concrete" system of Oriental philosophy because that would have been incoherent and also inconvenient. The earliest systems of philosophy had to be "the most abstract," "simplest," "easiest," and "poorest," while later philosophies were more "concrete" with the most recent system being "essentially the [latest] result of the foregoing labors of thinking Spirit."[109] It may seem that Spirit sometimes takes a backward step, but such a seeming regression indicates that Spirit is done with a stage.[110] We find in Rixner's *Handbuch* that Epicureanism is explained in this way: as "a harbinger and prelude to the decay of classical antiquity, on whose ruins a new era of humanity . . . was to blossom."[111] Hegel could express this idea more tersely: "Spirit is not idle."[112]

The exclusion of Africa and Asia was not a feature general to histories of philosophy of the late eighteenth and early nineteenth centuries. One can make the more limited claim that particular historians of philosophy in this period excluded Egypt and Asia. As we have seen, this exclusion was not even a feature general to the school of Absolute Idealism.

Hegel's embrace of the Kantian position is surprising because it is so wayward. It was a wayward step from Absolute Idealism, with which Hegel was united in many other ways. During lectures, Hegel acknowledged the many strengths of Ast's *Grundriss der Geschichte der Philosophie* and Rixner's *Handbuch der Geschichte der Philosophie* and recommended them to his students.[113] This was high praise from Hegel, who judged most historians of philosophy harshly.

In Ast's and Rixner's histories, the philosophical spirit descends upon India, moves through Asia and Egypt and on to Greece in real and ideal moments of self-apprehension. In Hegel's history, the philosophical spirit passes over the vast tracts of Asian and African humanity before descending upon the Greeks.

7

The Comparative History of Philosophy in August Tholuck's Polemic against Hegel

Among historians of philosophy of his generation, Hegel was exceptional in his antipathy toward the Orient, which went far beyond his disdain for the moral teachings of Confucius and the abstract thought in Indian texts. His judgment of Oriental (including Egyptian) religion and art was resoundingly negative as well. Scholars who have studied Hegel's relationship with Asia have all noted a great antipathy. It was more than fifty years ago that Helmuth von Glasenapp exposed Hegel as the arch-Orientalist that he was (in Edward Said's sense).[1] In 1979, Michel Hulin said of Hegel, "[N]o thinker contributed more to destroying the image, both traditional and Romantic, of the Orient as the source of wisdom and science."[2] In *India and Europe*, Halbfass ambivalently concludes that the exclusion of Indian and other Asian philosophical traditions from modern histories of philosophy is a legacy of Hegel's.[3] More recently, Stuart Jay Harten and Saverio Marchignoli have noted that Hegel was opposed even to the very notion of cross-cultural interpretation and appropriation.[4] Some scholars have tried more sympathetically to understand the reasons for Hegel's positions, which involved them in a search to find their coherence within his over-arching system. There is an apologetic aspect to some of their work as when they deal with Hegel's inconsistent statements and shifting opinions. Halbfass, for example, regards Hegel's shifting opinions on Indian philosophy as evidence of his open-mindedness in the face of changing information.[5] I would urge that one consider the possibility that they reveal a deep ambivalence, perhaps even an inner conflict, which Harten

133

has already begun to show.[6] In any case, the scholars whose work I mention above all agree on at least one explanation for Hegel's shortcomings of judgment: Not enough information on Chinese and Indian thought was available in Europe.

As I have shown, however, lack of information never stopped historians of philosophy from taking positions on questions that defined their field, including questions of the beginning point and domain of the history of philosophy. A lack of authenticated sources or reliable information as an explanation for academic philosophers' misjudgments of Asian thought is untenable.

This chapter presents an important context for reading Hegel's relationship with the Orient. We shall see that his statements were reactions to certain historical claims made by theologically motivated critics hostile to his philosophical project; that he was compelled to defend his philosophy from dangerous historicist attacks. One of his enemies was the Romantic philosopher and convert to Roman Catholicism, Friedrich Schlegel. We saw in Chapter 3 how Schlegel utilized his knowledge of Indian thought in a historical critique of all philosophy.[7] But he was not the only Christian thinker in Restoration Germany to have a deep investment in Oriental studies for what it could bring to the study of European thought. The Lutheran theologian and Orientalist August Tholuck (1799–1877) also utilized his knowledge of Asian thought in a sometimes subtle and sometimes overt polemic against speculative philosophy. In his 1826 work, *Die speculative Trinitätslehre des späteren Orients* (*The Speculative Doctrine of the Trinity of the Late Orient*), Tholuck combined philological and comparative-historical methods to produce a historical critique of philosophical attempts to know God through a speculative doctrine of the Trinity.[8]

Tholuck derived some early fame from his epistolary novel, *Die Lehre von der Sünde und vom Versöhner, oder Die wahre Weihe des Zweiflers* (*The Doctrine of Sin and the Redeemer, or The True Consecration of the Skeptic*), published originally in 1823.[9] Printed nine times during his lifetime and translated into French, English, Dutch, and Swedish, this work has been called the "standard tract" of the "German Awakening" (*Erweckungsbewegung*). It contains a polemic against "pantheism," which culminates in a synoptic history of both Eastern and Western thought for the purpose of demonstrating the futility and arrogance of speculative-philosophical approaches to Christian truth. When Tholuck was not battling theological "rationalists," the neo-Pietist was battling Hegelians. In one episode, he defended Christian orthodoxy against David Friedrich Strauss's de-mythologizing critique of the Gospels.[10]

Friedrich August Gotttreu Tholuck was born in 1799 in Breslau, the sickly son of a goldsmith.[11] Tholuck was a child of extraordinary intellectual gifts. By age seventeen, he was able to write in nineteen languages. He happily gave up the idea of entering his father's trade and began the study of Oriental philology at the University of Breslau. In 1816, he transferred to the University of Berlin, where he added theological studies. In the Prussian capital, he acquired several spiritual and academic mentors: Heinrich Friedrich von Diez (1751–1817), the Prussian diplomat and Orientalist; Hans Ernst von Kottwitz (1757–1843), the aristocratic patron of the German Awakening, and August Neander (1789–1850), the church historian and professor of theology at the university. Through them, Tholuck was introduced to neo-Pietist circles in Berlin. He taught at Johannes Jänicke's missionary school from 1821 to 1826 and served as the director of the Central Bible Society from 1821 to 1825 as well as the secretary for the Society for the Promotion of Christianity among the Jews. In 1823, he traveled to England as the German representative of the London Missionary Society.

During these same years, Tholuck was establishing an academic career. In 1821, he was appointed *Privatdozent* in theology at Berlin. In 1822, he was awarded a doctorate from the University of Jena for a dissertation on Sufism, which led to his promotion as *ausserordentlicher Professor* at Berlin.[12] Favored by Minister Altenstein and the conservative policies of Frederick William III's government, Tholuck was given a professorial chair in theology at the University of Halle. With the appointment of Tholuck, the government hoped to counteract the rationalism of Halle's theological faculty. Save for two trips to England and a year (1828–9) in Rome as the chaplain attached to the Prussian embassy, Tholuck spent the rest of his life in Halle. He died on June 10, 1877.

Tholuck's work was grounded in the knowledge of Near-Eastern languages, namely, Arabic, Turkish, Syriac, Persian, and Hebrew. He drew from the literature accumulating in Europe on Asian religions and philosophies, to which he himself contributed. In the introductions and prefaces to his several works of Oriental philology, he recommends the study of Oriental thought because of its relevance to contemporary theological issues. In the preface to *Blüthensammlung aus der morgenländischen Mystik* (*Bouquet of Oriental Mysticism*) (1825), an anthology of poems, Tholuck claims that the contents of Arabic, Persian, and Turkish manuscripts are very relevant to historians of both philosophy and religion.[13] He was especially intrigued by what he observed to be a close affinity between the mystical writings of the

Sufis and literary trends of his own time. He hoped that his translations "would raise prosaic minds to a higher level of religious consciousness," but he also addressed himself to "those caught in the
endless spiral over the barren field of metaphysics," "those who stood
nearest to Christianity without possessing the kernel of it," "those
who stood outside of Christian revelation" and "those who completely refused to accept the edifying mercy of God."[14] He would rebuke
such persons by holding a mirror up to them—by showing them that
they were no more ingenious than Muslim philosophers and mystics.

In the preface to *Die speculative Trinitätslehre*, Tholuck explains
the relevance of Oriental philosophy for academic theology:

> What one hesitantly calls Near-Eastern or Oriental phi-
> losophy has roused special interest in modern times for
> many reasons. The interest is partly due to the frequent
> attempts carried out in the new theology to derive certain
> Christian doctrines from *gnosis*, but it is also and especially
> due to the strong religious and philosophical inclination
> of our time if not toward the process and method of the
> so-called Oriental philosophy, then certainly toward the
> results thereof.[15]

In a parallel to trends in comparative-linguistic inquiry, Tholuck
hypothesized that the geographic origin of speculative philosophy lay
in a region east of the Levant. He was hopeful that increased access
to Islamic, Hindu, and Parsi sources would support his theory.[16] He
mentioned the recent publication in Calcutta of a Persian text called
Dabistan, which was also available in a German translation by Johann
Friedrich Hugo von Dalberg.[17] This work, presenting the religious
beliefs of various Indian sects, seemed to support his theory that theosophy in Islam and Judaism (and, by implication, Christianity) has
origins in the pagan religions of the East.[18] The aim of *Die speculative Trinitätslehre* was to separate the elements of Gnosticism from
the "positive religion" of the Muslims and trace such elements back
to a presumed Persian or Indian source. Thus, *Die speculative Trinitätslehre* deals a lot with the history of Islamic sects. Tholuck found
in this history the interesting phenomenon of the fusion of positive
religion with speculative philosophy.[19] But Tholuck's more audacious,
barely disguised aim was to separate philosophical conceptions of
God, based on a speculative Trinity, from the religion of the Bible.[20]
Die speculative Trinitätslehre suggests subtly that Hegel's account of
God is not Christian, but Oriental and pagan.[21]

Tholuck sent a copy of *Die speculative Trinitätslehre* to his former colleague at Berlin. In a belated reply of July 3, 1826, Hegel thanked Tholuck for "[t]he disclosures which you have first communicated to the public in this work."[22] Hegel appreciated learning about the influence of Greek, Jewish, and neo-Platonic philosophies on Muslim thinkers, which for him confirmed that the Arab nation did not develop any sciences independently. It did not surprise Hegel that he found himself disagreeing with Tholuck regarding the latter's interpretations of Aristotle and Plotinus. Tholuck was right that the Trinity appears in Plato's dialogues *Timaeus* and *Philebus*; however, it appears in a "very abstract" form. Hegel thought that Tholuck's citations of specific passages from Chinese and Indian sources were inadequate as there existed more reliable and relevant information. Hegel found particularly objectionable Tholuck's comment that early Christian theologians, under the influence of Platonic and Aristotelian ideas, arrived at a speculative theorem of the Trinity which they correlated with certain Bible passages of indeterminate meaning and that this was done in the manner of certain Muslim divines. Hegel wrote:

> Does not the sublime Christian knowledge of God as Triune merit respect of a wholly different order than comes from ascribing it merely to such an externally historical course? In your entire publication I have not been able to feel or find any trace of a native understanding of this doctrine. *I am a Lutheran, and through philosophy have been at once completely confirmed in Lutheranism.* I do not allow myself to be put off such a basic doctrine by externally historical modes of explanation. There is a higher spirit in it than merely that of such human tradition. I detest seeing such things explained in the same manner as perhaps the descent and dissemination of silk culture, cherries, smallpox, and the like.[23]

Was there even a question as to the Lutheranism of Hegel's philosophizing? In *Die speculative Trinitätslehre*, there apparently was.

Tholuck scholars never mention that *Die Lehre von der Sünde* also deals with Oriental thought.[24] Given its title, one might expect nothing other than a tract in theological dogmatics. The author states in the foreword that his book's aim is to clarify and reassert the fundamental Christian doctrines of sin and redemption. But there is more. This story of the spiritual journey of a university student is combined with a philosophical thesis on the problem of evil, which forms the main thrust of Tholuck's polemic against "pantheism." Through six supplements (reduced to five in later editions) appended to the end of the novel, Tholuck defends the Bible as historical truth and provides a commentary on the account of man's fall into sin as well as lessons on the use of apologetics, dogmatics, and "inner experience" in cultivating the conviction of the truth of Christianity. The second supplement, which I discuss in detail below, is particularly relevant to my study of the historiography of philosophy. There, Tholuck presents a synoptic history of "pantheistic" philosophies, beginning in ancient China and culminating in his contemporary Germany.

Tholuck adopted a line of argumentation used by Friedrich Schlegel: The problem of evil is the problem with pantheism. In Tholuck's novel, Julius has recently awakened to the truth of Christianity and hopes to save his friend, Guido, from his corrosive skepticism and spiritual despair through a meditation on evil: "Allow me, Dear One! to write down in great detail what I think of evil, its nature, and its origin."[25] Julius describes for Guido the three ways in which one can conceptualize evil. One can think, like the Persians, that evil has its own source, in the same way that the good has its source in God. This is similar to how Platonic philosophers conceived of evil: as arising from matter, which is by its nature unordered and eternally resistant to order. Julius tells Guido that two rulers cannot govern the same universe. Wanting unity, the mind seeks to know the ultimate basis of everything. Two gods who delimit each other's power is not satisfying. One thus arrives at the second way to conceptualize evil: If God is the unitary and absolute basis of being for everything, then He is the source of evil as well as the good. If He is the ground and condition of all that exists, He is also the father of evil. If all being is His being, if all things are themselves part of His consciousness, then evil is part of Creation. One must then view the individual as a defect of sorts and evil as a necessary outcome of Creation. If God is the ground of being of everything that is, if He is what conditions everything, then man, too, is conditioned by Him. This means that God is the one and only agent in the world and, therefore, in man; not only is the good in man the action of God, but the evil in man is also the action of God. For Tholuck's Julius, the moral consequences of precisely this negation of the distinction between good and evil is the central problem with pantheism.

In the introduction to *Blüthensammlung*, Tholuck claims provocatively that all speculative philosophy must result in either pantheism or polytheism. Sharper philosophical minds usually arrive at the first proposition while the second proposition does not really enter into consideration. The philosophers of the first proposition, however, often do not realize its "pernicious consequences." These are that man's moral standard is likewise not true in the absolute sense and that good and evil are a distinction based not in reality, but in an apparent reality.[26] It is in regard to the moral consequences of pantheism that Julius exclaims colorfully:

> The Medusa-head of the Absolute—this gradual, self-generating and self-annihilating, infinite chaos, which man cannot think, let alone love—deadens and paralyses the holiest stirrings of my soul, and, I do strongly state this, that besides the fanatic, only Satan can revel in the immeasurable abyss in which good and evil are as nothing.[27]

"I cannot set evil next to God," writes Julius to his friend, "and I also cannot set evil in God. Evil was not created by God and is no necessary defect in man."[28] Julius heeds the Bible in this matter:

> God, who is the law for Himself, is also the law for all created, including man. In his state of purity, man knew no other will but the will of his Creator and foundation of being, and it was this agreement with the holiest will that brought with it its blessings. Then, man wanted to be like God, he wanted to become the law and foundation for himself and to be the source of his own happiness, he wanted a will other than God's will, and so it happened— the fall of the first man.[29]

Man's first arrogant act resulted in sinfulness, error, and misery. The idea that error is inherent to the human condition illuminated in one stroke the entire history of philosophy.

Through comparison, the intellectual artifacts of antiquity shed light on modern philosophy while the intellectual artifacts of Asia shed light on European phenomena. Through a kind of morphological comparison of philosophical systems, Tholuck determined several classes of pantheism. The classification of pantheistic philosophies in itself was not the goal. Rather, Tholuck's intention was to utilize these comparisons and classifications in his polemics, which is apparent from the title of the second supplement attached to *Die Lehre von der Sünde*: "On the necessity by which the understanding is led logically to the denial of the self-conscious God, the existence of the individual, freedom and morality; on the age of these doctrines and their constant return in man's intellectual history; [and] on the belief in a self-conscious God in comparison to the belief in a pantheistic God."[30] Here and elsewhere, Tholuck used his study of religious and philosophical history as an occasion for distinguishing the "positive" doctrines of Christianity from speculative or pagan ideas.

Echoing an earlier polemic by F. H. Jacobi, the second supplement states, "It is conclusive from the most recent trend in philosophy that an idealist pantheism is the only true philosophy."[31] Immediately following is an interesting footnote on the usage of the term "pantheism":

> All the various pantheistic schools reject this appellation [pantheism], though Schelling himself admits it; but in certain respects all true philosophy must be pantheism. In any case, one will concede that the French materialists ought to be called such. One does not understand why the idealists should not also be called pantheists since they do not recognize a God who is separate from the world. It is on this very point that the materialist is no different from the idealist.[32]

But what is pantheism if the term encompasses both idealism and materialism? How does one classify such diverse pantheisms? Tholuck distinguished three classes of pantheism (conceptual pantheism, pantheism of fantasy, and pantheism of feeling) and explained that, historically, these pantheisms thrived within the positive religions of Judaism, Christianity, and Islam. Often one type of pantheism was combined with another. In the second (1825) edition of *Die Lehre von der Sünde*, Tholuck identifies the systems of the Eleatics, Spinoza, Fichte, and Hegel as species of conceptual pantheism. The pantheism of fantasy is found among the Orientals (e.g., Kabbalists and neo-Platonists), in the medieval philosophers Scotus Erigena and Jacob Böhme, and in the modern philosopher Schelling. Lastly, the pantheism of feeling is descriptive of many mystics both Christian and Muslim.[33]

Having supplied his readers with the classification of pantheistic thought, Tholuck proceeded with a "condensed"—and rather breathtaking—"overview of the various systems," covering China and Japan, India, Persia, Greece, and Europe (early Christian, medieval, and modern). Tholuck was aware of three varieties of philosophy in China: the "Inkia" based on the text called *I-Ching*, "Tao-tse" (Daoism) based on the book *Tao Te Ching* by Lao Tzu, and the religion of

"Fohi" (Buddhism). He regarded all three schools as pantheistic, the third being "the most logically resultant" pantheism of them all.[34] He related that the Shinto and "Budso" schools of Japan were as pantheistic as the Chinese "Syuto" school. In India there are three major religious sects (Brahmin, Buddhist, and Jain) and seven philosophical schools, but all are based on the same fundamental pantheistic doctrine.[35] A comment about the Jains is typical of Tholuck's approach. The Jains seem to have arrived at an elaborate version of Spinoza's system though they antedate the European philosopher by several hundred years.[36] Turning to Buddhism, Tholuck noted that no one of adequate philosophical capacity had yet given a good exposition of this system of thought. But it was known from existing accounts that the Buddhists were "less exuberating and more reflective, that they accepted the reality of matter, whose evolution they explained as the life of God and as eternal. . . . Hence, they are not emanationists, like the Brahmins, but genuine pantheists."[37] Moving on to Persia, Tholuck provided the reader with a list of references on Persian pantheism (for him, synonymous with Sufism). This list included Anquetil du Perron's *Oupnek'hat*, Francis Gladwin's translation *Ayeen-Akbary* (1800), Tholuck's own dissertation on *Sufismus*, and his anthology *Blüthensammlung*.[38] Tholuck asserted that pantheistic metaphysical thought results quite logically in the strange practices of Persian and Indian theosophers, who try to bring about in themselves a state of complete non-consciousness by either constantly twirling their bodies or staring at a spot. They believe that by such means they can block the sensory channels of the body, and after spending a duration in this numb condition, they claim to see God.[39] Moving on to ancient Greece, Tholuck claimed that pantheistic doctrines were the basis of all Greek philosophies; from the hylozoism of the Ionian philosophers to the full-blown pantheism of the Eleatic Xenophanes. The latter philosopher took that final step: He declared that All is One and that plurality is a deception of the senses. "After the Eleatic school, pantheism would never again express itself with such finality."[40] Thereafter, Greek philosophers had enough sense not to put forward this doctrine with such daring, that is, until the neo-Platonists.

"Only with the neo-Platonists, and indeed partly under Oriental influences, was a system again developed which was in every regard similar to the Indian, Chinese, and Sufi systems."[41] Neo-Platonism occupies a special place in Tholuck's history of philosophy. This school is important because it was the historical bridge between Oriental and Greek thought and between speculative philosophy and the positive content of the Old Testament. In addition, neo-Platonism is the bridge between ancient and modern philosophy insofar as certain modern systems share key features with neo-Platonism.

For Tholuck, neo-Platonism was no less a pantheism. Yet unlike the simplistic Eleatic doctrine of the All-Is-One, neo-Platonism is a system of emanation. In this system, completely unconditioned and absolute Being, through a primordial movement, becomes Spirit (or pure consciousness). Spirit, which contains the Ideas, undergoes self-copying and self-delimiting in stages or moments, resulting in the world of determinate or phenomenal being. The practical consequences of this system are the same as with all pantheistic systems: The individual is but an illusion, and evil is viewed as a necessary outcome of Creation. Plotinus, the key neo-Platonist, taught that true knowledge of God was attainable not through speculation, but through direct perception. To attain true knowledge of God meant, in fact, to become one with Him. This, according to Tholuck, is "in complete agreement with the Indian enthusiasts."[42]

Tholuck's interest in neo-Platonism and its influence on Jewish, Christian, and Islamic theologies culminated in his *Commentatio de VI guam Graeca philosophia in theologiam tum Muhammedanorum tum Judaeorum exercuerit, Particula II: De orut Cabbalae* of 1837.[43] But as early as 1825, Tholuck was convinced that neo-Platonism was a foreign element interpolated into revelation. And if neo-Platonic philosophy is alien to revelation, it should be possible to separate the one from the other through analysis. Tholuck's discussion of Dionysius the Areopagite demonstrates the objective:

> Within Christianity, neo-Platonism became in most cases the basis of contemplative mysticism. The first and, therefore, the most peculiar monument of this kind is the writings of Dionysius the Areopagite, falsely attributed to be the Dionysius of Apostolic history by a quasi-neo-Platonist of the fifth century (as there were many of them at that time). In this text, the highest goal of the Christian is said to be unification with God—but not that genuine and exclusively Christian faith, humility, and love attainable through overcoming one's own will, but an exaggerated, enthusiastic sort, attained through abstraction from all sensibility and ending up in—as Dionysius calls it—θεῖος γνοφος, where one sees God in a state of ecstasy.[44]

Dionysius was the only thinker able to develop a purely conceptual pantheism in the midst of the strict dogmatism of the Church while those "more inclined to their hearts" turned toward contemplative mysticism (the "cloudy pantheism of feeling") and empty theosophical speculations, combined further with theurgy and magic. Tholuck named Scotus Erigena and Amalric of Bena conceptual pantheists and supposed that Dionysius was a major influence on them.[45] Medieval mystics could also have found a model in Dionysius.

> [I]n the writings of these men the effect of Platonic pantheism is more or less evident along with an overestimation of man's relatedness to the divine, the neglect of Scripture, a vague brooding and a fanatical overexcitement. The pantheistic element distinctly reemerged in mystics such as Jacob Böhme, Robert Fludd, Paracelsus, and Helmont, who, besides the needs of their heart, had the gift of speculation. The systems of these men were based more or less on a pantheism of fantasy . . . to which magic and theurgy were added.[46]

Finally, the modern era has witnessed the complete triumph of pantheism, a state of affairs that indicted modern philosophy. *Die Lehre von der Sünde* gives the following account:

> A new era of speculation, unlike any other since pagan times, began with Descartes. He supplied Spinoza with the elements for the most complete, logically ultimate, and most manifestly pantheistic system that has ever existed. . . . Hume's radical skepticism concerning all certainty in knowledge called forth Kant's critique of the human faculty of knowledge. Kant's admission that the external world is an unknown X . . . his admission that a God who is separate from the world is only the postulate of practical reason allowed Fichte to take the next step. The predicateless thing-in-itself, which Kant left standing in the world, Fichte then put in the inner world of man and conceded that nothing but the limits of the Ego remained. . . . Fichte was however not yet the Messiah, as Jacobi called him, but the John the Baptist of speculative reason. The final step toward the sublation [*Aufhebung*] of the incomprehensible was taken by Schelling.[47]

The world tour of pantheism ends with Schelling and the following summation: "Pantheism, which is the beginning and consummation of the speculation of (fallen) man . . . has in most recent times appeared in its completely logical consistency."[48]

Tholuck's account of philosophy's history was designed to inflict maximum injury on the reputation of philosophy. It was also an affront to academic philosophy's version of its history in several ways: It defined philosophy broadly so as to include so-called religious ideas without distinguishing philosophy from religious thought. In contrast to the Kantians or Hegel, Tholuck antedated the beginning of philosophy, giving it an ancient Asian pedigree. In treating (albeit superficially) the philosophical or religious sects of China, Japan, India, and Persia together with the sects of Europe, Tholuck effected a parity between Eastern and Western thought. He exuberantly juxtaposed the Upanishads with Schelling's philosophy, Jainism with Spinozism, neo-Platonism with Hegelianism, and so on. Finally, Tholuck's history subverted the narrative of progressive development which was so vital to academic philosophy's legitimacy and self-representation. In Tholuck's view, there was no progress in philosophy—only "repetition" (*Wiederkehr*).

Hegel responded to Tholuck's attacks directly in his *Enzyklopädie der philosophischen Wissenschaften im Grundrisse* of 1827 and indirectly in his lectures on the philosophy of religion of the same year.[49] In a letter of May 29, 1827 to Carl Daub in Heidelberg, he mentions that the preface he just composed for the new edition of his *Enzyklopädie* runs longer than he intended and that Tholuck was the cause.[50] In the footnotes to this preface, Hegel censures Tholuck, who is labeled an "ardent representative of the Pietistic trend," for interpreting the doctrine of the Trinity in terms of its extrinsic, historical origins only; as the product of philosophical speculation by early Christian theologians enthused by Platonic and Aristotelian ideas. Hegel charged that Tholuck treated this fundamental dogma "cavalierly" by describing it as "decorative timbering" (*Fachwerk*) and by comparing it to a mirage! Hegel then quoted Tholuck, who had written that the Christian faith could never be grounded in the doctrine of the Trinity.[51]

Hegel was forced into the interesting position of defending the doctrine of the Trinity. He reminded his readers that the Trinity, the holiest doctrine of Christianity, was much older than Scholastic theology. The Trinity constitutes the very subtance of the Nicene Creed. Does Tholuck regard this fundamental creed of the faith as merely subjective? "Without this dogma, how can the doctrine of redemption, which . . . Herr Th[oluck] seeks to bring to the emotions with so much energy, have more than a moral or, if one will, more than a heathen meaning—how can it have a Christian meaning?"[52]

Hegel openly suspected Tholuck of disregarding other central dogmas of Christianity. He noted that Tholuck repeatedly brought up the suffering and death of Christ, but never mentioned the Resurrection. Tholuck seemed to equate the guilt-consciousness and wretchedness of the sinner with punishment for sin. He called God (and not Christ) the sole source of eternal beatitude. Hegel was alleging that Tholuck was no orthodox believer because his conception of the punishment of sin was none other than the "natural punishment of sin" of Enlightenment theologians. Hegel then unleashed the following:

> Some time ago, in the upper house of the English Parliament a bill concerning the sect of the Unitarians failed; on this occasion an English gazette put out a notice on the great number of Unitarians in Europe and America and added: "on the European continent Protestantism and Unitarianism are for the most part synonymous." Theologians can determine whether Herr Tholuk's dogmatics differentiates itself from the standard theology of the Enlightenment on no more than one or, at most, two points, and if they were looked at more closely, whether even in regard to these, [his dogmatics is any different] from the standard theology of the Enlightenment.[53]

Hegel struck back by accusing pious Tholuck of anti-Trinitarian natural theology.

Hegel also responded to the pernicious idea that pantheism is the only true philosophy especially since his own philosophy was implicated. In the longest of the footnotes in the *Enzyklopädie* preface, Hegel cites passages in *Blüthensammlung* and *Die Lehre von der Sünde* to argue that Tholuck's presentation of philosophy is facile and very biased if not false.[54] He added that Tholuck's perspective was not unique, but could be found in a hundred books by theologians.

Hegel criticized the "peculiar clumsiness and distortion" with which Tholuck, in *Die Lehre von der Sünde*, set out only two ways in which one could philosophically conceive of God: as unconditioned Being (which Tholuck called pantheistic) and as a multiplicity of gods, each with a separate nature. Hegel contended that the second view should, in fact, be called pantheistic, for in that view all beings are divine while monotheism is reflected in the first view.[55] (Hegel's point is that Tholuck is not much of a philosopher.) In case the reader desired an additional clarification, he was referred to a further note on pantheism near the end of the *Enzyklopädie*.[56] In that final note, Hegel, in reference to *Blüthensammlung*, informs the reader that Tholuck used the word pantheism in its usual, "unclear" sense in describing the poetry of Rūmī and other Muslim mystics and that he seemed unable to help himself, being "seized by a wonderful enthusiasm" for his subject. Hegel added, "Where the author engages in philosophizing (p. 12f.) however, he does not get beyond the ordinary standpoint of the metaphysics of the understanding and its uncritical categories."[57]

"'Pantheism' in the proper sense means that everything, the whole, the universe, this complex of everything existing, these infinitely many individual things—that all this is God." This was how, in his lectures on the philosophy of religion, Hegel explicated "[t]he usual"—that is, the confused and unphilosophical—"representation of pantheism." He continued, "And the accusation made [by Tholuck] against philosophy is that it maintains that everything is God, 'everything' meaning here this infinite multiplicity of individual things—not the universality that has being in and for itself but the individual things in their empirical existence, as they exist immediately but not in their universality."[58] Hegel dismissed this accusation as shallow and false:

> Now it is a wholly false contention that pantheism of this sort is effectively present in any philosophy [textual variant: religion] whatsoever. It has never occurred to anyone to say that everything, all individual things collectively, in their individuality and contingency, are God—for example, that paper or this table is God. No one has ever held that. Still less has this been maintained in any philosophy.[59]

He took up the example of Spinozism, a modern system commonly labeled pantheism. He disagreed with the characterization of Spinozism as pantheism because in that philosophy no actuality is ascribed to individual things ("in Spinozism this world or this 'all' simply is *not* [*ist gar nicht*]").[60] It is better to call it *acosmism*. In his lectures on the history of philosophy of 1825/26, Hegel said: "[O]ne could in fact call [Spinozism] acosmism because all things natural are merely modifications. Spinoza claims [that] what one calls a world is not at all; it is only a form of God, nothing in and for itself; the world has no true reality."[61] Spinozism cannot be characterized as atheism either; the accusation that Spinoza does not differentiate God from the finite is null because the finite, according to him, is not real.[62] When we think the idea that "God is the actual being, this abiding with self, the one truth, the absolute actuality," we think and define God above all as substance. It is "entirely correct that substance is this identity with itself," but it is "entirely superficial" to say that philosophy is an identity system; that speculative philosophy amounts to pantheism. Those who say this know "abstract identity, or unity in general" and not "the inherent determination of this unity."[63]

Hegel also addressed the accusation that speculative philosophy negates morality. He stayed with Spinozism as his example and proxy: "It is said that in Spinozism the distinction of good and evil has no intrinsic validity, that morality is annulled, and so it is a matter of indifference whether one is good or evil." While affirming the Christian doctrine that God is good, Hegel conceded that the good-evil distinction is "sublated in God as the sole true actuality"; that the good-evil distinction "is not present in this One, in this substance." "The distinction of good and evil makes its entrance together with the distinction of God from the world, in particular from human beings."[64] It is not the case that morality is absent from Spinozism. Hegel explained,

> With regard to the distinction of God and humanity, the basic determination of Spinozism is that human beings have God alone as their goal. For the distinction, i.e., for human beings, the law is the love of God, that they be directed solely toward this love and not grant validity to their distinction or wish to persist in it, but have their orientation toward God alone. This is the most sublime morality, that evil is what is null, and human beings ought not to let this distinction, this nullity, be valid within themselves nor make it valid at all. We can will to persist in this distinction, can push it to the point of opposition to God, the universal in and for itself. In so doing we are evil. But we can also deem our distinction to be null and void, and can posit our essential being solely in God and in our orientation toward God. In so doing we are good. [Unverified transcripts of the 1827 lectures add: Thus the distinctiveness of good and evil certainly enters into Spinozism. God and the human being confront one another, and indeed do so with the specification that evil is to be deemed null and void. Therefore it is so far from being the case that morality, ethics, and the distinction between good and evil are absent from this standpoint that, on the contrary, this distinction here stands entirely in its place.]

> This distinction is not [applicable] within God as such,
> within God under this definition as substance. But for hu-
> man beings there is this distinction, since distinctiveness in
> general enters with human existence, and more specifically
> the distinction between good and evil.[65]

With such thorough explications of the moral distinctions of Spinozism, Hegel hoped to put the accusations of amorality to rest.

Tholuck's comparative study of philosophy is another species of
the genus described in Chapters 2 and 3 above. It is a third species of
comparative history of philosophy after de Gérando's and Schlegel's
and a distinctly polemical one. The critical uses of the comparative
history of philosophy are demonstrated by de Gérando and Schlegel;
the polemical uses by Tholuck. The Lutheran theologian was neither
the first comparativist of philosophy nor the last. The comparative
history of philosophy was not advanced, however, by the polemical
uses he made of it.

As a major target of Tholuck's polemics, Hegel had good reason
to be hostile toward comparative history of philosophy. He was put
in a difficult position by Tholuck, who compared him to Arab and
Muslim theosophers on the one hand and Spinoza on the other and
who told the history of philosophy in a post-lapsarian narrative of
error and misery. The comparisons to theosophers, pantheists, and
Orientals could have brought down on Hegel the charge of atheism,
but he was deft in resisting the charge. One of the ways in which he
resisted was to write Africa and Asia out of the history of philosophy.

Conclusion

The historiographers of philosophy are nearly unanimous that the writing of the history of philosophy changed fundamentally in the late eighteenth century. I argued above that Kantian philosophers were the central agents of "reform." The methods that characterize modern historical practice, such as textual criticism and writing history from authenticated primary sources, were already in use in German universities and academies and were not the substance of the reform that took place at the end of the eighteenth century. What was new about this reform was that the empirical-historical record of philosophy was subordinated to an *a priori* schema whose principles were derived from Kantian philosophy. Despite the blatant sectarianism of such an approach, historiographers have tended to see this development as an important step in philosophy's scientization (*Verwissenschaftlichung*).

Scientization is the metanarrative at work in the historiographies as well as the histories of philosophy that have been the subject of this book. This metanarrative is premised on the view that changes in science proceed in unilinear development driven by internally generated causes. The science metanarrative preempts ideology critique. It covers over the contestations, missed opportunities, and ideological uses that riddle the history of philosophy. Does scientization explain the exclusion of Africa and Asia from the history of philosophy? It certainly can by subsuming exclusion under scientization, by divorcing the history of race and racism from the history of domination, and by divorcing philosophical developments from their human agents.

My approach has been different. I have argued that Christoph Meiners was the precise founder of a movement in historiography to exclude Africa and Asia and that this movement was carried forward by Tennemann and Hegel. Meiners's direct influence on them is apparent in their arguments for excluding the Orient from the history of philosophy. The most central arguments were

149

racial-anthropological ones, carried over from Meiners's publications and repeated without much change. Kant never produced a work of history of philosophy, but he sketched the outlines of one in his logic lectures. There, one can behold Kant's own words authorizing the exclusion of the Orientals. His reasons for the exclusion were ones he got from Meiners.

Thus, when the first Kantian histories of philosophy appeared in the 1790s, the campaign to exclude Africa and Asia from the history of philosophy had already begun. Kantian histories of philosophy united *a priori* construction and race-based Eurocentrism, which are fundamental features of Hegel's history of philosophy. In this regard, both he and Tennemann are of the same school, both he and Tennemann were heirs of Meiners's exclusionary historiography.

Like Meiners and Tennemann, Hegel tried to explain away persistent stories of Egyptian and Phoenician colonies in early, uncivilized Greece. Like Meiners and Tennemann, Hegel did not deny the historical existence of Asiatic colonies in Greece, but questioned the extent to which they influenced the Greek people. In phrases virtually identical to Tennemann's, Hegel extolled the originality and genius of the Greeks, which transformed what was foreign into something peculiarly their own.

Hegel and Tennemann are of the same school of historiography in a further way. When the first volume of his *Geschichte der Philosophie* appeared in 1798, Tennemann was criticized for excluding the Orientals. He resisted the critics, some of whom were armed with the latest information on Asian philosophies drawn from Asian texts. By 1816, the year of the second edition of his *Grundriss der Geschichte der Philosophie*, Tennemann presented an additional argument in the defense of his position: Oriental thought does not fall within the domain of philosophy. Hegel was making essentially the same point in defense of the same position when he pointed out that Oriental philosophy was no different from Oriental religion.

Tennemann and Hegel are of the same school in another respect. When it became too difficult to exclude the Orient outright, they adopted the compromise solution proposed by Carus: the thought of the non-Europeans is to be accounted for, but *not* in connection to the historical development of Greek philosophy. Tennemann and Hegel eventually included an account of the philosophemes of various Oriental peoples, which they placed deliberately within their introductory remarks (therefore, *not* in the body of their histories of philosophy). Notwithstanding this compromise, Tennemann and Hegel were still insisting that philosophy began in Greece.

The denial of Oriental philosophy was just one facet of a particularly difficult relationship that Hegel had with contemporary trends in Oriental philology. In *Ueber die Sprache und Weisheit der Indier*, Schlegel had implicitly compared Schelling's speculative idealism to Indian pantheism to the ill-repute of both. Hegel became the target of similar attacks, but from a foe more formidable than Schlegel. Tholuck compared Hegel's system to the systems of medieval Muslim divines in a comparative-historical critique of speculative philosophy in monotheistic civilizations. In Tholuck's polemical presentation, the history of philosophy is a serial repetition of pantheistic systems.

What the editors Walter Jaeschke and Pierre Garniron took to be Hegel's increasing interest, over the decade of the 1820s, in Oriental philosophies I interpret rather as his increasing effort to counterargue the Orientalists' claims about philosophy in Asia. Part of Hegel's strategy was to deny over and over again that the Orientals ever had philosophy. The other stratagem was to refute the very possibility of cross-cultural interpretation and appropriation on which the Oriental Renaissance was premised.

Hegel's exclusion of Africa and Asia from the history of philosophy was the culmination of a movement within academic philosophy that had been gaining momentum for two decades before he gave his first lecture on the history of philosophy in 1805. Thus, my work revises Halbfass's thesis that the exclusion of Asia from the history of philosophy is a legacy of Hegel's. The racial exclusion of Africa and Asia from the history of philosophy is ultimately a legacy of Meiners's.

In the nineteenth century, the history of philosophy was one of the subjects most regularly covered in philosophy lectures at German universities. Courses and handbooks on the history of philosophy were the vehicles through which students were initiated into the discipline. The history of philosophy ingrained in them the canons of philosophy, which in turn reenforced a particular vision of German and European identity.

When one day the history of philosophy ceases to do what it does in the service of philosophy, philosophers will cease to teach it.

Notes

Preface

1. See Sergio Moravia, *La scienza dell'uomo nel Settecento* (Bari: Laterza, 1970), 209f.; Britta Rupp-Eisenreich, "Des choses occultes en histoire des sciences humaines: le destin de la 'science nouvelle' de Christoph Meiners," in *L'Ethnographie* 90–91 (1983): 131–83, and "C. Meiners et J. M. Gérando: un chapitre du comparatisme anthropologique," in *L'homme des Lumières et la découverte de l'autre: Études sur le XVIIIe siècle*, ed. Daniel Droixhe and Pol-Pierre Gossiaux (Brussels: Université libre de Bruxelles, 1985), 21–47.

2. Christoph Meiners, *Geschichte des Ursprungs, Fortgangs und Verfalls der Wissenschaften in Griechenland und Rom* (Lemgo: Meyer, 1781).

3. Meiners is completely passed over by Peter Hanns Reill in his work on *The German Enlightenment and the Rise of Historicism* (Berkeley: University of California Press, 1975) and by Karl J. Fink in his essay "Storm and stress anthropology," *History of the Human Sciences* 6, no. 1 (1993): 51–71. Meiners *sans* racism comes up in Hans-Jürgen Schings's *Melancholie und Aufklärung: Melancholiker und ihre Kritiker in Erfahrungsseelenkunde und Literatur des 18. Jahrhunderts* (Stuttgart: Metzler, 1977) and Annette Meyer's *Von der Wahrheit zur Wahrscheinlichkeit: Die Wissenschaft vom Menschen in der schottischen und deutschen Aufklärung* (Tübingen: Niemeyer, 2008).

4. Georg G. Iggers, "The University of Göttingen 1760–1800 and the Transformation of Historical Scholarship," *Storia della storiografia* 2 (1982): 11–37 (see p. 33); and Johan van der Zande, "Popular philosophy and the history of mankind in eighteenth-century Germany," *Storia della storiografia* 22 (1992): 37–56 (see p. 52). In more recent conversations with me, van der Zande was more doubtful that the term racism could be used to describe eighteenth-century phenomena.

5. Michael C. Carhart, *The Science of Culture in Enlightenment Germany* (Cambridge, MA: Harvard University Press, 2007). Because Carhart separates "Meiners's cultural theory" from "his racial theory" and discusses the former without discussing the latter, his is a distorted portrait of Meiners (see pp. 243–47 in his book). Carhart is less apologetic on Meiners in his more recent study, "Polynesia and polygenism: the scientific use of travel

literature in the early 19th century" (*History of the Human Sciences* 22, no. 2 [2009]: 58–86).

6. These few studies are a forty-six-page essay by Friedrich Lotter, "Christoph Meiners und die Lehre von der unterschiedlichen Wertigkeit der Menschenrassen," in *Geschichtswissenschaft in Göttingen: Eine Vorlesungsreihe,* ed. Hartmut Boockmann und Hermann Wellenreuther (Göttingen: Vandenhoeck und Ruprecht, 1987), 30–75; a twelve-page section in Luigi Marino's *Praeceptores Germaniae: Göttingen 1770–1820* (Göttingen: Vandenhoeck und Ruprecht, 1995), 110–21; and Susanne Zantop's essay on Meiners, "The Beautiful, the Ugly, and the German: Race, Gender, and Nationality in Eighteenth-Century Anthropological Discourse," in *Gender and Germanness,* ed. Patricia Herminghouse and Magda Mueller (Providence, RI: Berghahn, 1997), 21–35. There are twenty pages and several notes on Meiners in Zantop's *Colonial Fantasies: Conquest, Family, and Nation in Precolonial Germany, 1770–1870* (Durham, NC; London: Duke University Press, 1997), 82–94 and passim. Martin Gierl is the latest to explore the ideological functions of Meiners's work in his essay "Christoph Meiners, Geschichte der Menschheit und Göttinger Universalgeschichte: Rasse und Nation als Politisierung der deutschen Aufklärung," in *Die Wissenschaft vom Menschen in Göttingen um 1800: wissenschaftliche Praktiken, institutionelle Geographie, europäische Netzwerke,* ed. Hans Erich Bödeker, Philippe Büttgen, and Michel Espagne (Göttingen: Vandenhoeck und Ruprecht, 2008), 419–33.

7. Michael Banton, *Race Relations* (New York: Basic Books, 1967), 7–8. Pierre-André Taguieff adopts Banton's tripartition of racism in *The Force of Prejudice: On Racism and Its Doubles* (Minneapolis: University of Minnesota Press, 2001), see p. 145.

8. David Hume, "Of National Characters," in his *Essays and Treatises on Several Subjects,* 4 vols. containing *Essays, Moral and Political,* 4th ed. (London: A. Millar; Edinburgh: A. Kincaid and A. Donaldson, 1753), 277–300. See Richard H. Popkin's essays on "Hume's Racism," in idem, *The High Road to Pyrrhonism,* ed. Richard A. Watson and James E. Force (San Diego: Austin Hill, 1980), 251–66, and "Hume's Racism Reconsidered," in idem, *The Third Force in Seventeenth Century Thought* (Leiden: E. J. Brill, 1992), 64–75; John Immerwahr, "Hume's Revised Racism," *Journal of the History of Ideas* 53, no. 3 (July–Sept. 1992): 481–86; Emmanuel Chukwudi Eze, "Hume, Race, and Human Nature," *Journal of the History of Ideas* 61, no. 4 (2000): 691–98; Eric Morton, "Race and Racism in the Works of David Hume," *Journal of African Philosophy* 1, no. 1 (2002): 1–27; and Andrew Valls, "A Lousy Empirical Scientist: Reconsidering Hume's Racism," in *Race and Racism in Modern Philosophy,* ed. Andrew Valls (Ithaca; London: Cornell University Press, 2005), 127–49.

9. Immanuel Kant, "Beobachtungen über das Gefühl des Schönen und Erhabenen," in AA 2: 205–56; "Observations on the Feeling of the Beautiful and Sublime," in idem, *Anthropology, History, and Education,* trans. by Günter Zöller and Robert I. Louden (Cambridge: Cambridge University Press, 2007), 23–64.

10. Londa Schiebinger, *Nature's Body: Gender in the Making of Modern Science* (New Brunswick: Rutgers University Press, 1993), 172ff.

11. Taguieff, 146.

12. For a reliable history of the word, see Chapter 3 of Taguieff's *The Force of Prejudice.*

13. Taguieff, 78 and 82.

14. Taguieff, 78.

15. See, for example, Carhart, *Science of Culture*, 13, and Meyer, 287.

Introduction

1. Ulrich Johannes Schneider, *Philosophie und Universität: Historisierung der Vernunft im 19. Jahrhundert* (Hamburg: Felix Meiner, 1999), 103ff.

2. Wilhelm Windelband, "Die Geschichte der Philosophie," in *Die Philosophie im Beginn des 20. Jahrhunderts, Festschrift für Kuno Fischer*, ed. Wilhelm Windelband (Heidelberg: C. Winter, 1904–5), 536; quoted in Schneider, *Philosophie und Universität*, 14.

3. "There is always a question—a philosophical question—as to how any specific definition of philosophy comes to be established and exclude whatever might otherwise be regarded as philosophy by displacing it as myth, religion, Volksgeist or Weltanschauung. . . . The narrowing of the history of philosophy to Greece and its legacy must be understood in relation to a certain narrowing of the conception of philosophy" (Robert Bernasconi, "Philosophy's Paradoxical Parochialism: The Reinvention of Philosophy as Greek," in *Cultural Readings of Imperialism*, ed. Keith Ansell-Pearson, Benita Parry, and Judith Squires [London: Lawrence & Wishart, 1997], 221).

4. "The decision to construe philosophy as a preeminently European or Western enterprise was made in the late eighteenth century" (Robert Bernasconi, "Heidegger and the Invention of the Western Philosophical Tradition," *Journal of the British Society for Phenomenology* 26, no. 3 [1995]: 240).

5. "The great social, political, and especially the cultural revolution that we call the Enlightenment marks an enormous increase in Europe's pursuit of knowledge about the East. While older traditions continued, the eighteenth century witnessed data collection on a new scale; it saw the creation of new institutions, or institutional roles, for philological scholars, especially in the places where the study of pagan cultures became more socially and culturally acceptable. There were large numbers of new travelogues and translations of nonwestern texts and more armchair readers able to read them. Of course, capitalist commerce also greatly expanded, as did, accordingly, the European consumption of oriental commodities such as coffee, tea, opium, and porcelain" (Suzanne Marchand, *German Orientalism in the Age of Empire*, 15; a complete citation given in the following note).

6. The term "Oriental Renaissance" comes from Raymond Schwab, author of *La renaissance orientale* (Paris: Payot, 1950); English translation by

Gene Patterson-Black and Victor Reinking, *The Oriental Renaissance: Europe's Rediscovery of India and the East, 1680–1880* (New York: Columbia University Press, 1984). The literature on the history of Asian studies in Germany ever increases. The following are works that I have consulted: Theodor Benfey, *Geschichte der Sprachwissenschaft und orientalischen Philologie in Deutschland seit dem Anfange des 19. Jahrhunderts mit einem Rückblick auf die früheren Zeiten* (München: J. G. Cotta, 1869); Ernst Windisch, *Geschichte der Sanskrit-Philologie und indischen Altertumskunde* (Strassburg: Trübner, 1917–20); Helmuth von Glasenapp, *Das Indienbild deutscher Denker* (Stuttgart: K. F. Koehler, 1960); René Gérard, *L'Orient et la pensée romantique allemande* (Paris: Marcel Didier, 1963); A. Leslie Willson, *A Mythical Image: The Ideal of India in German Romanticism* (Durham: Duke University Press, 1964); Wilhelm Halbfass, *Indien und Europa: Perspektiven ihrer geistigen Begegnung* (Basel: Schwabe, 1981) with an English edition, *India and Europe: An Essay in Understanding* (Albany: SUNY Press, 1988); J. J. Clarke, *Oriental Enlightenment: The Encounter between Asian and Western Thought* (London; New York: Routledge, 1997); Indra Sengupta, *From salon to discipline: state, university and Indology in Germany, 1821–1914* (Würzburg: Ergon, 2005); Bradley L. Herling, *The German Gītā: Hermeneutics and Discipline in the German Reception of Indian Thought, 1778–1831* (New York; London: Routledge, 2006); Pascale Rabault-Feuerhahn, *L'archive des origines: Sanskrit, philologie, anthropologie dans l'Allemagne du XIXe siècle* (Paris: Cerf, 2008); Nicholas A. Germana, *The Orient of Europe: The Mythical Image of India and Competing Images of German National Identity* (Newcastle upon Tyne, UK: Cambridge Scholars, 2009); Suzanne Marchand, *German Orientalism in the Age of Empire: Religion, Race, and Scholarship* (Cambridge; New York: Cambridge University Press, 2009); Douglas T. McGetchin, *Indology, Indomania, and Orientalism: Ancient India's Rebirth in Modern Germany* (Madison, NJ: Fairleigh Dickinson University Press, 2009); and Robert Cowan, *The Indo-German Identification: Reconciling South Asian Origins and European Destinies, 1765–1885* (Rochester, NY: Camden House, 2010).

7. Andrea Polaschegg, *Der andere Orientalismus: Regeln deutsch-morgenländischer Imagination im 19. Jahrhundert* (Berlin: Walter de Gruyter, 2005), 146–56; Marchand, 16–17.

8. William Jones, "The Third Anniversary Discourse on the Hindus," in *The Works of Sir William Jones* (Delhi: Agam Prakashan, 1977), 3: 24–46.

9. The first occupant of the chair was Antoine-Léonard de Chézy.

10. Sengupta, *From salon to discipline*, 26–27.

11. August Wilhelm Schlegel, *Bhagavad-Gita. Id est Thespesion Melos, sive almi Crishnae et Arjunae colloquium de rebus divinis* (Bonnae: Academia Borussica Rhenana Typiis Regis, Prostat apud E. Weber, 1823).

12. Franz Bopp, *Vergleichende Grammatik des Sanskrit, Zend, Griechischen, Lateinischen, Litthauischen, Gothischen und Deutschen* (Berlin: F. Dümmler, 1833–52).

13. McGetchin, *Indology, Indomania, and Orientalism*, 17.

14. Sheldon Pollock, "Deep Orientalism? Notes on Sanskrit and Power Beyond the Raj," in *Orientalism and the Postcolonial Predicament: Perspectives on*

South Asia, ed. Carol A. Breckenridge and Peter van der Veer (Philadelphia: University of Pennsylvania Press, 1993), 82.

15. McGetchin, *Indology, Indomania, and Orientalism,* 104 and 111; Marchand, 96.

16. G. M. Müller, ed., *Life and Religion: An Aftermath from the Writings of F. M. Müller* (New York: Doubleday, Page and Co., 1905), 100; quoted in Halbfass, 133.

17. Julius Bergmann, *Geschichte der Philosophie,* 2 vols. (Berlin: Mittler, 1892–3), I: 8; trans. by Halbfass, 154.

18. Friedrich Michelis, *Geschichte der Philosophie von Thales bis auf unsere Zeit* (Braunsberg, 1865), 2; trans. by Halbfass, 152.

19. Albert Schwegler, *Geschichte der Philosophie im Umriss: ein Leitfaden zur Uebersicht,* 5th ed. (Stuttgart: Franck, 1863), 4; trans. by Halbfass, 152.

20. Edward Zeller, *Die Philosophie der Griechen in ihrer geschichtlichen Entwicklung,* 5th ed., 2 vols. (Leipzig: O. R. Reisland, 1892) I: 41; trans. by Halbfass, 152.

21. Friedrich Ueberweg and Max Heinze, *Grundriss der Geschichte der Philosophie,* 8th ed., 4 vols. (Berlin: E. S. Mittler, 1894) I: 16f.; trans. by Halbfass, 153.

22. George Henry Lewes, *The History of Philosophy from Thales to Comte,* 4th ed., 2 vols. (London: Longmans, Green, 1871), I: 1; quoted in Halbfass, 154.

23. Seymour Guy Martin, Gordon Haddon Clark, Francis P. Clarke, and Chester Townsend Ruddick, *A History of Philosophy* (New York: Crofts, 1941), 9; quoted in Halbfass, 154.

24. Bertrand Russell, *A History of Western Philosophy* (New York: Simon and Schuster, 1945), 3; quoted in Halbfass, 154.

25. Martin Heidegger, *What Is Philosophy?,* trans. William Kluback and Jean T. Wilde (London: Vision Press, 1956), 29–31; quoted in Bernasconi, "Heidegger and the Invention of the Western Philosophical Tradition," 241.

26. Lucien Braun, *Histoire de l'histoire de la philosophie* (Paris: Ophrys, 1973); Lutz Geldsetzer, *Die Philosophie der Philosophiegeschichte im 19. Jahrhundert, Zur Wissenschaftstheorie der Philosophiegeschichtsschreibung und -Betrachtung* (Meisenheim am Glan: Anton Hain, 1968).

27. Martial Guéroult, *Dianoématique, Livre I: Histoire de l'histoire de la philosophie,* 3 vols. (Paris: Aubier Montaigne, 1984–8).

28. Giovanni Santinello, Gregorio Piaia, et al., *Storia delle storie generali della filosofia,* 5 vols. in 8 (Brescia: La Scuola [later Padova: Editrice Antenore], 1979–2004); Ulrich Johannes Schneider, *Die Vergangenheit des Geistes, Eine Archaeologie der Philosophiegeschichte* (Frankfurt am Main: Suhrkamp, 1990) and *Philosophie und Universität: Historisierung der Vernunft im 19. Jahrhundert* (Hamburg: Felix Meiner, 1999).

29. Wilhelm Halbfass, *India and Europe,* 145–59 ("On the Exclusion of India from the History of Philosophy"); Richard King, *Indian Philosophy: An Introduction to Hindu and Buddhist Thought* (Washington, DC: Georgetown University Press, 1999), 1–41; Robert Bernasconi, "Philosophy's Paradoxical Parochialism," 212–26; idem, "On Heidegger's other sins of omission: his

exclusion of Asian thought from the origins of Occidental metaphysics and his denial of the possibility of Christian philosophy," *American Catholic Philosophical Quarterly* 69, no. 2 (Spring 1995): 333–50; idem, "Heidegger and the Invention of the Western Philosophical Tradition," *Journal of the British Society for Phenomenology* 26, no. 3 (October 1995): 240–54; idem, "Krimskrams: Hegel and the Current Controversy about the Beginning of Philosophy," in *Interrogating the Tradition,* ed. C. E. Scott and J. Sallis (Albany: SUNY Press, 2000), 189–206; idem, "Religious Philosophy: Hegel's Occasional Perplexity in the Face of the Distinction Between Philosophy and Religion," *The Bulletin of the Hegel Society of Great Britain* 45/46 (2002): 1–15; and idem, "With What Must the History of Philosophy Begin? Hegel's Role in the Debate on the Place of India within the History of Philosophy," in *Hegel's History of Philosophy: New Interpretations,* ed. David A. Duquette (Albany: SUNY Press, 2003), 35–49.

30. Halbfass was primarily concerned with the status of Indian philosophy.

31. Halbfass, 150.

32. Bernasconi, "Philosophy's Paradoxical Parochialism," 213–4.

33. Bernasconi, "Philosophy's Paradoxical Parochialism," 218. See also Bernasconi's chapter on "Ethnicity, Culture, and Philosophy," in *The Blackwell Companion to Philosophy,* ed. Nicholas Bunnin and E. P. Tsui-James (Malden, MA: Blackwell, 2003), 569. Dieterich Tiedemann, *Geist der spekulativen Philosophie von Thales bis Sokrates,* 6 vols. (Marburg: Neue akademische Buchhandlung, 1791–7); Wilhelm Tennemann, *Geschichte der Philosophie,* 11 vols. (Leipzig: Johann Ambrosius Barth, 1798–1819).

34. Bernasconi, "Philosophy's Paradoxical Parochialism," 224, and "Religious Philosophy," 2; Martin Bernal, *Black Athena: The Afroasiatic Roots of Classical Civilization,* vol. 1: *The Fabrication of Ancient Greece 1785–1985* (New Brunswick: Rutgers University Press, 1987), 216–17.

35. Bernasconi, "Philosophy's Paradoxical Parochialism," 224. For some trenchant criticisms of Bernal's *Black Athena* project, see the volume of essays edited by Mary R. Lefkowitz and Guy Maclean Rogers, *Black Athena Revisited* (Chapel Hill: University of North Carolina Press, 1996), and Suzanne Marchand and Anthony Grafton, "Martin Bernal and His Critics," *Arion* 5, no. 2 (1997): 1–35. Bernal's replies are collected in *Black Athena Writes Back: Martin Bernal Responds to His Critics,* ed. David Chioni Moore (Durham, NC; London: Duke University Press, 2001). Due to the shoddy historical research and highly questionable argumentation of *Black Athena,* and the mountain of criticism that has erupted in response, the historical investigation of racism in eighteenth-century historiography has suffered a setback that is now in its third decade. Any historian who wishes to establish that racist ideas and attitudes were a determining factor in the exclusion of Africa and Asia from modern histories of philosophy must not rely on Bernal's work.

36. See Note 29 above for complete citations to Bernasconi's publications.

37. For Heidegger, see his essay *Was heisst Denken?* (Tübingen: Niemeyer, 1954), 136; Robert Bernasconi, "On Heidegger's other sins of omission," 340.

38. Bernasconi, "Heidegger and the Invention of the Western Philosophical Tradition," 248.

39. Bernasconi, "Religious Philosophy," 10.

40. Ibid., 11.

41. Robert Bernasconi, "Hegel at the Court of the Ashanti," in *Hegel after Derrida*, ed. Stuart Barnett (London; New York: Routledge, 1998), 41–63; and "With What Must the Philosophy of World History Begin? On the Racial Basis of Hegel's Eurocentrism," *Nineteenth-Century Contexts* 22 (2000): 171–201.

42. See note 26 above.

43. Dieterich Tiedemann, *Geist der spekulativen Philosophie*, 6 vols. (Marburg: Akademische Buchhandlung, 1791–7), 1: xviii.

44. In a 1997 essay, Bernasconi identified Tiedemann's *Geist der spekulativen Philosophie* as the first history of philosophy to begin with the Greeks (Bernasconi, "Philosophy's Paradoxical Parochialism," 218). But, as I show in Chapter 4, historical priority goes to Christoph Meiners's *Grundriss der Geschichte der Weltweisheit*, 1st ed. (Lemgo: Meyer, 1786).

45. Georg Wilhelm Friedrich Hegel, *Vorlesungen: Ausgewählte Nachschriften und Manuskripte* (Hamburg: Felix Meiner, 1983–), 6: 365.

Chapter 1

1. Tennemann, *Geschichte der Philosophie*, 1: LII.

2. Karl Leonhard Reinhold, "Ueber den Begrif der Geschichte der Philosophie," in *Beyträge zur Geschichte der Philosophie*, ed. Georg Gustav Fülleborn (Züllichau; Freystadt: Friedrich Frommann), vol. 1 (1791–4), first section. Reinhold studied philosophy at Leipzig. Through his *Briefe über die kantische Philosophie* (1786), Reinhold was able to win a larger following for Kant. In 1787, Reinhold was appointed to a chair of philosophy at Jena. Reinhold's *Ueber die bisherigen Schicksale der Kantische Philosophie* (1789), *Ueber das Fundament des philosophischen Wissens* (1791), *Beiträge zur Berichtung bisheriger Mißverständnisse der Philosophen* (1790–4), and *Versuch einer neuen Theorie des menschlichen Vorstellungsvermögens* (2nd ed., 1795) either defend or expound upon Kant's philosophy. In 1793, he was called to the chair of philosophy at Kiel, vacated by J. N. Tetens. My citations of "Ueber den Begrif der Geschichte der Philosophie" are to the version in the 2nd edition of Fülleborn's *Beyträge zur Geschichte der Philosophie*, vol. 1 (1796), 3–36.

3. Reinhold, "Ueber den Begrif der Geschichte der Philosophie," 11–12.

4. Ibid., 11: "Wissenschaft des bestimmten von der Erfahrung unabhängigen Zusammenhanges der Dinge."

5. Ibid., 12.

6. Ibid., 12–13.

7. Ibid., 13.

8. Ibid., 14–15.

9. Ibid., 15.

10. Ibid., 20.

11. Ibid., 28.

12. Ibid., 17: "der dargestellte Inbegrif der Veränderungen, welche die Wissenschaft des nothwendigen Zusammenhanges der Dinge von ihrer Entstehung bis auf unsre Zeiten erfahren hat."

13. Ibid., 26–27: "The biography of philosophers does absolutely not belong in the history of philosophy, which troubles itself simply with the inner destiny of the science, but in no way with its caretaker and carrier." See Braun, 226.

14. Reinhold, "Ueber den Begrif der Geschichte der Philosophie," 26–27.

15. Ibid., 28.

16. Ibid., 26.

17. Geldsetzer, 19.

18. The subtitle of the second part of *Der Streit der Facultäten* (1798), in AA 7: 1–116.

19. Geldsetzer, 13.

20. Georg Gustav Fülleborn, ed., *Beyträge zur Geschichte der Philosophie*, 7 vols. (Züllichau; Freystadt: Friedrich Frommann, 1794–99).

21. Geldsetzer, 17.

22. Joseph-Marie de Gérando, *Histoire comparée des systèmes de philosophie, relativement aux principes des connaissances humaines* (Paris: Chez Henrichs/ Ancienne Librairie de Du Pont, 1804), 1: 58. De Gérando praised the histories by Christian Thomasius, J. Gundling, Heineccius, Grotius, and Jacob Brucker. Also worthy of his mention were Tiedemann, Buhle, Meiners, Tennemann, Eberhard, Bardili, Gurlitt, Fülleborn, Garve, Platner, Heyne, Hissmann, Stäudlin, and the published proceedings of both Göttingen Society of Sciences and Berlin Academy of Sciences. Of these he singles out three works "of eminent worth": Stäudlin's *Geschichte und Geist des Skepticismus*; Tiedemann's *System der stoischen Philosophie*; and the French translation of Meiners's *Geschichte des Ursprungs, Fortgangs und Verfalls der Wissenschaften in Griechenland und Rom*.

23. Wilhelm G. Tennemann, "Vorrede des Uebersetzers," in Joseph-Marie de Gérando, *Vergleichende Geschichte der Systeme der Philosophie mit Rücksicht auf die Grundsätze der menschlichen Erkenntnisse*, trans. Wilhelm Tennemann (Marburg: Neue Academische Buchhandlung, 1806), 1: VII.

24. Braun, 94; see Ulrich Johannes Schneider, *Die Vergangenheit des Geistes*, 10.

25. Immanuel Berger, *Geschichte der Religionsphilosophie oder Lehren und Meinungen der originellsten Denker aller Zeiten über Gott und Religion* (Berlin, 1800), 1.

26. A similar account is offered by Schneider in *Die Vergangenheit des Geistes*, 9: "Philosophy participates in a fundamental revolution in the late eighteenth century, which transforms its concept, its self-understanding and its history."

27. The first printed Latin edition of the work is *Laertii Diogenis vitae et sententiae eorvm qvi in philosophia probati fvervnt* (Venice, 1475).

28. A doxography is a compilation of and commentary on the opinions of philosophers, typically ancient Greek philosophers. There are ancient dox-

ographies by Theophrastus, Cicero, and Plutarch. The word is derived from modern Latin and was coined by Hermann Diels for the title of his work, *Doxographi Graeci* (Berolini: G. Reimer, 1879). Braun (p. 34) comments: "Diogène domine l'histoire de la philosophie comme personne ne l'a dominée, puisqu'il commande toute la littérature historique de la philosophie jusqu'au milieu du XVIIIe siècle. Il était devenu le modèle à imiter, et tout le monde l'imitait sans que cela fît problème. Et son souvenir est encore vivant. On compte une trentaine d'éditions de son oeuvre dans les temps modernes." As late as 1758, a French translation of Diogenes' *Lives and Opinions* was published in Amsterdam: *Les vies des plus illustres philosophes de l'Antiquité avec leurs dogmes, leurs systèmes et leurs sentences les plus remarquables*, 3 vols., translator anonymous, with an *abrégé* of the lives of women philsophers (Amsterdam: J. H. Schneider).

29. Thomas Stanley, *The history of philosophy: containing the lives, opinions, actions and discourses of the philosophers of every sect* (London, editions of 1655–62, 1687, 1701, and 1743); see Richard H. Popkin, ed., *The Columbia History of Western Philosophy* (New York: MJF Books, 1999), 759.

30. Pierre Bayle, *Dictionnaire historique et critique* (Rotterdam: Reinier Leers, 1697) with a German edition by Johann Christoph Gottsched appearing in 1741–4, *Historisches und critisches Wörterbuch; nach der neuesten Auflage von 1740 ins Deutsche übersetzt* (Leipzig: Breitkopf).

31. Gerardus Joannes Vossius, *De philosophorum sectis liber* (Lipsiae: Impensis Joh. Casp. Meyeri; Jenae: Charactere Nisiano, Impr. Henricus Beyerus, 1705). The original edition was published in 1657–8.

32. Christoph August Heumann, *Acta philosophorum; das ist gründliche Nachrichten aus der Historia philosophica, nebst beygefügten Urtheilen von denen dahin gehörigen alten und neuen Büchern*, 3 vols. (Halle: Magdeburg, 1715–26); see Braun, 103. "[E]ighteenth-century German historians of philosophy like C. A. Heumann studied the influence of climate, environment, race, nationality, psychology, gender, and historical periods" (Donald R. Kelley, *The Descent of Ideas: The History of Intellectual History* [Aldershot, UK; Burlington, VT: Ashgate, 2002], 5).

33. André-François Boureau-Deslandes, *Histoire critique de la philosophie, où l'on traite de son origine, de ses progrez et des diverses revolutions qui lui sont arrivées jusqu'à notre temps* (Amsterdam: François Changuion, 1737).

34. Johann Jacob Brucker (1696–1770), born in Augsburg, studied theology and philosophy at Jena. After returning to Augsburg, he taught history, geography, genealogy, and other subjects at the *Gymnasium*. He became pastor in 1744, but continued to teach the history of philosophy and other subjects until his death. He was a member of the Berlin Royal Academy of Sciences.

35. Johann Jacob Brucker, *Historia critica philosophiae, a mundi incunabilis ad nostram usque aetatem deducta*, 5 vols. (Lipsiae: Breitkopf, 1742–4). Other eighteenth-century histories that draw heavily on Brucker's work are those by Jean-Henri-Samuel Formey, Anton Friedrich Büsching, Franz Nikolaus Steinacher, Karl Adolph Cäsar, Christian Gottlieb Stöwe, Johann Gottfried Gurlitt, and Franz Xavier Gmeiner; see Constance W. T. Blackwell, "Skepticism as a Sect, Skepticism as a Philosophical Stance: Johann Jacob Brucker

Versus Carl Friedrich Stäudlin," in *The Skeptical Tradition Around 1800: Skepticism in Philosophy, Science, and Society,* ed. Johan van der Zande and Richard H. Popkin (Dordrecht: Kluwer), 346 n. 17. Near the end of the eighteenth century, William Enfield published *The History of Philosophy From the Earliest Periods, Drawn Up From Brucker's historia critica philosophiae* (London: J. Johnson, 1791; subsequent reprints of 1792, 1819, 1837, and 1839). Also heavily dependent on Brucker is Agatopisto Cromaziano's (Appiano Buonafede's) seven-volume *Della istoria e della indole di ogni filosofia* (Lucca: Giovanni Riccomini, 1766–81).

36. Dieterich Tiedemann, *Geist der spekulativen Philosophie* (Marburg: Neue Akademische Buchhandlung, 1791–7).

37. Braun, 121.

38. Ibid.

39. Denis Diderot, Jean Le Rond d'Alembert, and Pierre Mouchon, eds., *Encyclopédie, ou dictionnaire raisonné des sciences, des arts et des métiers par une société de gens de lettres,* 17 vols. with 11 vols. of plates (Paris: Briasson [etc.], 1751–65) and five volumes of supplements (1776–7). Articles related to the history of philosophy were also published separately as *Histoire générale des dogmes et des opinions philosophiques depuis les plus anciens temps jusqu'à nos jours* (Londres, 1769). Braun, 153: "On sait que les articles relatifs à l'histoire de la philosophie sont presque tous tirés de l'*Historia critica,* dont ils ne constituent souvent que la simple traduction."

40. On the use of Brucker's *Historia critica* by the *encyclopédistes,* see Braun, 121 and 153–54, and Rainer Jehl, "Jacob Brucker und die 'Encyclopédie,'" in *Jacob Brucker (1696–1770): Philosoph und Historiker der europäischen Aufklärung,* ed. Wilhelm Schmidt-Biggemann and Theo Stammen (Berlin: Akademie Verlag, 1998), 238–56.

41. On the European reception of Brucker's work and its effect on later as well as contemporary historiography of philosophy, see Gregorio Piaia, "Jacob Bruckers Wirkungsgeschichte in Frankreich und Italien," in Schmidt-Biggemann and Stammen, 218–37.

42. De Gérando, *Histoire comparée,* 1: 146.

43. Reinhold, "Ueber den Begrif der Geschichte der Philosophie," 32.

44. Ibid., 32.

45. There were eight editions in French and two in English.

46. Georg Friedrich Daniel Goess, *Über den Begriff der Geschichte der Philosophie und über das System des Thales: Zwo philosophische Abhandlungen* (Erlangen: Palm, 1794), 27.

47. According to Goess (p. 30), the history of philosophy is often confused with the history of the sciences because, previously, human knowledge in general was thought to come under philosophy: "Von ihr muss Geschichte der Mathematik und Naturgeschichte sowohl, als Geschichte der Menschheit, der Religionen u. s. w. sorgfältig getrennt werden."

48. Johann Gottlieb Gerhard Buhle, *Lehrbuch der Geschichte der Philosophie und einer kritischen Literatur derselben* (Göttingen: Vandenhöck und Ruprecht, 1796), 1: 2–3. Buhle states that religion can be an object of philosophy and,

therefore, of the history of philosophy to the extent that it concerns "the concept of the relation in which man stands to the Divinity."

49. Ibid.

50. Kelley, *The Descent of Ideas*, 6 and 78–79.

51. Morhof's "Polyhistor philosophicus" is divided into (a) "Polyhistor philosophicus-historicus" (history of philosopy), covering the philosophical schools of antiquity, the Scholastics, and the "Novatores," and (b) "Polyhistor physicus" (history of natural philosophy), beginning with "metaphyics" in the Aristotelian sense. These are followed by a critical review of the literature on the *artes divinatoriae* and magic. The "Polyhistor philosophicus" ends with chapters on mathematics and the theory of knowledge. Morhof was Professor of Poetry and Eloquence at Kiel.

52. See Constance Blackwell, "Jacob Brucker's theory of knowledge and the history of natural philosophy," in *Jacob Brucker (1696–1770): Philosoph und Historiker der europäischen Aufklärung,* ed. Schmidt-Biggemann and Stammen, 198–217.

53. Originally planned by Morhof in 1686, the three-part *Polyhistor* was realized by his colleagues at Kiel, Moller and Muhler, with the 1708 edition.

54. See Paul Nelles, "Historia Litteraria and Morhof: Private Teaching and Professorial Libraries at the University of Kiel," in *Mapping the World of Learning: The Polyhistor of Daniel Georg Morhof,* ed. Françoise Waquet (Wiesbaden: Harrassowitz, 2000), 31–56.

55. Daniel Georg Morhof, *Polyhistor sive De notitia auctorum et rerum commentarii,* 1st ed. (Lubecae: Petri Böckmanni, 1688); see Françoise Waquet's introduction to *Mapping the World of Learning,* 7–11, and Jean-Marc Chatelain, "Philologie, pansophie, polymathie, encyclopédie: Morhof et l'histoire du savoir global," in *Mapping the World of Learning,* ed. Waquet, 15–29.

56. Nelles, 40.

57. In Gottlieb Stolle's *Anleitung zur Historie der Gelahrheit* (Jena, 1718), the history of philosophy is placed within the history of learning in general. It comes after the history of the liberal arts and also is distributed into the particular branches of learning, e.g., logic, psychology, moral philosophy, and natural law. See Kelley, *The Descent of Ideas*, 79–80.

58. Goess (p. 26) defined the history of philosophy as "the portrayed quintessence of all changes that the science of the necessary and universally valid forms, rules and principles of the original faculties of the human mind has suffered and of those things that are made determinate by these; from the beginning to our times."

59. Buhle, *Lehrbuch*, 1: 1.

60. Buhle, *Lehrbuch*, 1: 3–4.

61. Carl Heinrich Heydenreich, "Einige Ideen über die Revolution in der Philosophie bewirkt durch I. Kant und besonders über den Einfluss derselben auf die Behandlung der Geschichte der Philosophie," a "sketch" appended to Agatopisto Cromaziano's (Appiano Buonafede's) *Kritische Geschichte der Revolution der Philosophie in den drey letzten Jahrhunderten,* trans. Carl Heinrich Heydenreich (Leipzig: Weygand, 1791), 2: 213–32.

62. Heydenreich, "Einige Ideen über die Revolution," in Cromaziano, 2: 229. Heydenreich (1764–1801) was a poet and philosopher. He studied philology and philosophy at Leipzig, earning a *Magister* in 1785. He became a professor of philosophy at Leipzig, where he taught until 1798.

63. Ibid., 231: "Eine pragmatische Geschichte der Bildung der Philosophie zu einem Systeme ist erst dadurch möglich geworden, daß Kant die wirklich innerlich systematische Philosophie dargestellt hat."

64. Ibid., 231.

65. Ibid.

66. Carl Heinrich Heydenreich, *Originalideen über die Kritische Philosophie* (Leipzig: Friedrich Gotthelf Baumgärtner, 1793), 1: 5.

67. Heydenreich, *Originalideen*, 1: 5: "Die Wissenschaft der menschlichen Natur, wie fern ihre Vermögen durch ursprüngliche, wesentliche, allgemeingültige Formen, Regeln und Prinzipien bestimmt sind, und die Wirksamkeit von jenen (Vermögen) durch das blosse Bewusstseyn von diesen (Formen, Regeln, Prinzipien) im Einzelnen und im Ganzen begriffen werden kann."

68. Ibid., 6.

69. Johann Georg Heinrich Feder, *Leben, Nature und Grundsätze: Zur Belehrung und Ermunterung seiner lieben Nachkommen* (Leipzig, 1825), 60.

70. Johann Georg Heinrich Feder, *Grundriss der philosophischen Wissenschaften, nebst der nötigen Geschichte, zum Gebrauche seiner Zuhörer* (Coburg: 1767; 2nd ed., 1769).

71. See Johan van der Zande, "The Moderate Skepticism of German Popular Philosophy," in *The Skeptical Tradition around 1800: Skepticism in Philosophy, Science, and Society*, ed. Johan van der Zande and Richard H. Popkin (Dordrecht; Boston; London: Kluwer, 1998), 69–80.

72. Ibid.

73. Heydenreich, *Originalideen*, 1: 3–4 and 6.

74. Immanuel Kant, *Prolegomena zu einer jeden künftigen Metaphysik, die als Wissenschaft wird auftreten können* (1783), in AA 4: 255–56. I quote from the revised English edition, *Prolegomena to Any Future Metaphysics* by Gary Hatfield (Cambridge: Cambridge University Press, 2004), 3.

75. Johann Georg Heinrich Feder and Christoph Meiners, eds., *Zugabe zu den Göttingischen Anzeigen von gelehrten Sachen* (Göttingen), 40–48.

76. Before it was published, Garve's review was heavily edited and augmented by Feder. The Anglo-Irish philosopher George Berkeley (1685–1753) was Bishop of Cloyne.

77. Frederick C. Beiser, *German Idealism: The Struggle against Subjectivism, 1781–1801* (Cambridge, MA; London: Harvard University Press, 2002), 89. Berkeley expounded his idealism in *Principles of Human Knowledge* (1710) and *Three Dialogues between Hylas and Philonous* (1713).

78. Upset by the review, Kant replied in the spring of 1783 (printed as the Appendix to the *Prolegomena*) that the reviewer's account of his philosophy was a "deliberate distortion and caricature." Kant explained that it was never his intention to expound a system of metaphysics, but rather to

place constraints on all metaphysics. According to Beiser, "[w]hat particularly bothered Kant, however, was the equation of his idealism with Berkeley's. He feared that such an insinuation could completely undermine the reception of the *Kritik*. Given the general reputation of Berkeley's philosophy in late-eighteenth-century Germany, this could serve as a cheap and popular *reductio ad absurdum* of his entire work" (Beiser, *German Idealism*, 90). For the following two decades Kant made repeated attempts to differentiate his position from Berkeley's.

79. Beiser, *German Idealism*, 606 n. 47.

80. Ibid., 22.

81. Johann August Eberhard (1739–1809) studied theology, philosophy, and classical philology at Halle. He then served for some years as tutor in the household of Baron v. d. Horst. In 1763, he became co-rector of the school of his youth, the Martineum, in Halberstadt and second pastor of the hospital church there. In 1763, he assumed a pastoral post in Berlin, where he also came into contact with Friedrich Nicolai and Moses Mendelssohn. In 1778 he was called to a chair of philosophy at Halle. In 1786 he was inducted into the Berlin Royal Academy. In 1808 he was awarded a doctorate by the theological faculty at Halle.

82. See Henry E. Allison, *The Kant-Eberhard Controversy: an English translation together with supplementary materials and a historical-analytic introduction of Immanuel Kant's "On a discovery according to which any new critique of pure reason has been made superfluous by an earlier one"* (Baltimore: Johns Hopkins University Press, 1973) and H. J. de Vleeschauwer, *La déduction transcendentale dans l'oeuvre de Kant* (Antwerp: De Sikkel, 1934).

83. Johann August Eberhard, ed., *Philosophisches Magazin*, 4 vols. (Halle: J. Gebauer, 1788–92). It was succeeded by two volumes of the *Philosophisches Archiv* (1793–4), which continued the compaign against Kantianism. The Kantians had their own journal, *Allgemeine Literatur-Zeitung*, edited by Schulze and Reinhold in Jena since 1785.

84. *Philosophisches Magazin* 1: 289.

85. Immanuel Kant, *Über eine Entdeckung nach der alle neue Kritik der reinen Vernunft durch eine ältere entbehrlich gemacht werden soll?* (1790), in AA, vol. 8; see Allison, 46–104.

86. Heydenreich, *Originalideen*, 1: 6–7.

87. Ibid., 11: "Wer kennt nicht den allgemeinen Kampf auf dem Schauplatze der Philosophie, bevor nicht die Vernunftkritik einen ewigen Frieden vermittelt!"

88. Ibid., 15.

89. Ibid., 29–30.

90. Ibid., 35–36.

91. Johann Christian August Grohmann (1769–1847) matriculated at the University of Leipzig in 1786 with intentions to study theology, but he turned to philosophy. He studied under Ernst Platner, but was converted to Kantianism. In 1790 he earned his doctorate in philosophy and moved to Dresden. There, he composed *Ideen zu einer physiognomischen Anthropologie*

(1791). In 1792, he became *Privatdozent* at Wittenberg and, in 1798, *Professor extraordinarius*. Five years later he was promoted to *Professor ordinarius* and named University Librarian. He is the author of several Kantian works. Among them are *Neue Beyträge zur kritischen Philosophie, insbesondere zur Logik* (1796), *Neue Beyträge zur kritischen Philosophie und insbesondere zur Geschichte der Philosophie* (1798), *Ueber das Verhältnis der kantischen Kritik zur Herderschen Metakritik* (1802), and *Dem Andenken Kant's oder die neueren philosophischen Systeme in ihrer Nichtigkeit dargestellt* (1804). In 1810, he moved to Hamburg to become Professor of Theoretical Philosophy and Eloquence at the *Gymnasium*. He continued to live in Hamburg after retirement, but returned to Leipzig and then to Dresden, where he died.

92. Grohmann, *Über den Begriff der Geschichte der Philosophie* (1797), 64. This text was reprinted in the following year after some changes, with the title "Was heisst: Geschichte der Philosophie?," in *Neue Beyträge zur kritischen Philosophie und insbesondere zur Geschichte der Philosophie*, ed. Johann Christian August Grohmann and Karl Heinrich Ludwig Pölitz (Berlin: Köngl. Preuss. Akademische Kunst- und Buchhandlung, 1798).

93. Ibid., 30.

94. Ibid., 41.

95. See the introduction to Immanuel Kant, *What real progress has metaphysics made in Germany since the time of Leibniz and Wolff?*, trans. Ted Humphrey (New York: Abaris, 1983).

96. Kant's manuscripts and fragments related to the prize-essay question became the basis of Friedrich Theodor Rink's edition of *Immanuel Kant über die von der Königl. Akademie der Wissenschaften zu Berlin für das Jahr 1791 ausgesetzte Preisfrage: Welche sind die wirklichen Fortschritte, die die Metaphysik seit Leibnitzens und Wolf's Zeiten in Deutschland gemacht hat?* (Königsberg, 1804), in AA 20: 255–351. These manuscripts have since been lost.

97. Immanuel Kant, "Löse Blätter zu den Fortschritten der Metaphysik," in AA 20: 333–51.

98. Ibid., 340–41.

99. Ibid., 341. Kant elsewhere demotes "empirical history" as not scientific.

100. See Giovanni Santinello et al., *Storia delle storie generali della filosofia,* 3 (*Il secondo illuminismo e l'età Kantiana*), Part II: 940–46.

101. AA 7: 79–80.

102. AA 12: 36.

103. AA 20: 343.

104. Ibid., 264.

105. See Braun, 205–24.

106. Carl Friedrich Stäudlin, *Geschichte und Geist des Skepticismus, vorzüglich in Rücksicht auf Moral und Religion*, 2 vols. (Leipzig, 1794). Kant's *Streit der Facultäten* (1798) is dedicated to Stäudlin.

107. John Christian Laursen, "Skepticism and the History of Moral Philosophy: The Case of Carl Friedrich Stäudlin," in *The Skeptical Tradition around 1800*, ed. Zande and Popkin, 374–75.

108. Richard H. Popkin, "Some Thoughts about Stäudlin's 'History and Spirit of Skepticism,'" in *The Skeptical Tradition around 1800*, ed. Zande and Popkin, 341.

109. See Schneider, *Philosophie und Universität*, 213.

110. Johann Gottlieb Gerhard Buhle, *Lehrbuch der Geschichte der Philosophie*, 8 vols. bound in 6 (Göttingen: Vandenhöck und Ruprecht, 1796–1804) and *Geschichte der neuern Philosophie seit der Epoche der Wiederherstellung der Wissenschaften*, 6 vols. (Gottingen: J. G. Rosenbusch's Wittwe, 1800–1804).

111. Wilhelm Tennemann, *Geschichte der Philosophie*, 11 vols. (Leipzig: Johann Ambrosius Barth, 1798–1819). Tennemann was born in Kleinbrembach in the vicinity of Erfurt. His father was the village pastor. A bout with smallpox during his fifth year delayed his physical and intellectual development. He and his siblings received a primary education from their father. Wilhelm attended the *Gymnasium* in Erfurt during 1778–9 and went on to the University of Erfurt, where, having been exposed to philosophy, he gave up plans to pursue theology. In the spring of 1781, he moved to Jena, where he attended Johann August Heinrich Ulrich's philosophical lectures and encountered Kant's *Critique of Pure Reason*. In the years thence, he grappled with Kantian philosophy in his writings on psychology and "immortality" and on the Socratics, especially Plato. He produced German translations of Hume's *Enquiry Concerning Human Understanding* with an introduction by K. L. Reinhold (1793) and Locke's *Essay Concerning Human Understanding* (3 vols., 1795–7). Tennemann was *Professor extraordinarius* of philosophy at Jena when, in 1804, he was called to a chair in philosophy at Marburg, vacant since the death of Tiedemann. While at Marburg, Tennemann produced a German translation of de Gérando's *Histoire comparée des systèmes de philosophie*. He died in Marburg on October 1, 1819. See the *Allgemeine Deutsche Biographie* 37 (1894): 566–67, http://www.deutsche-biographie.de/pnd119092603.html?anchor=adb.

112. Wilhelm Tennemann, *Grundriss der Geschichte der Philosophie* (Leipzig: Johann Ambrosius Barth, 1812; subsequent editions of 1816, 1820, 1825, and 1829). "The *Grundriss* was used widely as a school text through the middle of the nineteenth century and translated into English, French, Italian, and even Modern Greek" (Popkin, ed., *The Columbia History of Western Philosophy*, 764).

113. Schneider, in *Philosophie und Universität* (pp. 213–14), calls Tennemann "the author of the first great modern history of philosophy."

114. Tennemann, *Geschichte der Philosophie*, 1: IV.

115. Ibid., III and LXXIV.

116. Ibid., LXXIV–LXXV.

117. Ibid., LXXV. Tennemann regarded Pierre Bayle as an exception.

118. Ibid., IV: The history of philosophy "has lacked the good fortune of finding an author who combines the historical craft with a philosophical mind and who can set the model for others."

119. Ibid., LXXVI.

120. Tennemann wanted to separate the history of philosophy from its special branches: history of the philosophy of particular peoples; history of the philosophy of particular time periods; history of a philosophical school; history of a system; history of a philosophical science; history of particular philosophical doctrines, principles etc.; history of philosophical debates; history of philosophical methods; history of philosophical language; biographies of philosophers (*Geschichte der Philosophie*, 1: LXX–LXXIII).

121. Tennemann, *Grundriss* (1816), 7.

122. Tennemann, *Geschichte der Philosophie*, 1: XLVI.

123. Ibid., LVI.

124. Ibid., LVII.

125. Ibid., LXIV.

126. Ibid., LXIV–LXV.

127. Ibid., XI.

128. Ibid., XIX–XX.

129. Tennemann, *Grundriss* (1816), 3.

130. Ibid., 6.

131. Ibid.

132. Tennemann, *Geschichte der Philosophie*, 1: XII.

133. Ibid., XIII.

134. Ibid., XIV–XV.

135. Ibid., XV.

136. Ibid., XVI.

137. Ibid., XVII.

138. Ibid., XXIX.

139. Friedrich Nicolai, *Philosophische Abhandlungen* (Berlin; Stettin: 1808), 2: 187.

140. Nicolai cites Tennemann's *Geschichte der Philosophie*, 1: XXIV and XXXVII.

141. Nicolai, *Philosophische Abhandlungen*, 2: 190.

142. Ibid., 191.

143. Ibid., 197.

144. Ibid., 198.

145. Ibid., 184.

146. Ibid., 206.

Chapter 2

1. Joseph-Marie de Gérando, *Histoire comparée des systèmes de philosophie*, 1: 4–5. See the following note.

2. Joseph-Marie de Gérando, *Histoire comparée des systèmes de philosophie relativement aux principes des connaissances humaines* (Paris: Henrichs, An XII = 1804). The second edition bears a slightly modified title, *Histoire comparée des systèmes de philosophie, considérés relativement aux principes des connaissances humaines*, 4 vols. (Paris: A. Eymery, 1822). Laurence L. Bongie (p. 26) calls de Gérando's work "the most comprehensive French history of philosophy

of [its] day" (Bongie, "Hume and Skepticism in Late Eighteenth-Century France," in *The Skeptical Tradition around 1800,* ed. Johan van der Zande and Richard H. Popkin, 15–29).

3. Friedrich Schlegel, *Die Entwicklung der Philosophie in zwölf Büchern,* in *KFSA,* vols. 12–13.

4. Joseph-Marie de Gérando, *Des signes et de l'art de penser considérés dans leurs rapports mutuels,* 4 vols. (Paris: Goujon fils; Fuchs; Henrichs, 1800) and *De la génération des connoissances humaines: Mémoire qui a partagé le prix de l'Académie Royale des Sciences de Berlin, sur la Question suivante: Démontrer d'une manière incontestable l'origine de toutes nos connoissances, soit en présentant des argumens non-employés encore, soit en présentant des argumens déjà employés, mais en les présentant d'une manière nouvelle et d'une force victorieuse de toute objection* (Berlin: George Decker, 1802).

5. De Gérando, *Histoire comparée* 1: xxij, xxiv–xxv.

6. Ibid., xxvij.

7. Ibid., xxvi.

8. Ibid., 10–12.

9. Ibid., 9.

10. Ibid., xxiv.

11. Ibid., xvj.

12. Toby A. Appel, *The Cuvier-Geoffroy Debate: French Biology in the Decades Before Darwin* (New York; Oxford: Oxford University Press, 1987), 48.

13. De Gérando, *Histoire comparée* 1: xxvj.

14. Ibid., xviij–xix. This question was the subject of de Gérando's earlier work, *De la génération des connoissances humaines* (1802), for which he won a Berlin Academy prize.

15. Brucker, *Historia critica Philosophiae,* 1st ed., 1: 21; quotation from William Enfield, *The History of Philosophy, from the Earliest Periods: Drawn Up from Brucker's* Historia Critica Philosphiæ, 2 vols., with an introduction by Knud Haakonssen (Bristol, UK; Sterling,VA: Thoemmes Press, 2001 [reprint of 1837 edition]), 1: 5.

16. Enfield, 1: 5.

17. De Gérando, *Histoire comparée* 1: 59.

18. Ibid., 60–61.

19. Ibid., 61.

20. Ibid., 62.

21. Ibid.

22. Ibid., xxx.

23. De Gérando, *Histoire comparée* 3: 180–81.

24. Ibid., 96.

25. Ibid., 201–2.

26. Ibid., 202.

27. Ibid., 203.

28. Ibid., 204.

29. Ibid., 206.

30. Ibid., 208.

31. Ibid., 212–13.

32. Ibid., 214.

33. De Gérando, *Histoire comparée* 2: 21, 3: 216.

34. De Gérando, *Histoire comparée* 3: 223–24.

35. Ibid., 224.

36. Ibid., 219–23.

37. Ibid., 225.

38. Ibid., 285–86.

39. De Gérando, *Histoire comparée* 2: 381–82.

40. Ibid., 103.

41. Ibid.

42. Ibid., 105.

43. Ibid., 382.

44. De Gérando, *Histoire comparée* 3: 286 and 306.

45. Ibid., 306–7.

46. Ibid., 307–8.

47. Ibid.

48. Ibid., 324.

49. Ibid.

50. Ibid., 325.

51. Ibid., 326.

52. De Gérando, *Histoire comparée* 2: 379.

53. De Gérando, *Histoire comparée* 3: 253–57.

54. Ibid., 258.

55. Ibid., 278–80.

56. Ibid., 263.

57. Ibid., 270.

58. Ibid., 271.

59. Ibid., 273–74.

60. Ibid., 274–75.

61. Ibid., 277.

62. Ibid., 284.

63. Ibid.

64. Ibid., 391.

65. Ibid., 443. Here, de Gérando cites Carl Friedrich Stäudlin's *Geschichte und Geist des Skepticismus, vorzüglich in Rücksicht auf Moral and Religion* (Leipzig: Crusius, 1794).

66. De Gérando, *Histoire comparée* 1: 445.

67. De Gérando, *Histoire comparée* 2: 383.

68. De Gérando, *Histoire comparée* 3: 388–90.

69. Ibid., 392–93.

70. Ibid., 437. De Gérando notes that Francis Bacon made the same distinction.

71. Ibid., 440–41.

72. Ibid., 441.

73. Ibid., 445. De Gérando's list of modern empiricists includes A. Ceesalpin, C. Cremonini, J. Chr. Magnenus, Telesio, Jerome Hirnhaym, Jules-César Vanini, Claude Berigard, and Hobbes.

74. De Gérando, *Histoire comparée* 2: 180–81.

75. De Gérando, *Histoire comparée* 3: 505ff.

76. Ibid.

77. De Gérando, *Histoire comparée* 2: 181 and 251.

78. Ibid., 247.

79. Ibid.

80. Ibid., 248.

81. Ibid., 249.

82. De Gérando, *Histoire comparée* 1: 186.

83. Ibid.

84. De Gérando, *Histoire comparée* 2: 251.

85. Ibid., 252.

86. Ibid.

87. Ibid., 265–66.

88. Ibid., 333.

89. Ibid., 335–36.

90. Ibid., 336.

91. De Gérando, *Histoire comparée* 3: 524–25.

92. De Gérando, *Histoire comparée* 2: 233 and 259–61.

93. Ibid., 269–70.

94. Ibid., 270.

95. De Gérando, *Histoire comparée* 3: 525.

96 Ibid., 528–29: "The philosophy of Descartes began with doubt and ended in dogmatism; the philosophy of Kant has done the very opposite."

97. De Gérando, *Histoire comparée* 3: 525–27.

98. De Gérando, *Histoire comparée* 2: 263.

99. Ibid., 269–70.

100. De Gérando, *Histoire comparée* 3: 568.

101. Ibid., 578.

102. Ibid., 579–80 and 580 n.

103. Ibid., 570.

104. François Picavet, *Les idéologues; essai sur l'histoire des idées et des théories scientifiques, philosophiques, religieuses, etc. en France depuis 1789,* reprint (New York: Burt Franklin, 1971), 515 n. 1.

105. On eclecticism in early modern philosophy, see Horst Dreitzel, "Zur Entwicklung und Eigenart der 'eklektischen Philosophie,'" *Zeitschrift für Historische Forschung* 18 (1991), 3: 281–343; and Michael Albrecht, *Eklektik: Eine Begriffsgeschichte mit Hinweisen auf die Philosophie- und Wissenschaftsgeschichte* (Stuttgart-Bad Cannstatt: Frommann-Holzboog, 1994).

106. De Gérando, *Histoire comparée* 2: 79.

107. Brucker, too, viewed modern philosophy as generally eclectic. The last segment of the *Historia critica philosophiae* is titled "Of Modern Eclectic Philosophy" and includes sections on Bruno, Cardano, Bacon, Campanella, Hobbes, Descartes, Leibniz, Thomasius, Wolff, Ramus, Arnold, Spinoza, Malebranche, Tschernhaus, Locke, Montaigne, Charron, Scultetus, Bodin, Machiavelli, Grotius, Selden, Pufendorf, Copernicus, Tycho Brahe, Kepler, Galileo, Gilbert, Boyle, and Newton.

Chapter 3

1. *KFSA* 18: 137: "Die Philosophie ist wohl allerdings nichts als *Geschichte d[er] Philosophie*, wenn man Geschichte recht versteht."

2. *KFSA* 12: 175.

3. Schwab, 71.

4. Friedrich Schlegel, *Ueber die Sprache und Weisheit der Indier* (Heidelberg: Mohr und Zimmer, 1808), in *KFSA* 8: 105–433.

5. Halbfass, 79.

6. On the history of the comparative method in philosophy, see Halbfass, 419–33.

7. Friedrich Schlegel, *Friedrich Schlegels Briefe an seinem Bruder August Wilhelm*, ed. Oskar F. Walzel (Berlin: Speyer & Peters, 1890), 511.

8. *Friedrich Schlegels Briefe*, 516.

9. Ibid., 523.

10. Friedrich Schlegel, *Philosophische Vorlesungen aus den Jahren 1804 bis 1806 nebst Fragmenten vorzüglich philosophisch-theologischen Inhalts*, ed. C. J. H. Windischmann, 4 vols. (Bonn: E. Weber, 1836–7).

11. *KFSA* 12: XIII.

12. See the introduction by Hans Eichner in *KFSA* 8: LXXI–LXXXVII; Frederick C. Beiser, *The Romantic Imperative: The Concept of Early German Romanticism* (Cambridge, MA: Harvard University Press, 2003), 119–30; and Elizabeth Millán-Zaibert, *Friedrich Schlegel and the Emergence of Romantic Philosophy* (Albany: SUNY Press, 2007), 123–29.

13. Beiser, *Romantic Imperative*, 120–21.

14. On Schlegel's ties to the Niethammer circle, see Manfred Frank, *"Unendliche Annäherung": Die Anfänge der philosophischen Frühromantik* (Frankfurt am Main: Suhrkamp, 1997), 569–93, 862–86.

15. *KFSA* 8: LXXIII; Beiser, *Romantic Imperative*, 121.

16. "Geist der Wissenschaftslehre 1797–1798" fragments in *KFSA* 18: 31–39 (nos. 126–227); Beiser, *Romantic Imperative*, 121–22.

17. See *KFSA* 18: 31–39; "Zur Wissenschaftslehre 1796," in *KFSA* 18: 3–15 (nos. 1–121); "Philosophische Fragmente 1796," Beilage I, in *KFSA* 18: 505–16; "Zur Logik und Philosophie," Beilage II, in *KFSA* 18: 517–21; and Beiser, *Romantic Imperative*, 122–23.

18. *KFSA* 18: 343; quoted in Beiser, *Romantic Imperative,* 121–22.

19. *KFSA* 18: 32: "Er ist zu . . . [mathematisch], aber nicht . . . [systematisch], d. h. nicht hist[orisch] genug."

20. Ibid., 85: "Sobald die . . . [Philosophie] Wiss[enschaft] wird, giebts Hist[orie]. Alles . . . [System] ist hist[orisch] und umgekehrt.—Die mathematische Methode ist grade die antisystematische."

21. Quoted in *KFSA* 8: LXXV.

22. Millán-Zaibert is right to connect Schlegel's historical insights to his developing anti-foundationalism. See page 124 in her book.

23. *Die Entwicklung der Philosophie in zwölf Büchern* (1804–5) in *KFSA,* vols. 12–13.

24. *KFSA* 12: 111; Millán-Zaibert, 124.

25. *KFSA* 12: 286.
26. See Millán-Zaibert, 124–25.
27. Ibid., 129.
28. Ibid., 128.
29. *KFSA* 12: 109.
30. Ibid.
31. Ibid., 109–10.
32. Ibid., 110
33. Ibid.
34. Ibid., 115.
35. Ibid., 111.
36. Ibid., 110; see Millán-Zaibert, 123–24.
37. Millán-Zaibert, 116.
38. Ibid., 127.
39. See pp. 33–34 above.
40. *KFSA* 12: 115–16.
41. Ibid., 152.
42. Ibid., 116.
43. Ibid., 117.
44. Ibid., 161.
45. Ibid., 118.
46. Ibid., 130.
47. Ibid., 126.
48. Ibid., 128. Schlegel is referring to the fideism of F. H. Jacobi (1743–1819).
49. Ibid., 129–30.
50. Ibid., 130 and 161.
51. Ibid., 131.
52. Ibid., 133–34.
53. Ibid., 130 and 161.
54. Ibid., 132 and 134.
55. Schlegel has much to say and condemn about pantheism in *Ueber die Sprache und Weisheit der Indier*; see Peter K. J. Park, "A Catholic Apologist in a Pantheistic World," in *Sanskrit and 'Orientalism': Indology and Comparative Linguistics in Germany, 1750–1958*, ed. Douglas T. McGetchin, Peter K. J. Park, and D. R. SarDesai (New Delhi: Manohar, 2004), 96–99.
56. *KFSA* 12: 132–3.
57. Ibid., 135.
58. Ibid., 136.
59. Ibid.
60. Ibid.
61. Ibid., 137.
62. Ibid., 138.
63. Ibid., 139.
64. Ibid., 140.
65. Ibid., 161. In *Ueber die Sprache und Weisheit der Indier*, Schlegel presented what he regarded as other evidence, taken from Indian textual

sources, of divine revelation; see my essay, "Catholic Apologist in a Pantheistic World," 94–95.

66. *KFSA* 12: 142 and 144.

67. Ibid., 144.

68. Ibid., 148: "Was hat z. B. das Wort Sinnlichkeit mit der Sache zu tun? Das Bild oder Wort, das einen Geist mit dem andern verbindet und in Gemeinschaft bringt, hat doch *selbst* gar nichts gemein mit dem Begriff, den dadurch ein Geist dem andern mitteilt, oder der Verbindung, in welche dadurch die beiden Geister miteinander treten. Ein Wort oder Bild ist also, ungeachtet es gar keine Ähnlichkeit hat mit dem Gegenstand, den es bedeutet, doch kein *leerer Schein*."

69. Ibid.

70. Ibid., 152.

71. Ibid., 170–71.

72. Ibid., 171.

73. Ibid., 171: "Der historischen Untersuchung der griechischen Philosophie kann noch die Frage vorausgehen, ob man durchaus mit der griechischen anfangen, nicht höher steigen, diese aus der frühern orientalischen herleiten soll, und ob überhaupt die orientalische Philosophie nicht in die Geschichte der Philosophie aufzunehmen sei."

74. Ibid., 171–72.

75. Ibid., 172.

76. Ibid.

77. Ibid., 173.

78. Ibid.

79. Ibid.

80. Abraham Hyacinthe Anquetil du Perron, *Zend-Avesta, ouvrage de Zoroastre*, 3 vols. (Paris: N. M. Tilliard, 1771).

81. *KFSA* 12: 174.

82. Ibid.

83. On the late eighteenth- and early nineteenth-century German reception of the *Bhagavadgītā*, see Marchignoli's "Canonizing an Indian Text?" and Herling's *The German Gītā*.

84. *KFSA* 12: 174.

85. Ibid., 175.

86. Ibid.: "Aus diesen Untersuchungen geht nun zur Genüge hervor, daß die Indier eine wirkliche Philosophie auch der *Form* und Methode nach hatten, und daß es uns einstweilen nur noch an hinlänglichen Urkunden fehlt, um sie in die Geschichte der Philosophie selbst aufzunehmen."

Chapter 4

1. Taguieff, 121.

2. *Lives* was rendered into Latin by Ambrogio Travesari and was available in several printed editions starting in the fifteenth century; see *Models*

of the History of Philosophy, vol. 1: *From Its Origins in the Renaissance to the "Historia philosophica,"* ed. Giovanni Santinello, C. W. T. Blackwell, and Philip Weller (Dordrecht: Kluwer, 1993), 154–60. I cite the English edition of *Lives of Eminent Philosophers* by R. D. Hicks (Cambridge, MA: Harvard University Press, 1972), I: 3–5.

3. *Lives of Eminent Philosophers*, I: 15.

4. Ibid., 5.

5. See Bernal, *Black Athena Writes Back*, 422 n. 8.

6. Constance Blackwell, "Thales Philosophicus: The Beginning of Philosophy as Discipline," in *History and the Disciplines: The Reclassification of Knowledge in Early Modern Europe*, ed. Donald R. Kelley (Rochester, NY: University of Rochester Press, 1997), 61.

7. Johannes Jacobus Frisius, *Bibliotheca philosophorum classicorum authorum chronologica : in qua veterum philosophorum origo, successio, aetas [et] doctrina compendiosa, ab origine mundi usque ad nostram aetatem, proponitur; quibus accessit Patrum, Ecclesiae Christi doctorum a temporibus apostolorum usque ad tempora scholasticorum ad a. usque D. 1140 secundum eandem temporis seriem, enumeratio* (Tiguri: Wolphius, 1592).

8. Georg Horn, *Historiae philosophicae libri VII, quibus de origine, successione, sectis et vita philosophorum ab orbe condito ad nostram aetatem agitur* (Lugduni: apud Johannem Elsevirium, 1655); Halbfass, 148.

9. Thomas Stanley, *The history of philosophy: containing the lives, opinions, actions and discourses of the philosophers of every sect* (London: Humphrey Moseley and Thomas Dring, 1655–62), 1: 1; see Popkin, ed., *The Columbia History of Western Philosophy*, 759.

10. Stanley, 1: 1–2.

11. Ibid. 3.

12. Stanley, 4: 757. In 1667, Johann Jacob Hezel published his dissertation, *De vero philosophiae origine*, in which he argues that philosophy's origin is Chaldean (Geldsetzer, 184 n. 108).

13. Gerardus Joannes Vossius, *De philosophia et philosophorum sectis* (Hagae-Comitis: apud Adrianum Vlacq, 1657); Bernasconi, "Ethnicity, Culture and Philosophy," 568–69; Halbfass, 147.

14. Thomas Burnet, *Archaeologiae philosophicae sive doctrina antiqua de rerum originibus* (London: Typis R. N., Impensis Gualt. Kettilby, 1692).

15. Abraham de Grau, *Historia philosophica, continens veterum phil. qui quidem praecipui fuerent, studia ac dogmata, modernorum quaestionibus in primis exagitata* (Franekerae Frisiorum: Excudit Johannes Wellens, 1674); Halbfass, 150.

16. Pierre Sylvain Régis, *Système de philosophie: contenant la logique, métaphysique, physique & morale* (Lyon: Anisson, Posuel & Rigaud, 1691); Halbfass, 150.

17. Johann Franz Buddeus, *Introductio ad historiam philosophiae Ebraeorum* (Halle, 1702; 2nd ed., 1720).

18. Halbfass, 59.

19. Laurentius Reinhardus, *Compendium historiae philosophiae* (Leipzig, 1725); Friedrich Gentzken, *Historia philosophiae in qua philosophorum celebrium*

vitae eorumque hypotheses notabiliores ac sectarum facta a longa rerum memoria ad nostra usque tempora succincte et ordine sistuntur (Hamburgi: Apvd Theodor. Christoph. Felginer, 1724; 2nd ed., 1731); see Geldsetzer, 184 n. 108.

20. Giambattista Capasso, Santolo Cirillo, and Giovanni Girolamo Frezza, *Historiae philosophiae synopsis sive De origine et progressu philosophiae: de vitis, sectis et systematibus omnium philosophorum libri IV* (Naples, 1728).

21. Jean-Henri-Samuel Formey, *Histoire abrégée de la philosophie* (Amsterdam: J. H. Schneider, 1760); Geldsetzer, 184 n. 109.

22. Johann Ernst Schubert, *Historia philosophiae* (Ienae: Cröker, 1742).

23. Jacob Brucker, *Historia critica philosophiae, a mundi incunabilis ad nostram usque aetatem deducta,* 1st ed., 5 vols. (Lipsiae: Breitkopf, 1742–4), 1: 41.

24. The second edition of the *Historia critica philosophiae* was issued with a sixth volume in 1766–7.

25. Brucker, *Historia critica philosophiae,* 1st ed., I: 50 and 458. See Halbfass, 149; Bernasconi, "Ethnicity, Culture and Philosophy," 569; and Blackwell, "Thales Philosophicus," 61–82. Blackwell overreaches when she claims that by the mid-eighteenth century, specifically with the arrival of Brucker's *Historia critica,* "a history of philosophy was agreed upon which claimed that Thales was the first real philosopher."

26. Friedrich Victor Leberecht Plessing, *Osiris und Sokrates* (Berlin; Stralsund, 1783); *Historische und philosophische Untersuchungen über die Denkart, Theologie und Philosophie der ältern Völker vorzüglich der Griechen bis auf Aristoteles Zeiten* (Elbingen, 1785); *Versuch zur Aufklärung der Philosophie des ältesten Alterthums* (Leipzig, 1788–90); and *Memnonium, oder Versuche zur Enthüllung der Geheimnisse des Alterthums* (Leipzig: Weygand, 1787). On Plessing, see Ulrich Johannes Schneider's *Die Vergangenheit des Geistes,* 229–31 and 238.

27. See D. P. Walker, *The Ancient Theology: Studies in Christian Platonism from the Fifteenth to the Eighteenth Century* (Ithaca: Cornell University Press, 1972).

28. The classic study of Renaissance hermeticism is by Frances A. Yates, *Giordano Bruno and the Hermetic Tradition* (Chicago: University of Chicago Press, 1964).

29. The Hermetic texts are thought to be circa-third-century compositions.

30. Johann August Eberhard, *Allgemeine Geschichte der Philosophie zum Gebrauch akademischer Vorlesungen* (Halle: Hemmerde und Schwetschke, 1788; 2nd ed., 1796).

31. John Zephaniah Holwell, *Interesting historical events, relative to the provinces of Bengal, and the empire of Indostan,* 3 vols. (London, 1766–71); see Thomas R. Trautmann, *Aryans and British India* (Berkeley; Los Angeles: University of California Press, 1997), 68–70. Holwell's work was translated into German: *Merkwürdige historische Nachrichten von Indostan und Bengalen, nebst einer Beschreibung der Religionslehren, der Mythologie, Kosmogenie, Fasten und Festtage, der Gentoos und einer Abhandlung über die Metempsychose, mit Anmerkungen und einer Abhandlung über die Religion und Philosophie der Indier,* trans. Johann Friedrich Kleuker (Leipzig: Weygand, 1778); see Willson, 24.

32. Alexander Dow, *The history of Hindostan from the earliest account of time, to the death of Akbar, translated from the Persian of Mahummud Casim Ferishta*

of Delhi; together with a dissertation concerning the religion and philosophy of the Brahmins; with an appendix, containing the history of the Mogul empire, from its decline in the reign of Mahummud Shaw, to the present times (London: T. Becket and P. A. de Hondt, 1768). Dow's preface was separately translated into German and French: *Abhandlungen zur Erläuterung der Geschichte, Religion und Staatsverfassung von Hindostan aus dem Englischen übersetzt* (Leipzig: Johann Friedrich Junius, 1773) and *Dissertation sur les moeurs, les usages, le langage, la religion et la philosophie des Hindous,* trans. Claude-François Bergier (Paris: Saugrain, 1780).

33. Willson, 27.

34. Jean Calmette and Guillaume-Emmanuel-Joseph Guilhem de Clermont-Lodève Sainte-Croix, *L'Ezour Vedam ou Ancien commentaire du Vedam, contenant l'exposition des opinions religieuses et philosophiques des Indiens* (Yverdon: M. de Felice, 1778). The German translation appeared in the following year: *Ezour-Vedam, oder die Geschichte, Religion und Philosophie der Indier* (Leipzig, 1779). See the introduction to *Ezourvedam: A French Veda of the Eighteenth Century,* ed. Ludo Rocher (Amersterdam; Philadelphia: J. Benjamins, 1984); Trautmann, 72; and Halbfass, 46 and 57.

35. Halbfass, 57–58.

36. Voltaire, François-Marie Arouet de, *Les oeuvres complètes de Voltaire/ The Complete Works of Voltaire,* ed. Theodore Bestermann et al. (Geneva: Institut et musée Voltaire; Toronto: University of Toronto Press; Banbury, Oxfordshire [etc.]: Voltaire Foundation, 1968–), 124: 92; quoted in Halbfass, 59.

37. Voltaire, *Les oeuvres complètes,* 126: 299; quoted in Halbfass, 58.

38. Herling, 60.

39. Ibid., 61.

40. Jean-Sylvain Bailly, *Lettres sur l'origine des sciences et sur celle des peuples de l'Asie, adressées à M. de Voltaire, et precedées des quelques lettres de M. de Voltaire à l'auteur* (London: M. Elmesly; Paris: Frères Debure, 1777) with a supplementary volume, *Lettres sur l'Atlantide de Platon et sur l'ancienne histoire de l'Asie: pour servir de suite aux lettres sur l'origine des sciences, addessées à M. de Voltaire* (London: M. Elmesly, 1779).

41. Jean-Sylvain Bailly, *Histoire de l'astronomie ancienne, depuis son origine jusqu'à l'etablissement de l'école d'Alexandrie,* 4 vols. (Paris: Frères Debure, 1775–82) with a supplementary volume, *Traité de l'astronomie indienne et orientale* (Paris: Frères Debure, 1787); see Trautmann, 85–86.

42. Trautmann, 84–85.

43. William MacIntosh, *Travels in Europe, Asia, and Africa describing characters, customs, manners, laws, and productions of nature and art; containing various remarks on the political and commercial interests of Great Britain; and delineating, in particular, a new system for the government and improvement of the British settlements in the East Indies; begun in the year 1777, and finished in 1781* (London: J. Murray, 1782), 1: 310; see Willson, 25.

44. Pierre de Sonnerat, *Voyage aux Indes Orientales et à la Chine, fait par ordre du roi, depuis 1774 jusqu'en 1781, dans lequel on traite des moeurs, de la religion, des sciences & des arts des Indiens, des Chinois, des Pegouins & des*

Madegasses; suivi d'observations sur le cap de Bonne-Esperance, les isles de France & de Bourbon, les Maldives, Ceylan, Malacca, les Philippines & les Moluques, & de recherches sur l'histoire naturelle de ces pays (Paris: chez l'auteur, Froule, Nyon, Barrois, 1782); see Willson, 25.

45. Edward Ives, *A voyage from England to India, in the year MDCCLIV; and an historical narrative of the operations of the Squadron and Army in India . . . in the years 1755, 1756, 1757 . . . interspersed with some interesting passages relating to the manners, customs, &c. of several nations in Indostan: also, a journey from Persia to England, by an unusual route; with an appendix, containing an account of the diseases prevalent in Admiral Watson's squadron; a description of most of the trees, shrubs, and plants, of India, with their real, or supposed medicinal virtues; also a copy of a letter written by a late ingenious physician, on the disorders incidental to Europeans at Gombroon in the Gulph of Persia; illustrated with a chart, maps, and other copper-plates* (London: Edward and Charles Dilly, 1773); Christian Wilhelm Dohm, *Reisen nach Indien und Persien in einer freyen Uebersetzung aus dem englischen Original geliefert, mit historisch-geographischen Anmerkungen und Zusätzen vermehrt von Christian Wilhelm Dohm. Mit einer Vorrede begleitet von D. Büsching* (Leipzig: M. G. Wiedmanns Erben und Reich, 1774–5).

46. Nathaniel Brassey Halhed, *A code of Gentoo laws, or, Ordinations of the pundits, from a Persian translation, made from the original, written in the Shanscrit language* (London, 1776), xliv; see Willson, 39. This text was translated into German and French: *Gesetzbuch der Gentoo's oder Sammlung der Gesetze der Pundits, nach der persischen Übersetzung des in der Sanscrit-Sprache geschriebenen Originals*, trans. Rudolph Erich Ratze (Hamburg, 1778) and *Code des loix des Gentous, ou Réglemens des brames, traduit de l'anglois, d'après les versions faites de l'original écrit en langue samskrete* (Paris: Stoupe, 1778).

47. Johann Gottfried Herder, *Abhandlung über den Ursprung der Sprache* (1770), in idem, *Sämmtliche Werke*, ed. Bernhard Ludwig Suphan et al. (Berlin: Weidmann), vol. 5 (see pp. 72, 139, and 143).

48. Johann Gottfried Herder, *Ideen zur Philosophie der Geschichte der Menschheit* (1784), in idem, *Sämmtliche Werke*, vols. 13–14. Herling (p. 76) describes *Ideen* as Herder's "most ambitious attempt to construct a comprehensive, universal history. It gave voice to a cultural distinctiveness and concreteness, while at the same time attempting to inscribe cultures into a coherent developmental scheme."

49. See Paul T. Hoffmann, *Der indische und der deutsche Geist von Herder bis zur Romantik*, dissertation (Tübingen, 1915); Willson, 51; and Halbfass, 69–72. "Asian sources pointed towards a primal monotheistic revelation, which expressed itself in different terms among the ancient cultures of Asia" (Herling, 59).

50. "It was [Majer's] conviction that the religious and philosophical situation in Europe could only be clarified and rectified through a return to the Indian origins, and that the sources of the Western tradition founded their integrating context and background in Indian thought" (Halbfass, 73).

51. Friedrich Majer, *Allgemeines Mythologisches Lexikon*, 2 vols. (Weimar, 1803–4). Majer makes similar claims in *Brahma oder über die Religion der Indier als Brahmaismus* (Leipzig, 1818); see Halbfass, 73.

52. Quoted in Halbfass, 63.

53. Letter of September 24, 1788, in *The Letters of Sir William Jones*, ed. Garland Cannon (Oxford: Clarendon, 1970), 2: 818.

54. William Jones, "The Third Anniversary Discourse, on the Hindus, delivered to the Asiatic Society, 2, February 1786," in *Asiatick researches, or, Transactions of the society instituted in Bengal, for inquiring into the history and antiquities, the arts, sciences, and literature of Asia* (London: Vernor and Hood, 1798); and multiple other editions).

55. Halbfass, 64.

56. Asiatic Society of Bengal, *Abhandlungen über die Geschichte und Alter-thümer, die Künste, Wissenschaften und Litteratur Asiens, von Sir William Jones und andern Mitgliedern der im Jahre 1784 zu Calcutta in Indien errichteten gelehrten Gesellschaft*, 3 vols., trans. by J. C. Fick and D. J. F. Kleuker (Riga, 1795–6), and *Recherches asiatiques, ou Mémoires de la Société établie au Bengale pour faire des recherches sur l'histoire et les antiquités, les arts, les sciences et la littérature de l'Asie* (Paris, 1802 and 1805).

57. Meiners was born in Warstade in the Duchy of Bremen. His father was the town's postmaster. The son attended the *Gymnasium* in Bremen from 1763 to 1767. He studied at the University of Göttingen from 1767 to 1770. He became *Professor extraordinarius* at the university in 1772, at age twenty-five, and full professor three years later. A member of the Göttingen Society of Sciences since 1776, Meiners was also Privy Councillor by 1788. From 1788 to 1791, he coedited the journal *Philosophische Bibliothek* with his colleague and close friend Johann Georg Heinrich Feder. From 1787 to 1791, he coedited the journal *Göttingisches historisches Magazin* with Ludwig Timotheus Spittler. He died on May 1, 1810, in Göttingen. See Christian Gottlob Heyne, "Memoria Christophori Meiners, 1810," in *Commentationes Societatis Regiae Scientiarum Gottingensis* (Göttingae: Henricum Dieterich, 1808–1811); and "Meiners, Christoph," in *Allgemeine Deutsche Biographie* 21 (1885): 224–26, http://www.deutsche-biographie.de/pnd116863498.html?anchor=adb.

58. Britta Rupp-Eisenreich, "Des choses occultes en histoire des sciences humaines: Le destin de la 'science nouvelle' de Christoph Meiners," *L'ethnographie* 90–91 (1983): 131–83, and "Christoph Meiners et Joseph-Marie de Gérando: un chapitre du comparatisme anthropologique," in *L'homme des Lumières et la découverte de l'autre*, ed. Daniel Droixhe and Pol-Pierre Jossiaux (Brussels: Université Libre de Bruxelles), 21–47.

59. Christoph Meiners, *Geschichte des Ursprungs, Fortgangs und Verfalls der Wissenschaften in Griechenland und Rom*, 2 vols. (Lemgo: Meyer, 1781–2); translated by J. Ch. Laveaux, *Histoire de l'origine, des progrès et de la décadence des sciences dans la Grèce*, 4 vols. (Paris: Laveaux et Compagnie, an VII = 1799). See Santinello et al., *Storia delle storie generali della filosofia*, Vol. 3, Part II: 725.

60. Hans-Jürgen Schings, *Melancholie und Aufklärung: Melancholiker und ihre Kritiker in Erfahrungsseelenkunde und Literatur des 18. Jahrhunderts* (Stuttgart: Metzler, 1977), 13; Helmut Pfotenhauer, *Literarische Anthropologie* (Stuttgart: Metzler, 1987), 1; John H. Zammito, *Kant, Herder, and the Birth of Anthropology* (Chicago: University of Chicago Press, 2002), 245 and 345. The most useful study of Meiners's racial anthropology of recent date is the 46-page essay by

Friedrich Lotter, "Christoph Meiners und die Lehre von der unterschiedlichen Wertigkeit der Menschenrassen," in *Geschichtswissenschaft in Göttingen: Eine Vorlesungsreihe,* ed. Hartmut Boockmann and Hermann Wellenreuther (Göttingen: Vandenhoeck und Ruprecht, 1987), 30–75.

61. Wilhelm Dilthey calls Göttingen "the center of historical studies in Germany" (idem, *Gesammelte Schriften,* ed. Paul Ritter [Stuttgart: Teubner, 1959], 3: 261). Reill (p. 8) describes Göttingen as the "most important single center of the Aufklärung."

62. Christoph Meiners, *Revision der Philosophie* (Göttingen; Gotha: Dieterich, 1772); Zammito, *Kant, Herder, and the Birth of Anthropology,* 248. Some historians of eighteenth-century Germany are given to think that Meiners was rejected or ignored by his contemporaries and therefore was not influential and that he became popular starting in the nineteenth century. Could this Göttingen professor and prolific writer of scores of books and hundreds of articles in popular journals really have been ignored by his contemporaries? J. F. Blumenbach and Georg Forster disagreed with him, but they could not ignore him (see Frank W. P. Dougherty, "Christoph Meiners und Johann Friedrich Blumenbach im Streit um den Begriff der Menschenrasse," in *Die Natur des Menschen: Probleme der physischen Anthropologie und Rassenkunde (1750–1850),* ed. Gunter Mann and Franz Dumont [Stuttgart; New York: Gustav Fischer, 1990], 89–111; and Lotter, 60–63). The comparative anatomist Samuel Thomas Sömmerring called him "the beloved philosopher of our Fatherland, Meiners" in *Ueber die körperliche Verschiedenheit des Negers vom Europäer* (Frankfurt; Mainz: Varrentrapp Sohn und Wenner, 1785), XIII.

63. See Zantop, "The Beautiful, the Ugly, and the German," 30–32.

64. Christoph Meiners, *Grundriss der Geschichte der Weltweisheit* (Lemgo: Meyer, 1786; 2nd ed., 1789). I cite from the second edition.

65. Christoph Meiners, *Geschichte des Ursprungs, Fortgangs und Verfalls der Wissenschaften in Griechenland und Rom* (see note 59 above) and *Grundriss der Geschichte der Menschheit* (Lemgo: Meyer, 1785; 2nd ed., 1793).

66. Meiners's preface to the second edition of *Weltweisheit*: "Seit einigen Jahren hat sich unter uns von neuem die unhistorische Schwärmerey zu regen angefangen, vermöge deren die abgezogensten Ideen und Systeme den rohen, oder wenig gebildeten Völkern des ältesten Alterthums zugeschrieben werden, allein es scheint, als wenn diese Krankheit des Geistes, die unter den Griechen und Römern, wie unter unsern Nachbarn jenseit des Rheins die Vorläuferinn, oder Wirkung des Verfalls aller ächten Gelehrsamkeit, und Kritik war, sich unter uns nicht weit über die Gränzen gewisser geheimer Schulen verbreiten werde."

67. Meiners, *Griechenland und Rom,* 3.

68. Ibid.

69. Ibid., 3–4: "Menschen . . . die einen desto unbezwinglichern Haß gegen Fremde hatten. . . . wurden von ihren ehemaligen Landsleuten eben sowohl, als andere geplündert und weggeschleppt. . . . außer ihren Göttern und gottesdienstlichen Gebräuchen, außer den ersten Anfängen des Acker-

baues, und der damals noch ganz unbrauchbaren Schrift, endlich außer einer gewissen Anzahl von Wörtern wenig oder gar nichts von bildenden Kenntnissen und Fertigkeiten überliefert haben."

70. Meiners, *Weltweisheit*, 6.

71. Ibid., 7.

72. Ibid., 7–8.

73. Ibid., 9: "zu den aufgeklärten Völkern."

74. Ibid., 9.

75. Ibid., 10: "Unter allen Völkern der alten Welt kann kein anderes mit grösserm Recht auf den Ruhm von Originalität und selbst von früher Cultur Anspruch machen, als die Aegyptier."

76. Ibid., 10–11: "aber in Rücksicht auf wahre Schönheit und Grösse...."

77. Ibid., 11: "Die späte Entstehung und der langsame Fortgang der Wissenschafften in Griechenland würde allein schon beweisen, daß die Griechen nicht einmal die Elemente derselben von den Aegyptiern entlehnt hätten a), wenn es auch nicht ausser allem Zweyfel wäre, daß die Geschichte und Geographie, die Naturkunde, Medicin, und die mathematischen Wissenschafften der Aegyptischen Priester vor ihrer Aufklärung durch die Griechen in einer beständigen Kindheit geblieben sind b)."

78. Martin Bernal, *Black Athena*, 1: 189–443 passim.

79. Meiners, *Weltweisheit*, 12–13.

80. Ibid., 13–14.

81. Ibid., 13–14: "halten keine genaue Prüfung aus."

82. Ibid., 15.

83. Ibid., 16–17: "Am wahrscheinlichsten ist es, daß die Hindus Schüler der Griechen waren. Wahrscheinlich wird dieses nicht nur dadurch daß viele Tausende von Griechen nach dem Alexander sich in Hindostan niederliessen, daß Griechische Könige eine Zeitlang über einen Theil von Hindostan herrschten, und daß die Griechische Sprache sich mehrere Jahrhunderte in diesem Lande erhielt; sondern auß auch noch viele andere unläugbare Spuren Griechischer und Christlicher Kenntnisse unter den Hindus übrig sind."

84. Ibid., 18.

85. Ibid., 19–20.

86. Ibid., 24.

87. Meiners's preface to *Menschheit*, 1st ed.: "daß das gegenwärtige Menschengeschlecht aus zween Hauptstämmen bestehe, dem Tatarischen oder Kaukasischen, und dem Mongolischen Stamm: daß der leztere nicht nur viel schwächer von Cörper und Geist, sondern auch viel übel gearteter und tugendleerer, als der Kaukasische sey: daß endlich der kaukasische Stamm wiederum in zwo Racen zerfalle, in die Celtische und Slawische, unter welchen wiederum die erstere am reichsten an Geistesgaben und Tugenden sey."

88. Meiners, *Menschheit*, 2nd ed., 5–6: "Ich habe daher die Nationen, welche in der ersten Ausgabe Mongolische hießen, in der gegenwärtigen dunkelfarbige, und häßliche; so wie die Kaukasischen weiße, oder hellfarbige,

und schöne Völker genannt. Diese Merkmahle sind zwar nicht die einzigen, wodurch die weißen und schönen, und die dunkelfarbigen und häßlichen Nationen sich von einander auszeichnen."

89. Ibid., 29–30.

90. Ibid., 75.

91. Ibid., 30–31: "warum große Gesetzgeber, Weise, und Helden, warum Künste und Wissenschaften nur unter gewissen Völkern entstanden und ausgebildet, warum die letztern von andern Nationen zwar aufgenommen, aber mehr verschlimmert als vervollkommt wurden, und warum sie unter andern Völkern aller Bemühungen ungeachtet keinen Eingang finden konnten: warum ein einziger Erdtheil und gewisse Völker fast immer die herrschenden, und alle übrige hingegen die dienenden waren: warum von jeher die Göttinn der Freyheit nur innerhalb so enger Gränzen wohnte, und der schrecklichste Despotismus hingegen seinen unerschütterlichen Thron unter den meisten Völkern der Erde aufschlug: warum endlich die Europäischen Nationen selbst im Zustande der Barbarey sich so sehr von den Wilden und Barbaren der übrigen Erdtheile durch ihre höhern Tugenden, durch ihre größere Empfänglichkeit gegen Aufklärung, durch ihre Verfassung, Gesetze, und Art zu kriegen, durch ihr Betragen gegen Weiber, Sclaven, und überwundene Feinde auszeichneten."

92. Tiedemann was born in Bremervörde in the Duchy of Bremen. His father was a Bürgermeister of the town. Dieterich attended schools in Bremervörde and Verden and then the *Gymnasium* in Bremen. In 1767, he matriculated at the University of Göttingen, where he studied theology, mathematics, and philosophy. He left Göttingen to become a tutor in the household of Baron Budberg in Livonia during 1769–73, but by 1774 he was back in Göttingen. He completed his training in classical philology under Christian Gottlob Heyne and in 1776 was appointed *Professor extraordinarius* of Latin and Greek at the Collegium Carolinum in Kassel. In December of 1785, he was promoted to the rank of *Professor ordinarius* of philosophy at the University of Marburg. He died in Marburg on May 24, 1803. Among his published works are *System der stoischen Philosophie*, 3 vols. (Leipzig: Weidmann, 1776); *Untersuchungen über den Menschen*, 3 vols. (Leipzig: Weidmann, 1777–8); *Griechenlands erste Philosophen, oder Leben und Systeme des Orpheus, Pherecydes, Thales und Pythagoras* (Leipzig: Weidmann, 1780); *Hermes Trismegist's Poemander und Asklepias, oder von der göttlichen Macht und Weisheit* (Berlin und Stettin, 1781); *Theätet, oder über das menschliche Wissen, ein Beitrag zur Vernunftkritik* (Frankfurt am Main: Varrentrapp und Wenner, 1794); and *Handbuch der Psychologie zum Gebrauche bei Vorlesungen und zur Selbstbelehrung bestimmt*, with a biography of the author, ed. L. Wachler (Leipzig: Johann Ambrosius Barth, 1804).

93. See the eulogy for Tiedemann by Karl Wilhelm Justi in *Der neue Teutsche Merkur* 3 (1803): 353–67; published also in *Hessische Denkwürdigkeiten*, ed. Karl Wilhelm Justi (Marburg: Neue Akademische Buchhandlung, 1805), Part 4, Section 2: 46–60; the article on Tiedemann in Friedrich Wilhelm Strieder, *Grundlage zu einer hessische Gelehrten- und Schriftsteller-Geschichte*, ed. D.

Ludwig Wachler (Marburg: Neue Akademische Buchhandlung, 1812) XVI: 182–98; and "Tiedemann, Dietrich," *Allgemeine Deutsche Biographie* 38 (1894): 276–77, http://www.deutsche-biographie.de/pnd117376280.html?achor=adb.

94. Dieterich Tiedemann, *Geist der spekulativen Philosophie von Thales bis Sokrates*, 6 vols. (Marburg: Neue Akademische Buchhandlung, 1791–7).

95. Tiedemann, *Geist der spekulativen Philosophie* 1: xviii.

96. Ibid., xviii–xix.

97. Ibid., xix.

98. Ibid.

99. Ibid.

100. Johann Gottlieb Buhle, *Lehrbuch der Geschichte der Philosophie und einer kritischen Literatur derselben* (Göttingen: Vandenhöck und Ruprecht, 1796–1804).

101. Buhle, *Lehrbuch* 1: 13–14; see Bernasconi, "Religious Philosophy," 2.

102. Ibid., 17–18: "Wenn sich auch nicht mit Gewißheit entscheiden läßt, welches Volk des Alterthums sich zuerst durch Cultur und Philosophie hervorgethan habe; so ist doch unleugbar, daß der zuverlässigen Geschichte nach die Aegyptier eines der ältesten Völker gewesen sind, welche auf die Ehre des Besitzes derselben in einem gewissen Grade Anspruch machen konnten. Dieses hat auch mehr ältere und neuere Gelehrte bewogen, grade die Aegyptier für das originale Volk zu erklären, von welchem sich alle Cultur, Religion, und Philosophie ursprünglich über andere Nationen verbreitet hätten."

103. Ibid., 19.

104. Ibid., 91.

105. Among the modern sources on Indian philosophy cited by Buhle are Abraham Roger, François Bernier, La Croze, and Niekamp; *Lettres edifiantes et curieuses des missions etrangères*; August. Anton. Georgius; the German edition of Holwell; Dow's translation of Firishta; Dow's "Dissertation"; Sinner's German edition of *Ezour-Vedam* including the introduction by St. Croix; Anquetil du Perron; the German edition of *A Code of Gentoo-Laws*; Gladwin; Wilkins's *Bhagvat-Geeta*; *Bagavadam*; Paulinus a S. Bartholomaeo; the German edition of *Asiatick Researches*; Hennings; Sonnerat; de Guignes; Abbé Mignot; the excerpt of the "Upnek'hat" in Anquetil du Perron's *Recherches historiques et geographiques sur l'Inde* (Berlin, 1786); an excerpt of the *Ambertkend* which de Guignes printed in *Mémoires de l'Académie des Inscriptions*, vol. XXVI; and translated excerpts of the "Vedangshaster," "Dirmshaster," and "Shastahbade" in *Sammlung asiatischer Originalschriften*, vol. 1 (Zürich, 1791).

106. Buhle, *Lehrbuch*, 1: 99: "Hier bemerkt man offenbar die sich kreuzenden Lehren der berühmtesten philosophischen Schulen unter den Griechen. Sie wurden theils durch den Zug des Alexander, und die Griechen, die nach demselben in Indien blieben, theils durch die Römer, und späterhin selbst durch die Araber, die griechische Literatur, vornämlich die Platonische und Aristotelische Philosophie, kennen gelernt hatten, in Indien verbreitet." See note 83 above.

107. Tennemann, *Geschichte der Philosophie,* 1: 3 and 5.

108. Ibid., 11. He adds, "It is true that here one finds some examples of the persecution and restriction of the freedom of thought, but this is true in respect to individual philosophers, not in respect to philosophy itself."

109. Immanuel Kant, *Lectures on Logic,* trans. J. Michael Young (Cambridge University Press, 1992), 20.

110. Tennemann, *Geschichte der Philosophie,* 1: 3.

111. Ibid., 5.

112. De Gérando, *Histoire comparée,* 1: 62: "Nous nous bornerons à annoncer ici, que . . . sept ou huit ont fixé davantage notre attention, et nous ont paru devoir être plus particulièrement recommandées. Ce sont celles de Tiedemann, de Buhle, de Meiners, de Tennemann, d'Eberhard, de Bardili, de Gurlitt; les *Mélanges* de Fulleborn, divers travaux de Garve, les notes qui accompagnent les *Aphorismes* de Platner, et les savantes Dissertations de Heyne; les Mémoires de la Société de Gœttingue, ceux de l'Académie de Berlin, le Magasin de Hismann, sont enrichis d'une foule de dissertations très-utiles à consulter."

113. Ibid., 12–13.

114. Ibid., 13–14.

115. On Carus's ideas on the history of philosophy in relation to the rest of his work, see Jörn Garber, "Von der 'anthropologischen Geschichte des philosophierenden Geistes' zur Geschichte der Menschheit (Friedrich August Carus)," in *Zwischen Empirisierung und Konstruktionsleistung: Anthropologie im 18. Jahrhundert,* ed. Jörn Garber and Heinz Thoma (Tübingen: Max Niemeyer, 2004), 219–61.

116. Friedrich August Carus, *Ideen zur Geschichte der Philosophie* (Leipzig: Iohann Ambrosius Barth und Paul Gotthelf Kummer, 1809).

117. Ibid., 143.

118. Ibid., 144–45.

119. Ibid., 145.

120. Ibid., 146.

121. Ibid.

122. Ibid., 146–47.

123. Ibid., 149.

124. Ibid., 163.

125. Ibid., 160–61.

126. Ibid., 164: "Man hat oft gesagt, dass die Griechen von den Aegyptiern viel Weisheit erhalten haben, mithin auch nicht originell heissen könnten. Welche geringen Anfänge von Cultur waren aber dies? Wo ist auch das Volk, das gar keinen Beitrag zu seiner Cultur von einer Andern mehr oder weniger empfangen hätte? Worauf die Griechen stolz seyn konnten, jene Systeme tiefgedachter Philosophie, jene Ideale der Kunst, das erhält ihnen den Titel von schöpferischen Genies."

127. Ibid., 164: "Sie, die erhabene Nation, gab dem Asiern und Afrikern die wenigen von ihnen erhaltenen Kenntnisse mit reichem Wucher zurük. Sie bleibt immer die Einzige, die sich selbst entwickelte, und dann sich humanisirter und zarter als alle Andere zeigte."

128. See pp. 90 and 128 above.

129. Carus, 171.

130. See p. 167 n. 112 above.

131. Tennemann, *Grundriss* (1816), 11. Carl Friedrich Bachmann, *Dissertationis philosophicae de peccatis Tennemanni in historia philosophiae particula I* (Jena, 1814).

132. Tennemann, *Grundriss* (1816), 11.

133. Ibid., 8.

134. Ibid., 9.

135. Ibid., 10.

136. Ibid., 10–11.

137. Ibid., 46–47.

138. Tennemann, *Grundriss* (1820), 10–11.

139. There are more than a couple of direct references to Meiners in Tennemann's *Grundriss der Geschichte der Philosophie.*

140. AA 24: 800–801; Kant, *Lectures on Logic*, 261.

141. On the dating of the logic lectures, see the translator's introduction to Kant, *Lectures on Logic*, xxv–xxvi.

142. AA 28: 531; Immanuel Kant, *Lectures on Metaphysics*, trans. Karl Ameriks and Steve Naragon (Cambridge: Cambridge University Press, 1997), 299: "We have said of rational cognitions that they are cognitions from principles <*ex principiis*>, they must thus be *a priori*. There are two cognitions that are *a priori* but which nevertheless have many noteworthy differences: namely *mathematics* and *philosophy.*"

143. AA 24: 894; Kant, *Lectures on Logic*, 340.

144. See p. 79 above.

145. Imannuel Kant, *Logik: ein Handbuch zu Vorlesungen*, ed. Gottlob Benjamin Jäsche (Königsberg: Friedrich Nicolovius, 1800), in AA 9: 1–150; translation in Kant, *Lectures on Logic*, 521–640.

146. AA 9: 27; Kant, *Lectures on Logic*, 540; see Bernasconi, "Religious Philosophy," 2.

147. AA 9: 28; Kant, *Lectures on Logic*, 540.

148. Emmanuel Chukwudi Eze, "The Color of Reason: The Idea of 'Race' in Kant's Anthropology," *Bucknell Review* 38 (1995): 200–41; Tsenay Serequeberhan, "Eurocentrism in Philosophy: The Case of Immanuel Kant," *The Philosophical Forum* 27, no. 4 (Summer 1996): 333–56; Robert Bernasconi, "Who Invented the Concept of Race? Kant's Role in the Enlightenment Construction of Race," in *Race*, ed. Robert Bernasconi (Malden, MA: Blackwell, 2001), 11–36; Bernasconi, "Kant as an Unfamiliar Source of Racism," in *Philosophers on Race: Critical Essays*, ed. Julie K. Ward and Tommy L. Lott (Malden, MA: Blackwell, 2002), 145–66; Bernasconi, "Will the Real Kant Please Stand Up: The Challenge of Enlightenment Racism to the Study of the History of Philosophy," in *Radical Philosophy* 117 (2003): 13–22; Bernasconi, "Kant and Blumenbach's Polyps: A Neglected Chapter in the History of the Concept of Race," in *The German Invention of Race*, ed. Sara Eigen and Mark Larrimore (Albany: SUNY Press, 2006), 73–90; Mark Larrimore, "Sublime Waste: Kant on the Destiny of the 'Races,' " *Canadian Journal of Philosophy* 25 / supp.

vol. titled *Civilization and Oppression* (1999): 99–125; Mark Larrimore, "Race, Freedom and the Fall in Steffens and Kant," in *The German Invention of Race*, 91–120; Mark Larrimore, "Antinomies of race: diversity and destiny in Kant," *Patterns of Prejudice* 42, nos. 4–5 (2008): 341–63; and Todd Hedrick, "Race, Difference, and Anthropology in Kant's Cosmopolitanism," *Journal of the History of Philosophy* 46, no. 2 (2008): 245–68. More than sixty years ago, Walter Scheidt argued that Kant created "the first theory of race which really merits that name" in an essay on "The concept of race in anthropology," in *This is race: An anthology selected from the international literature on the races of man*, ed. E. W. Count (New York: Schuman, 1950), 354–91 (quotation taken from p. 372). Pauline Kleingeld and Bernasconi have debated whether Kant persevered in his racial and racist views. Kleingeld argues that he changed his views by the last decade of his life in "Kant's Second Thoughts on Race," *Philosophical Quarterly* 57 (2007): 573–92. Bernasconi presents arguments to the contrary in "Kant's Third Thoughts on Race," in *Reading Kant's Geography*, ed. Stuart Elden and Eduardo Mendieta (Albany: SUNY Press, 2011), 291–318.

149. So claims Bernasconi in "Who Invented the Concept of Race?" and "Kant as an Unfamiliar Source of Racism."

150. Kant, "Beobachtungen über das Gefühl des Schönen und Erhabenen," in AA 2: 205–56; "Observations on the Feeling of the Beautiful and Sublime," in idem, *Anthropology, History, and Education*, ed. Günter Zöller and Robert I. Louden (Cambridge: Cambridge University Press, 2007), 23–64.

151. AA 2: 253.

152. Ibid., 254–55.

153. "Von den verschiedenen Racen der Menschen," in AA 2: 427–43; "Bestimmung des Begriffs einer Menschenrace" (1785), in AA 8: 89–106; and "Über den Gebrauch teleologischer Principien in der Philosophie" (1788), in AA 8: 157–84.

154. Christoph Girtanner, *Ueber das kantische Prinzip für die Naturgeschichte: Ein Versuch diese Wissenschaft philosophisch zu behandeln* (Göttingen: Vandenhoeck und Ruprecht, 1796).

155. AA 2: 432: "Sie sind 1) die Race der Weißen, 2) die Negerrace, 3) die hunnische (mungalische oder kalmuckische) Race, 4) die hinduische oder hindustanische Race."

156. AA 8: 93: "Wir kennen mit Gewißheit nicht mehr erbliche Unterschiede der Hautfarbe, als die: der Weißen, der gelben Indianer, der Neger und der kupferfarbig-rothen Amerikaner."

157. Bernasconi, "Who Invented the Concept of Race?," 22.

158. Bernasconi, "Kant as an Unfamiliar Source of Racism," 155.

159. Frank W. P. Dougherty, "Christoph Meiners und Johann Friedrich Blumenbach im Streit um den Begriff der Menschenrasse," 102 n. 52.

160. Christoph Meiners, "Ueber die Bevölkerung von America," in *Göttingisches historisches Magazin*, ed. Christoph Meiners and Ludwig Timotheus Spittler 3 (1788): 193–218; AA 25.2: 1187–8.

161. Christoph Meiners, "Ueber die Natur der Afrikanischen Neger," in *Göttingisches historisches Magazin* 6 (1790): 385–456; AA 15: 877–79 (*Reflexion 1520*).

162. AA 25.2: 665.

163. Ibid., 1187–8. Also, AA 15: 877–79 (*Reflexion 1520*): "Von der race der Weissen, die alle revolutionen in der Welt hervorgebracht hat. . . . Die drey übrige racen gar keine."

164. AA 15.2: 880.

165. Ibid.

166. Christoph Meiners, "Ueber die Ursachen des Despotismus," in *Göttingisches historisches Magazin* 2 (1788): 193–229.

167. Ibid., 203: "Eben die Schwäche, Gefühllosigkeit, und Beschränktheit des Geistes, welche die Mongolischen Hirten-Völker zu Sclaven ihrer Fürsten machten, erhoben auch die Häupter und Könige aller übrigen Mongolischen Nationen unter ähnlichen Umständen zu unumschränkten Herren des Lebens und Eigenthums, der Freyheit und Ehre ihrer Unterthanen."

168. Ibid., 208: "Eine ähnliche Schwäche, Gefühllosigkeit, und Dummheit ist die Ursache, daß die Negern bey der grössten Armuth und der grössten Leichtigkeit zu entfliehen sich von jeher eben so willkührlich beherrschen liessen, als die angeführten Völker in America."

169. Ibid., 200: "In allen Theilen der Erde also, und zu allen Zeiten verhielt sich die Freyheit oder Sclaverey von Völkern, wie der innere Werth und Unwerth deselben, und nie ist eine Nation von einem Despoten unterdruckt worden, ohne daß sie nicht dieses Schicksal verdient, und sich ihre Fesseln vorher selbst geschmiedet hätte."

170. Tennemann, *Grundriss* (1820), 9.

171. AA 15.2 ("Reflexionen zur Anthropologie"): 494–899.

172. AA 15.2: 877–79: "Unsere (alte) Geschichte der Menschen geht mit Zuverläßigkeit nur auf die Race der Weissen. Egypter. Perser. Thracier. Griechen. Celten. Scythen. (nicht Indier, Neger.)"

173. Ibid., 880: "Celtischer Stamm."

174. Larrimore, "Sublime Waste," 115.

Chapter 5

1. Friedrich Ast, *Grundriss einer Geschichte der Philosophie* (Landshut: Joseph Thomann, 1807), 6.

2. On Carus, see the essay by Jörn Garber, "Von der 'anthropologischen Geschichte des philosophierenden Geistes' zur Geschichte der Menschheit (Friedrich August Carus)."

3. F. W. J. von Schelling, *Sämmtliche Werke* (Stuttgart; Augsburg: J. G. Cotta, 1856), 1: 461–73.

4. Schelling, *Sämmtliche Werke* 1: 467 and 471. "[T]hat which can be predicted *a priori*, that which occurs following necessary laws, is not the object

of history; and the obverse, that which is the object of history must not be predictable *a priori*" (ibid., 467). "Thus, if man can have history only insofar as it is not determined *a priori*, it follows from this that an *a priori* history is a contradiction in itself. . . ." (ibid., 437).

5. Christian Weiss, *Über die Behandlungsart der Geschichte der Philosophie auf Universitäten* (Leipzig, 1799), 44.

6. Schelling, *Sämmtliche Werke*, 1: 472–73.

7. Geldsetzer (p. 74) quotes Schelling's contemporary, Christian August Brandis: "Were there to be a complete [*vollständiges*] system of philosophy, one would have to claim necessarily that all history has stopped."

8. Hegel, *Differenz des Fichteschen und Schellingschen Systems der Philosophie* (1801); see the first part ("Mancherlei Formen, die bei dem jetzigen Philosophieren vorkommen") in the section "Geschichtliche Ansicht philosophischer Systeme," in idem, *Gesammelte Werke* (Hamburg: Felix Meiner, 1968–), vol. 4.

9. Hegel, *Gesammelte Werke*, 4: 9.

10. Ibid., 9–10: "Dieses [the amassing of knowledge of past opinions] halt sich auf seinem gegen Wahrheit gleichgültigen Standpunkte fest; und behält seine Selbstandigkeit, es mag Meynungen annehmen, oder verwerfen, oder sich nicht entscheiden; es kann philosophischen Systemen kein anderes Verhältniß zu sich geben, als daß sie Meynungen sind; und solche Accidenzien, wie Meynungen können ihm nichts anhaben, es hat nicht erkannt, daß es Wahrheit gibt."

11. Carus, 5–6.

12. Schelling, *Sämmtliche Werke*, 1: 458–59.

13. Carus, 6–7 and 21.

14. Friedrich Ast, *Grundriss der Geschichte der Philosophie* (Landshut: Joseph Thomann, 1825), 7–8.

15. Ibid.

16. Carus, 5.

17. Thaddä Anselm Rixner, *Handbuch der Geschichte der Philosophie* (Sulzbach: Seidel, 1822–3), 1: 2 and 6.

18. Rixner, 1: 3.

19. Carus, 20.

20. Ibid., 9; Rixner, 1: V–VI.

21. Carus, 9.

22. Ibid., 14.

23. Ast (1807), I and 4–5; Ast (1825), 3–5.

24. Rixner, 1: 3–4.

25. Ast (1807), 2; Ast (1825), 1–2.

26. Rixner, 1: IV.

27. Ibid., 4.

28. Carus, 8.

29. Rixner, 1: 6.

30. Ast (1807), 6; Ast (1825), 5–6.

31. Ast (1807), 7; Ast (1825), 9.

32. Ast (1807), IV–VI.

33. Ast (1807), 10–11; Ast (1825), 9.

34. Ast (1807), 11 and 13.

35. Rixner, 1: 11.

36. Ast (1807), 12–13; Ast (1825), 12.

37. Rixner, 1: 11.

38. Rixner pointed to Dante Alighieri's *Divine Comedy* as an example of the complete fusion of epic and lyric forms of poetry as well as of tragic and comic drama.

39. Rixner, 1: 12.

40. Ast (1807), 12–13; Ast (1825), 12.

41. Ast (1807), 18; Ast (1825), 17.

42. Ast (1807), 18.

43. Ibid.

44. Rixner, 1: 17.

45. Ast (1807), 17–18; Ast (1825), 16; Rixner, 1: 17–18.

46. Ast (1807), 7; Ast (1825), 7.

47. Ast (1807), 19–20.

48. Ibid., 19–20 and 36.

49. Ast (1825), 18.

50. Ast (1807), VII; Rixner, 1: 18–19.

51. Rixner, 1: 21.

52. Ast (1807), 36; Ast (1825), 33; Rixner, 1: 29.

53. Rixner, 1: 19.

54. Rixner does not however cite his own German translation of portions of Anquetil du Perron's Latin *Oupnek'hat* with notes, Sanskrit glossary, and brief account of the life of the Frenchman who translated it from the Persian text: *Versuch einer neuen Darstellung der uralten indischen All-Eins-Lehre* (Nürnberg: Stein, 1808).

55. Ast (1807), 41; Ast (1825), 37.

56. Ast (1807), 44–47. Ast viewed the religion of the ancient Scandinavians as a further development of Oriental myth, which may have occurred with the emigration of an Asiatic tribe led by the historical Odin.

57. Ast (1807), 51; Ast (1825), 46.

58. Rixner, 1: 36–37.

59. Ast (1807), 18.

60. Rixner, 1: 19.

61. Ast (1807), 52; Ast (1825), 46.

62. Ast (1807), 52–53; Ast (1825), 46–47.

63. Ast (1807), 53; Ast (1825), 47–48.

64. Ast (1807), 53 and 53 n; Ast (1825), 47–48.

65. Rixner, 1: 37.

66. Here, Rixner cites Herodotus and F. W. J. von Schelling's *Über die Gottheiten von Samothrake* (1815).

67. Rixner, 1: 37–38.

68. Ast (1807), 53; Ast (1825), 47–48.

69. Ast (1807), 54–55; Ast (1825), 48–49.
70. Ast (1825), 59–60.
71. Ibid., 60.
72. Ast (1807), 84.
73. Ast (1825), 75.
74. Ibid., 82.
75. Ast (1807), 55; Ast (1825), 49.
76. Ast (1807), 95–96; Ast (1825), 83.
77. Rixner, 1: 133.
78. Ibid., 38, 134, and 175.
79. Ibid., 294.
80. Ast (1807), 206; Ast (1825), 181.
81. Ast (1807), 208.
82. Ast (1807), 210–11; Ast (1825), 184.
83. Ast (1825), 182.
84. Rixner, 3: 3; Ast (1825), 183 and 312; Ast (1807), 354.
85. Rixner, 3: 32; Ast (1825), 324.
86. Ast (1825), 321.
87. Ast (1807), 380; Ast (1825), 336.
88. Rixner, 3: 116.
89. Ast (1807), 442; Ast (1825), 394–95.
90. Ast (1807), 443; Ast (1825), 395.
91. Rixner, 3: 280, 283, and 330.
92. Ast (1807), 475.
93. Ast (1807), 477; Ast (1825), 428.
94. Rixner, 3: 358.
95. Ast (1825), 438–39.
96. Ibid., 439–40.

Chapter 6

1. *Vorlesungen* 6: 114 (Kolleg 1819, 9).
2. *Vorlesungen* 6: 5 (Synopsis des Ms. 1820, 10a).
3. *Vorlesungen* 6: 347 (Kolleg 1829/30, 26a).
4. See Saverio Marchignoli, "Canonizing an Indian Text?"
5. *Vorlesungen* 7: 1 (Kolleg 1825/26, 122).
6. *Vorlesungen* 6: 365 (Kolleg 1825/26, 87).
7. Darrel Moellendorf, "Racism and Rationality in Hegel's Philosophy of Subjective Spirit," *History of Political Thought* 13, no. 2 (Summer 1992): 243–55; G. W. F. Hegel, *Philosophy of Subjective Spirit*, trans. M. J. Petry, 3 vols. (Dordrecht: D. Reidel, 1978 [reprinted with corrections, 1979]). Moellendorf cites the additions to paragraphs 393 and 435 and the remark on paragraph 482 in the *Philosophy of Subjective Spirit* as the relevant passages.
8. Moellendorf, 248–49.
9. Ibid., 243, 249, and 251.

10. Ibid., 243.

11. Bernasconi, "Hegel at the Court of the Ashanti.

12. Bernasconi, "Hegel at the Court of the Ashanti," 63 and 41.

13. Bernasconi, "Hegel at the Court of the Ashanti," 55–60.

14. Robert Bernasconi, "With What Must the Philosophy of World History Begin?," 187–88.

15. Michael H. Hoffheimer, "Hegel, Race, Genocide," *The Southern Journal of Philosophy* 39, Issue S (2001): 35–61 and "Race and Law in Hegel's Philosophy of Religion," in *Race and Racism in Modern Philosophy*, ed. Andrew Valls (Ithaca; London: Cornell University Press, 2005), 194–216.

16. Hoffheimer, "Hegel, Race, Genocide," 35.

17. Karlheinz Barck, "Amerika in Hegels Geschichtsphilosophie," *Weimarer Beiträge* 38, no. 2 (1992): 274–78.

18. Hoffheimer, "Race and Law in Hegel's Philosophy of Religion," 207.

19. Michael H. Hoffheimer, "Does Hegel Justify Slavery?" *Owl of Minerva* 25 (1993): 118–19.

20. Johannes Hoffmeister, ed., *Dokumente zu Hegels Entwicklung* (Stuttgart: Fr. Fromanns, 1936), 108 and 418–19; Michel Hulin, *Hegel et l'Orient* (Paris: J. Vrin, 1974), 31. Hegel's personal papers from the *Gymnasium* period (1784–8) contain excerpts of Meiners's *Revision der Philosophie, Briefe über die Schweiz*, Parts I & II (Berlin: Spener, 1784–5), and *Grundriss der Geschichte der Menschheit*. Hegel kept a diary of his voyage into the Alps above Bern during July and August of 1796, which contain several references to Parts II (1785) and III (1790) of Meiners's *Briefe über die Schweiz*. On Meiners's influence on the young Hegel, Hoffmeister (p. 419) states, "The empirical material that Meiners brings forth on 'races,' degrees of culture, forms of government, and everything else remaining of the cultural-historical inventory, which a compilation out of travel accounts can provide, was ample enough to captivate an inquisitive student such as Hegel."

21. Bernasconi, "Krimskrams," 198. Bernasconi cites Hegel's *Frühe Exzerpte*, specifically his excerpts of Meiners's *Revision der Philosophie*, Part 1 (Göttingen und Gotha, 1772); G. W. F. Hegel, *Gesammelte Werke*, 3: 113–14 and 175–76.

22. *Vorlesungen* 6: XI.

23. Ibid., XVII.

24. Ibid., XVIII.

25. See Chapter 2 of Stuart Jay Harten's dissertation, *Raising the Veil of History: Orientalism, Classicism and the Birth of Western Civilization in Hegel's Berlin Lecture Courses of the 1820's* (Cornell University, 1994). "It is true that Hegel busied himself in further textual research as the decade wore on, and that he revised the classificatory status of Hinduism and substantially altered his interpretation of pantheism; nonetheless, some of the major changes were induced by the religious controversies of the mid 1820's and Hegel appears to have partially retracted these in the last year or two of his life" (Harten, 49).

26. See pp. 88–89 above.

27. *Vorlesungen* 6: 110 (Kolleg 1819, 4).

28. Ibid., 19 (Synopsis des Ms. 1820, 14b).

29. Ibid., 18 (Synopsis des Ms. 1820, 14a).

30. Ibid., 29 (Synopsis des Ms. 1820, 20a).

31. *Vorlesungen* 6: 27 (Synopsis des Kollegs 1820/21, 3); G. W. F. Hegel, *The Encyclopaedia Logic: Part I of the Encyclopaedia of Philosophical Sciences with the Zusätze*, trans. by T. F. Geraets, W. A. Suchting, and H. S. Harris (Indianapolis: Hackett, 1991), 138.

32. *Vorlesungen* 6: 25 and 27–28. "I claim that the succession of the systems of philosophy in history is the same as the succession of the logical deduction of the concept-determinations of the Idea. I claim that, if one purely strips the fundamental concept of the systems appearing in the history of philosophy from those historical systems, in terms of its external formation, its application to the particular and similar, one obtains the various stages of the determination of the idea itself in its logical concept" (*Vorlesungen* 6: 27 [Synopsis des Manuskriptes 1820: 18b–19a]).

33. *Vorlesungen* 6: 323.

34. Ast (1807), 7.

35. *Vorlesungen* 6: 217 (Kolleg 1825/26, 16).

36. *Vorlesungen* 6: 218 (Kolleg 1825/26, 17–18).

37. Hegel, *The Encyclopaedia Logic*, 39.

38. Rixner, 1: 3–4; *Vorlesungen* 6: 209–10 (Kolleg 1825/26, 7).

39. Ast (1807), 2; Ast (1825), 1; Rixner, 1: IV; *Vorlesungen* 6: 25 (Synopsis des Ms. 1820, 18a).

40. *Vorlesungen* 6: 99 (Synopsis des Kollegs 1820/21, 33); and see pp. 100–101 above.

41. Ibid.

42. Ibid.: "Die neueuropäische Philosophie und die neueuropäische Welt gehen überhaupt von den germanischen Völkern aus."

43. *Allgemeine deutsche Real-Encyclopädie für die gebildeten Stände (Conversations-Lexicon)*, 5th ed., 10 vols. (Leipzig: S. A. Brockhaus, 1819–20), 169–76. There are no noticeable changes to the article on "Germanien und Germanen" in either the 6th (1824) or the 7th (1827) edition.

44. *Vorlesungen* 12: 444–55.

45. *Vorlesungen* 12: 445.

46. Ibid.

47. G. W. F. Hegel, *Die Vernunft in der Geschichte*, ed. Johannes Hoffmeister, 5th ed. (Hamburg: Felix Meiner, 1955), 240.

48. *Vorlesungen* 12: 43 and 443–44.

49. Meiners, *Menschheit*, 2nd ed., 75; see pp. 81–82 above.

50. AA 15: 880.

51. Hegel regarded Tennemann's work as mere compilation with bad translations and rambling excerpts (see *Vorlesungen* 6: 362–63 [Kolleg 1825/26, 84]). Of Tennemann's so-called non-partisanship he said contemptuously, "This non-partisanship is simply negative; it is nothing at all. If one has no interest in the thought; if one does not recognize the purpose of the history of philosophy, the development of thought, then he cannot represent it.

Tennemann is such a historian of philosophy. The reproach was leveled at him that a particular representation was not correct. He explained in response that he was a Kantian philosopher, that he knew that no knowing was possible. It is inconceivable how a man can plod ahead in this way without a purpose. With this kind of non-partisanship as the truth, there is no subordination, no discrimination—that which has a relation to a purpose does not exist" (*Vorlesungen* 6: 330 [Kolleg 1829/30, 13a–b]).

52. *Vorlesungen* 9: 71 (Kolleg 1825/26: 148).

53. Quoted in Geldsetzer, 50.

54. *Vorlesungen* 6: 213 (Kolleg 1825/26, 12).

55. Ibid., 215 (Kolleg 1825/26, 14).

56. See p. 102 above.

57. *Vorlesungen* 6: 31 (Synopsis des Ms. 1820, 21b.33a).

58. Ibid., 58 (Synopsis des Ms. 1820, 25a–b) and 35–36 (Synopsis des Kollegs 1820/21, 6).

59. Ibid., 48 (Synopsis des Kollegs 1820/21, 10).

60. Ibid., 58 (Synopsis des Kollegs 1820/21, 15).

61. Carus, 114.

62. Tennemann, *Grundriss* (1816), 10.

63. *Vorlesungen* 6: 266 (Kolleg 1825/26, 68).

64. Ibid., 94 (Kolleg 1820/21, 29).

65. Ibid., 94–95 (Synopsis des Kollegs 1820/21, 29).

66. Ibid., 95 (Synopsis des Kollegs 1820/21, 30).

67. Ibid., 133 (Kolleg 1819, 30) and 349 (Kolleg, 1829/30, 28a).

68. Ibid., 133–34 (Kolleg 1819, 30–31 [31.53]): "no philosophy existed among them, or at least we have no concept of it; or generally they cannot claim to have a place in the history of European learning."

69. Ibid., 266–68 (Kolleg 1825/26, 68–70).

70. Ibid., 266–67 (Kolleg 1825/26, 68–69).

71. Ibid., 267 (Kolleg 1825/26, 69).

72. Ibid., 267 (Kolleg 1825/26, 70).

73. Ibid., 268 (Kolleg 1825/26, 70).

74. Ibid., 268 (Kolleg 1825/26, 71).

75. Ibid., 268–69 (Kolleg 1825/26, 71–72).

76. See p. 103 above.

77. *Vorlesungen* 6: 365 (Kolleg 1825/26: 87) and 374 (Kolleg 1825/26, 96).

78. Bernasconi, "Religious Philosophy," 5–10.

79. Bernasconi, "With What Must the History of Philosophy Begin?," 44.

80. *Vorlesungen* 6: 366 (Kolleg 1825/26, 88).

81. Ibid., 365 (Kolleg 1825/26, 88).

82. Ibid., 378 (Kolleg 1825/26, 99).

83. Ibid., 378 (Kolleg 1825/26, 100).

84. Ibid., 369 (Kolleg 1825/26, 91).

85. Ibid., 94–95 (Synopsis des Kollegs 1820/21, 28).

86. Ibid., 371 (Kolleg 1825/26, 93).

87. Ibid., 369 (Kolleg 1825/26, 91–92).

88. Ibid., 374 (Kolleg 1825/26, 95).

89. *Vorlesungen* 7: 1 (Kolleg 1825/26, 122).

90. Ibid., 2 (Kolleg 1825/26, 123). On Hegel's use of the trope of creative genius or "creative transformation," see Harten, 59–60, 318, and 363–68.

91. *Vorlesungen* 7: 2–3 (Kolleg 1825/26, 124).

92. *Vorlesungen* 6: 270 (Kolleg 1825/26, 73).

93. *Vorlesungen* 7: 5–6 (Kolleg 1825/26, 127).

94. *Vorlesungen* 6: 105–6 (Synopsis des Kollegs 1820/21, 39).

95. Ibid., 136 (Kolleg 1819, 56).

96. Ast (1807), 51; Ast (1825), 46; Rixner, 1: 36–37.

97. *Vorlesungen* 6: 99 (Synopsis des Kollegs 1820/21, 33–34) and 138 (Kolleg 1819, 59).

98. Ibid., 374 (Kolleg 1825/26, 96).

99. Ibid., 99 (Synopsis des Kollegs 1820/21, 33v34) and 107 (Synopsis des Kollegs 1820/21, 40).

100. *Vorlesungen* 9: 69 (Kolleg 1825/26, 147).

101. *Vorlesungen* 6: 107–8 (Synopsis des Kollegs 1820/21, 40–42) and 138 (Kolleg 1819, 59).

102. See p. 14 above.

103. *Vorlesungen* 6: 47–48 (Synopsis Ms. 1820, 38b) and 119 (Kolleg 1819, 14).

104. Geldsetzer, 50.

105. *Vorlesungen* 6: 54–55 (Synopsis des Kollegs 1820/21, 12–13); Hegel, *The Encyclopaedia Logic*, 138.

106. *Vorlesungen* 6: 227 (Kolleg 1825/26, 27).

107. Ibid., 117–18 (Kolleg 1819, 13).

108. Ibid., 31 (Synopsis des Kollegs 1820/21, 4) and 24–25 (Synopsis des Ms. 1820, 17a–18a).

109. Ibid., 218 (Kolleg 1825/26, 18), 270 (Kolleg 1825/26, 72), and 44 (Synopsis des Ms. 1820, 37a).

110. Ibid., 116 (Kolleg 1819, 11).

111. Rixner (1822), 294 and 315.

112. *Vorlesungen* 6: 116 (Kolleg 1819, 11).

113. Ibid., 363 (Kolleg 1825/26, 84).

Chapter 7

1. See Helmuth von Glasenapp, *Das Indienbild deutscher Denker* (Stuttgart: K. F. Koehler, 1960), 39–60; Edward W. Said, *Orientalism* (New York: Pantheon, 1978); Ignatius Viyagappa, *G. W. F. Hegel's Concept of Indian Philosophy* (Rome: Pontificia Universitas Gregoriana, 1980); Halbfass, 84–99; and Marchignoli, "Canonizing an Indian Text?"

2. Hulin, 139.

3. Halbfass, 98–99, 146, and 151.

4. Harten, 173–74; Marchignoli, 259–65.

5. See Halbfass, 84–99.

6. See Harten, 52–53 and 242–46.

7. Halbfass (p. 85) perceived that Hegel's antipathy toward the Orient had something to do with his disdain for the Romantics and their glorification of the Orient, but did not explore this further. For a book-length discussion of Hegel's critique of Romanticism, see Otto Pöggeler, *Hegels Kritik der Romantik: Philosophie an der Jahrtausendwende* (München: Fink, 1998).

8. August Tholuck, *Die speculative Trinitätslehre des späteren Orients, Eine religions-philosophische Monographie aus handschriftlichen Quellen der Leydener, Oxforder und Berliner Bibliothek* (Berlin: Ferdinand Dümmler, 1826).

9. August Tholuck, *Die Lehre von der Sünde und vom Versöhner, oder Die wahre Weihe des Zweiflers*, 1st ed. (Hamburg: Perthes, 1823).

10. August Tholuck, *Die Glaubwürdigkeit der evangelischen Geschichte, zugleich eine Kritik des Lebens Jesu von Strauss für theologische und nicht theologische Leser* (Hamburg: F. Perthes, 1837).

11. On Tholuck's life and work, see Leopold Witte's biography, *Das Leben D. Friedrich August Gotttreu Tholuck's*, 2 vols. (Bielefeld: Velhagen & Klasing, 1884–6); Emanuel Hirsch, *Geschichte der neueren evangelischen Theologie*, 4th ed. (Gütersloh: Gerd Mohn, 1968), 5: 103–15; Peter Maser, "Orientalische Mystik und evangelische Erweckungsbewegung: Eine biographische Studie zu Briefen von und an F. A. G. Tholuck," *Zeitschrift für Religions- und Geistesgeschichte* 33 (1981): 221–49; Gunther Wenz, "'Gehe Du in Dich, mein Guido': August Tholuck als Theologe der Erweckungsbewegung," *Pietismus und Neuzeit: Ein Jahrbuch zur Geschichte des neueren Protestantismus* (Göttingen: Vandenhoeck und Ruprecht, 2001), 27: 68–80; Martin Kähler, "Tholuck, Friedrich August Gotttreu," in *Realencyklopädie für protestantische Theologie und Kirche*, ed. Albert Hauck, 3rd ed. (Leipzig: J. C. Hinrichs, 1896–1913), 19: 695–702; and David Crowner and Gerald Christianson, *The Spirituality of the German Awakening* (Mahwah, NJ: Paulist Press, 2003), 45–51.

12. August Tholuck, *Ssufismus, sive, Theosophia Persarum pantheistica, quam e mss. Bibliothecae regiae Berolinensis: Persicis, Arabicis, Turcicis* (Berolini: F. Duemmleri, 1821).

13. August Tholuck, *Blüthensammlung aus der morgenländischen Mystik, nebst einer Einleitung über Mystik überhaupt und morgenländische insbesondere* (Berlin: F. Dümmler, 1825).

14. Ibid., II–III.

15. Tholuck, *Die speculative Trinitätslehre*, V.

16. Ibid., VI–VII.

17. Mirza Muḥammad Fānī, *Dabistāni Mazāhib* (Calcutta, 1807); Mirza Muḥammad Fānī, Francis Gladwin, and Johann Friedrich Hugo von Dalberg, *Scheik Mohammed Fani's Dabistan oder von der Religion der ältesten Parsen: Nebst Erläuterungen und einem Nachtrage die Geschichte der Semiramis aus indischen Quellen betreffend* (Aschaffenburg: Carl Christian Erlinger, 1809).

18. Tholuck, *Die speculative Trinitätslehre*, VII.

19. Ibid., VII–IX.

20. Studies of Hegel's "Trinitarian ontology of God" include Patricia Marie Calton, *Hegel's Metaphysics of God: The Ontological Proof as the Development of a Trinitarian Divine Ontology* (Aldershot, UK; Burlington, VT: Ashgate, 2001); Dale M. Schlitt, *Hegel's Trinitarian Claim: A Critical Reflection* (Leiden: E. J. Brill, 1984), and "Trinity and Spirit," *American Catholic Philosophical Quarterly* 64 (1990): 457–89; Jörg Splett, *Die Trinitätslehre G. W. F. Hegels* (München: Alber, 1965); and James Yerkes, *The Christology of Hegel* (Albany: SUNY Press, 1983).

21. "Tholuck was convinced that the doctrine of the triad was widespread in Islamic thought and in late Greek philosophy, and that the Christian doctrine of the Trinity is closely linked with Neoplatonism" (editorial introduction to G. W. F. Hegel's *Lectures on the Philosophy of Religion, One-volume Edition: The Lectures of 1827*, ed. Peter C. Hodgson and trans. R. F. Brown, P. C. Hodgson, and J. M. Stewart with the assistance of H. S. Harris [Oxford; New York: Oxford University Press, 2006], 83 n. 17).

22. G. W. F. Hegel, *Briefe von und an Hegel*, ed. Friedhelm Nicolin (Berlin: Akademie, 1982) IV.2: 60–61; translation in *Hegel: The Letters*, trans. Clark Butler and Christiane Seiler (Bloomington: Indiana University Press, 1984), 519–20.

23. *Hegel: The Letters*, 520; italics mine.

24. I cite from the second edition (1825) of *Die Lehre von der Sünde* unless I indicate otherwise.

25. Tholuck, *Die Lehre von der Sünde*, 16.

26. Tholuck, *Blüthensammlung*, 12–13.

27. Tholuck, *Die Lehre von der Sünde*, 18.

28. Ibid., 24.

29. Tholuck, *Die Lehre von der Sünde* (1823), 17.

30. Tholuck, *Die Lehre von der Sünde*, 223.

31. Ibid., 224. On the pantheism controversy between Jacobi and Moses Mendelssohn, see Frederick C. Beiser, *The Fate of Reason: German Philosophy from Kant to Fichte* (Cambridge, MA: Harvard University Press, 1987), 44–108.

32. Tholuck, *Die Lehre von der Sünde*, 224 n. 9.

33. Ibid., 231–32.

34. Ibid., 232. Tholuck provides a translation of an excerpt of Philippe Couplet's *Confucius Sinarum philosophus, sive scientia Sinensis Latine exposita* (Paris: D. Horthemels, 1687).

35. In expounding the "fundamental pantheistic doctrine," Tholuck quotes from William Ward's *A View of the History, Literature and Religion of the Hindoos, including a minute description of their manners and customs, and translations from their principal works*, 3rd ed. (London: Black, Parbury, and Allen, 1817).

36. Tholuck, *Die Lehre von der Sünde*, 236–37.

37. Ibid., 234–35.

38. Abraham Hyacinthe Anquetil du Perron, *Oupnek'hat, id est, Secretum tegendum; opus ipsa in India rarissimum, continens antiquam et arcanam, seu*

theologicam et philosophicam, doctrinam, è quatuor sacris Indorum libris, Rak Beid, Djedjr Beid, Sam Beid, Athrban Beid, excerptam; ad verbum, e Persico idiomate, Samskreticis vocabulis intermixto, in Latinum conversum; dissertationibus et annotationibus, difficiliora explanantibus, illustratum (Argentorati: Typis et impensis fratrum Levrault; Parisiis: Apud eosd. bibliopolas, 1801–2); Abū al-Faḍl ibn Mubārak and Francis Gladwin, *Ayeen Akbery or, The Institutes of the Emperor Akber* (London: G. Auld, 1800).

39. Tholuck, *Die Lehre von der Sünde*, 236.

40. Ibid., 241.

41. Ibid., 241–42.

42. Ibid., 242. For Plotinus, Tholuck cites *Plotini Enneades* (Basel, 1530).

43. August Tholuck, *Commentatio de VI guam Graeca philosophia in theologiam tum Muhammedanorum tum Judaeorum exercuerit, Particula II: De orut Cabbalae* (Hamburgi: F. Perthes, 1837).

44. Tholuck, *Die Lehre von der Sünde*, 243–44.

45. Ibid., 243–45.

46. Ibid., 246.

47. Ibid., 247–48.

48. Ibid., 248.

49. G. W. F. Hegel, *Gesammelte Werke*, vol. 19; and *Vorlesungen über die Philosophie der Religion*, ed. Walter Jaeschke (vols. 3–5 of Hegel, *Vorlesungen: Ausgewählte Nachschriften und Manuskripte*). On the polemical exchange between Hegel and Tholuck, see pp. 21–22 in the editorial introduction to Hegel, *Lectures on the Philosophy of Religion*.

50. G. W. F. Hegel and Friedhelm Nicolin, "Hegels Briefwechsel mit Karl Daub," *Hegel-Studien* 17 (1982): 47.

51. Hegel, *Gesammelte Werke* 19: 13f.

52. Ibid.

53. Ibid.

54. Ibid., 8ff.

55. Ibid.

56. Ibid., 411.

57. Ibid.

58. Hegel, *Lectures on the Philosophy of Religion*, 123 (the editor Hodgson cites the controversy with Tholuck as the subtext of this passage).

59. Ibid.

60. Ibid., 125. On Hegel's "erroneous interpretation of Spinoza," see G. H. R. Parkinson, "Hegel, Pantheism, and Spinoza," *Journal of the History of Ideas* 38, no. 3 (July–Sept. 1977): 449–59.

61. *Vorlesungen* 9: 111.

62. Ibid.

63. Hegel, *Lectures on the Philosophy of Religion*, 122 and 127.

64. Ibid., 126.

65. Ibid., 126–27. Hegel is referring to Spinoza's *Ethics*, Part V, Prop. 36.

Bibliography

Primary Sources

Allgemeine deutsche Real-Encyclopädie für die gebildeten Stände (Conversations-Lexicon). Multiple editions. Leipzig: S. A. Brockhaus.

Anquetil du Perron, Abraham Hyacinthe. *Oupnek'hat, id est, Secretum tegendum; opus ipsa in India rarissimum, continens antiquam et arcanam, seu theologicam et philosophicam, doctrinam, è quatuor sacris Indorum libris, Rak Beid, Djedjr Beid, Sam Beid, Athrban Beid, excerptam; ad verbum, e Persico idiomate, Samskreticis vocabulis intermixto, in Latinum conversum; dissertationibus et annotationibus, difficiliora explanantibus, illustratum.* Argentorati: Typis et impensis fratrum Levrault; Parisiis: Apud eosd. bibliopolas, 1801–2.

———. *Zend-Avesta, ouvrage de Zoroastre, contenant les idées théologiques, physiques & morales de ce législateur, les cérémonies du culte religieux qu'il a établi, & plusieurs traits importans relatifs à l'ancienne histoire des Perses.* 3 vols. Paris: N. M. Tilliard, 1711.

Asiatic Society of Bengal. *Abhandlungen über die Geschichte und Alterthümer, die Künste, Wissenschaften und Litteratur Asiens, von Sir William Jones und andern Mitgliedern der im Jahre 1784 zu Calcutta in Indien errichteten gelehrten Gesellschaft.* Translated and annotated by J. C. Fick and J. F. Kleuker. Riga, 1795–6.

———. *Asiatic Researches, or, Transactions of the Society Instituted in Bengal, for Inquiring into the History and Antiquities, the Arts, Sciences, and Literature of Asia.* Calcutta: The Society (also London: Vernor and Hood), 1788–1839.

———. *Recherches asiatiques, ou Mémoires de la Société établie au Bengale pour faire des recherches sur l'histoire et les antiquités, les arts, les sciences et la littérature de l'Asie.* Translated by Antoine-Gabriel Griffet de La Baume, L. Langlès, Georges Cuvier, J. B. J. Delambre, Jean Baptiste Pierre Antoine de Monet de Lamarck and G. A. Olivier. Paris, 1802 and 1805.

Ast, Friedrich. *Grundriss einer Geschichte der Philosophie.* Landshut: Joseph Thomann, 1807.

———. *Grundriss der Geschichte der Philosophie.* Landshut: Joseph Thomann, 1825.

Bachmann, Carl Friedrich. *Dissertatio philosophica de peccatis Tennemanni in historia philosophiae*. Jena, 1814.

Bailly, Jean Sylvain. *Histoire de l'astronomie ancienne, depuis son origine jusqu'à l'etablissement de l'école d'Alexandrie*. Paris: Frères Debure, 1775; 2nd ed., 1781.

———. *Lettres sur l'Atlantide de Platon et sur l'ancienne histoire de l'Asie: pour servir de suite aux lettres sur l'origine des sciences, addressées à M. de Voltaire*. London: M. Elmesly, 1779.

———. *Lettres sur l'origine des sciences et sur celle des peuples de l'Asie, adressées à M. de Voltaire, et precedées des quelques lettres de M. de Voltaire à l'auteur*. London: M. Elmesly; Paris: Frères Debure, 1777.

———. *Traité de l'astronomie indienne et orientale: ouvrage qui peut servir de suite à l'histoire de l'astronomie ancienne*. Paris: Debure, 1787.

Bayle, Pierre. *Dictionnaire historique et critique*. Rotterdam: Reinier Leers, 1697.

Bayle, Pierre, Johann Christoph Gottsched, and Pierre Desmaizeaux. *Historisches und critisches Wörterbuch, nach der neuesten Auflage von 1740 ins Deutsche übersetzt*. 4 vols. Leipzig: Breitkopf, 1741–4.

Berger, Immanuel. *Geschichte der Religionsphilosophie oder Lehren und Meinungen der originellsten Denker aller Zeiten über Gott und Religion*. Berlin: Lang, 1800.

Bergmann, Julius. *Geschichte der Philosophie*. Berlin: Mittler, 1892.

Bopp, Franz. *Vergleichende Grammatik des Sanskrit, Zend, Griechischen, Lateinischen, Litthauischen, Gothischen und Deutschen*. Berlin: F. Dümmler, 1833–52.

Boureau-Deslandes, André-François. *Histoire critique de la philosophie, où l'on traite de son origine, de ses progrez et des diverses revolutions qui lui sont arrivées jusqu'à notre temps*. Amsterdam: François Changuion, 1737.

Brucker, Johann Jacob. *Historia critica philosophiae, a mundi incunabilis ad nostram usque aetatem deducta*. 5 vols. Lipsiae: Breitkopf, 1742–4; 2nd ed. in 6 vols., 1766–7.

Buddeus, Joannes Franciscus. *Introductio ad historiam philosophiae Ebraeorvm*. Halae Saxonvm: Typis & impensis Orphanotrophii Glavcha-Halensis, 1702; 2nd ed., 1720.

Buhle, Johann Gottlieb Gerhard. *Geschichte der neuern Philosophie seit der Epoche der Wiederherstellung der Wissenschaften*. 6 vols. Göttingen: J. G. Rosenbusch, 1800.

———. *Lehrbuch der Geschichte der Philosophie und einer kritischen Literatur derselben*. 8 vols. in 6. Göttingen: Vandenhöck und Ruprecht, 1796–1804.

Burnet, Thomas. *Archaeologiae philosophicae sive doctrina antiqua de rerum originibus*. Londini: Typis R. N., Impensis Gualt. Kettilby, 1692.

Calmette, Jean, and Guillaume-Emmanuel-Joseph Guilhem de Clermont-Lodève Sainte-Croix. *L'Ezour vedam ou ancien commentaire du vedam, contenant l'exposition des opinions religieuses et philosophiques des indiens*. Yverdon: M. de Felice, 1778.

Capasso, Giambattista, Santolo Cirillo, and Giovanni Girolamo Frezza. *Historiae philosophiae synopsis sive de origine et progressu philosophiae: de vitis, sectis et systematibus omnium philosophorum libri IV*. Neapoli: Typis Felicis Muscae, 1728.

Carus, Friedrich August. *Ideen zur Geschichte der Philosophie* (vol. 4 of *Nachgelassene Werke*). Leipzig: Iohann Ambrosius Barth & Paul Gotthelf Kummer, 1809.

Chézy, Antoine-Léonard de. "[Review of] Bhagavad-Gita, Id Est Thespesion Melos, Etc., Bonnae 1823." *Journal des Savants* (Jan. 1825): 37–48.

Colebrooke, Henry Thomas. *Miscellaneous Essays by H. T. Colebrooke, a New Edition with Notes*. Edited by E. B. Cowell. 2 vols. London: Truebner & Co., 1873.

Commentationes Societatis Regiae Scientiarum Gottingensis. Göttingae: Henricum Dieterich, 1808–11.

Cromaziano, Agatopisto (Appiano Buonafede). *Della istoria e della indole di ogni filosofia*. 7 vols. Lucca: Giovanni Riccomini, 1766–81.

———. *Kritische Geschichte der Revolution der Philosophie in den drey Jahrhunderten*. Translated by Carl Heinrich Heydenreich. 2 vols. Leipzig: Weygand, 1791.

Diderot, Denis, Jean Le Rond d'Alembert, and Pierre Mouchon, eds. *Encyclopédie, ou, Dictionnaire raisonné des sciences, des arts et des métiers*. 17 vols. Paris: Briasson [etc.], 1751–65; 5 supp. vols., 1776–7.

Diderot, Denis, and Jean Louis Castillon. *Histoire générale des dogmes et opinions philosophiques, depuis les plus anciens temps jusqu'à nos jours, tirée du Dictionnaire encyclopédique des arts & des sciences*. 3 vols. Londres, 1769.

Diels, Hermann. *Doxographi graeci*. Berolini: G. Reimer, 1879.

Diogenes Laertius. *Les vies des plus illustres philosophes de l'antiquité, avec leurs dogmes, leurs systêmes, leur morale, & leurs sentences les plus remarquables*. 3 vols. Amsterdam: J. H. Schneider, 1758.

———. *Lives of Eminent Philosophers*. Translated by R. D. Hicks. 2 vols. Cambridge, MA: Harvard University Press; London: William Heinemann Ltd., 1925.

———. *Vitae et sententiae eorvm qvi in philosophia probati fvervnt*. Translated by Ambrogio Traversari. Venice: Nicolas Jenson, 1475.

Dohm, Christian Wilhelm. *Reisen nach Indien und Persien in einer freyen Uebersetzung aus dem englischen Original geliefert, mit historisch-geographischen Anmerkungen und Zusätzen vermehrt von Christian Wilhelm Dohm. Mit einer Vorrede begleitet von D. Büsching*. Leipzig: M. G. Wiedmanns Erben und Reich, 1774–5.

Dow, Alexander. *Abhandlungen zur Erläuterung der Geschichte, Religion und Staatsverfassung von Hindostan aus dem Englischen übersetzt*. Leipzig: Johann Friedrich Junius, 1773.

———. *Die Geschichte von Hindostan*. 3 vols. Leipzig: Johann Friedrich Junius, 1772–4.

———. *Dissertation sur les moeurs, les usages, le language, la religion et la philosophie des Hindous*. Translated by Claude-François Bergier. Paris: Saugrain, 1780.

———. *The History of Hindostan from the Earliest Account of Time, to the Death of Akbar, Translated from the Persian of Mahummud Casim Ferishta of Delhi;*

Together with a Dissertation Concerning the Religion and Philosophy of the Brahmins; with an Appendix, Containing the History of the Mogul Empire, from Its Decline in the Reign of Mahummud Shaw, to the Present Times. London: T. Becket and P. A. de Hondt, 1768.

Eberhard, Johann August. *Allgemeine Geschichte der Philosophie zum Gebrauch akademischer Vorlesungen.* Halle: Hemmerde und Schwetschke, 1788; 2nd ed., 1796.

Eberhard, Johann August, ed. *Philosophisches Magazin.* 4 vols. Halle: J. Gebauer, 1788–92.

Enfield, William. *The History of Philosophy, from the Earliest Times to the Beginning of the Present Century; Drawn Up from Brucker's* Historia critica philosophiae. 2 vols. London: J. Johnson, 1791; reprint, Bristol, UK; Sterling, VA: Thoemmes Press, 2001.

Fānī, Mirza Muḥammad. *Dabistāni Mazāhib.* Calcutta, 1807.

Fānī, Mirza Muḥammad, Francis Gladwin, and Johann Friedrich Hugo von Dalberg. *Scheik Mohammed Fani's Dabistan oder von der Religion der ältesten Parsen: Nebst Erläuterungen und einem Nachtrage die Geschichte der Semiramis aus indischen Quellen betreffend.* Aschaffenburg: Carl Christian Erlinger, 1809.

Feder, Johann Georg Heinrich. *Grundriss der philosophischen Wissenschaften, nebst der nötigen Geschichte, zum Gebrauche seiner Zuhörer.* Coburg: Johann Carl Findeisen, 1767; 2nd ed., 1769.

———. *Leben, Nature und Grundsätze: Zur Belehrung und Ermunterung seiner lieben Nachkommen.* Leipzig: Schwickert, 1825.

Feder, Johann Georg Heinrich, and Christoph Meiners, eds. *Zugabe zu den Göttingischen Anzeigen von gelehrten Sachen.* Göttingen, 1782.

Formey, Jean-Henri-Samuel. *Histoire abrégée de la philosophie.* Amsterdam: J. H. Schneider, 1760.

Fries, Jakob Friedrich. *Die Geschichte der Philosophie dargestellt nach den Fortschritten ihrer wissenschaftlichen Entwickelung.* 2 vols. Halle: Verlag der Buchhandlung des Waisenhauses, 1837.

Frisius, Johannes Jacobus. *Bibliotheca philosophorum classicorum authorum chronologica: in qua veterum philosophorum origo, successio, aetas [et] doctrina compendiosa, ab origine mundi usque ad nostram aetatem, proponitur; quibus accessit patrum, ecclesiae Christi doctorum a temporibus apostolorum usque ad tempora scholasticorum ad a. usque d. 1140 secundum eandem temporis seriem, enumeratio.* Tiguri: Wolphius, 1592.

Fülleborn, Georg Gustav, ed. *Beyträge zur Geschichte der Philosophie.* 7 vols. Züllichau; Freystadt: Friedrich Frommann, 1794–9.

Gentzken, Friedrich. *Historia philosophiae in qua philosophorum celebrium vitae eorumque hypotheses notabiliores ac sectarum facta a longa rerum memoria ad nostra usque tempora succincte et ordine sistuntur.* Hamburgi: Apvd Theodor. Christoph. Felginer, 1724; 2nd ed., 1731.

Gérando, Joseph-Marie de. *De la génération des connoissances humaines: Mémoire qui a partagé le prix de l'Académie Royale des Sciences de Berlin, sur la question suivante: Démontrer d'une manière incontestable l'origine de toutes nos connoissances, soit en présentant des argumens non-employés encore, soit en présentant des argumens déjà employés, mais en les présentant d'une manière nouvelle et d'une force victorieuse de toute objection.* Berlin: George Decker, 1802.

———. *Des signes et de l'art de penser considérés dans leurs rapports mutuels.* 4 vols. Paris: Goujon fils; Fuchs; Henrichs, 1800.

———. *Histoire comparée des systèmes de philosophie, considérés relativement aux principes des connaissances humaines.* 2nd ed. 4 vols. Paris: A. Eymery, 1822.

———. *Histoire comparée des systèmes de philosophie, relativement aux principes des connaissances humaines.* 1st ed. 3 vols. Paris: Henrichs, 1804.

———. *Vergleichende Geschichte der Systeme der Philosophie mit Rücksicht auf die Grundsätze der menschlichen Erkenntnisse.* Translated by Wilhelm Tennemann. 2 vols. Marburg: Neue akademische Buchhandlung, 1806.

Girtanner, Christoph. *Ueber das kantische Prinzip für die Naturgeschichte, Ein Versuch diese Wissenschaft philosophisch zu behandeln.* Göttingen: Vandenhoeck und Ruprecht, 1796.

Goess, Georg Friedrich Daniel. *Ueber den Begriff der Geschichte der Philosophie und über das System des Thales: zwo philosophische Abhandlungen.* Erlangen: Palm, 1794.

Grau, Abraham de. *Historia philosophica, continens veterum phil. qui quidem praecipui fuerent, studia ac dogmata, modernorum quaestionibus in primis exagitata.* Franekerae Frisiorum: Johannes Wellens, 1674.

Grohmann, Johann Christian August. *Über den Begriff der Geschichte der Philosophie,* 1797.

———. "Was heisst: Geschichte der Philosophie?" In *Neue Beyträge zur kritischen Philosophie und insbesondere zur Geschichte der Philosophie,* edited by Johann Christian August Grohmann and Karl Heinrich Ludwig Pölitz, 1–78. Berlin, 1798.

Grohmann, Johann Christian August, and Karl Heinrich Ludwig Pölitz, eds. *Neue Beyträge zur kritischen Philosophie und insbesondere zur Geschichte der Philosophie.* Berlin, 1798.

Halhed, Nathaniel Brassey. *Code des loix des Gentous, ou réglemens des Brames, traduit de L'Anglois, d'après les versions faites de l'original écrit en langue samskrete.* Paris: Stoupe, 1778.

———. *A Code of Gentoo Laws, or, Ordinations of the Pundits, from a Persian Translation, Made from the Original, Written in the Shanscrit Language.* London, 1776.

———. *Gesetzbuch der Gentoo's; oder Sammlung der Gesetze der Pundits, nach einer persianischen Uebersetzung des in der Schanscrit-Sprache geschriebenen Originales.* Translated by Rudolph Erich Ratze. Hamburg: Carl Ernst Bohn, 1778.

Hegel, Georg Wilhelm Friedrich. *Briefe von und an Hegel.* Vol. 4. Edited by Friedhelm Nicolin. Berlin: Akademie, 1982.

———. *Die Vernunft in der Geschichte*. Edited by Johannes Hoffmeister. 5th ed. Hamburg: Felix Meiner, 1955.

———. *The Encyclopaedia Logic: Part I of the Encyclopaedia of Philosophical Sciences with the Zusätze*. Translated by T. F. Geraets, W. A. Suchting, and H. S. Harris. Indianapolis: Hackett, 1991.

———. *Gesammelte Werke*. Edited by the Nordrhein-Westfälische Akademie der Wissenschaften und der Künste in association with the Deutsche Forschungsgemeinschaft. 40 vols. projected. Hamburg: Felix Meiner, 1968–.

———. *Hegel: The Letters*. Translated by Clark Butler and Christiane Seiler. Bloomington: Indiana University Press, 1984.

———. *Lectures on the Philosophy of Religion, One-volume Edition: The Lectures of 1827*. Edited by Peter C. Hodgson. Translated by R. F. Brown, P. C. Hodgson, and J. M. Stewart with the assistance of H. S. Harris. Oxford; New York: Oxford University Press, 2006.

———. *Vorlesungen: Ausgewählte Nachschriften und Manuskripte*. Multiple editors. 17 vols. Hamburg: Felix Meiner, 1983–.

———. *Wissenschaft der Logik*. Edited by Georg Lasson. Berlin: Akademie, 1971.

Hegel, Georg Wilhelm Friedrich, and Friedhelm Nicolin. "Hegels Briefwechsel mit Karl Daub." *Hegel-Studien* 17 (1982): 47.

Herder, Johann Gottfried. *Herders sämmtliche Werke*. Edited by Jakob Balde, Bernhard Ludwig Suphan, Carl Christian Redlich, Otto Hoffmann, and Reinhold Steig. 33 vols. Berlin: Weidmann, 1877–1913.

Heumann, Christoph August. *Acta philosophorum: das ist gründliche Nachrichten aus der Historia philosophica, nebst beygefügten Urtheilen von denen dahin gehörigen alten und neuen Büchern*, 3 vols. Halle: Renger, 1715–26.

Heydenreich, Carl Heinrich. "Einige Ideen über die Revolution in der Philosophie bewirkt durch I. Kant und besonders über den Einfluss derselben auf die Behandlung der Geschichte der Philosophie." In Agatopisto Cromaziano (Appiano Buonafede), *Kritische Geschichte der Revolution der Philosophie in den drey Jahrhunderten*, translated by Carl Heinrich Heydenreich, vol. 2: 213–32. Leipzig: Weygand, 1791.

———. *Originalideen über die Kritische Philosophie*. 3 vols. Leipzig: Friedrich Gotthelf Baumgärtner, 1793.

Hoffmeister, Johannes, ed. *Dokumente zu Hegels Entwicklung*. Stuttgart: Fr. Fromanns, 1936.

Holwell, John Zephaniah. *Interesting Historical Events, Relative to the Provinces of Bengal, and the Empire of Indostan*, 3 vols. London: T. Becket and P. A. de Hondt, 1765–71.

———. *Merkwürdige historische Nachrichten von Indostan und Bengalen, nebst einer Beschreibung der Religionslehren, der Mythologie, Kosmogenie, Fasten und Festtage, der Gentoos und einer Abhandlung über die Metempsychose, mit Anmerkungen und einer Abhandlung über die Religion und Philosophie der Indier*. Translated by Johann Friedrich Kleuker. Leipzig: Weygand, 1778.

Horn, Georg. *Historiae philosophicae libri VII, quibus de origine, successione, sectis et vita philosophorum ab orbe condito ad nostram aetatem agitur.* Lugduni: apud Johannem Elsevirium, 1655.

Hume, David. "Of National Characters." In idem, *Essays, Moral and Political,* 4th ed., 277–300. London: A. Millar; Edinburgh: A. Kincaid and A. Donaldson, 1753.

Ibn Mubārak, Abū al-Faḍl, and Francis Gladwin. *Ayeen Akbery or, The Institutes of the Emperor Akber.* London: G. Auld, 1800.

Ives, Edward. *A Voyage from England to India, in the Year MDCCLIV; and an Historical Narrative of the Operations of the Squadron and Army in India . . . In the Years 1755, 1756, 1757 . . . Interspersed with Some Interesting Passages Relating to the Manners, Customs, & C. Of Several Nations in Indostan: Also, a Journey from Persia to England, by an Unusual Route; with an Appendix, Containing an Account of the Diseases Prevalent in Admiral Watson's Squadron; a Description of Most of the Trees, Shrubs, and Plants, of India, with Their Real, or Supposed Medicinal Virtues; Also a Copy of a Letter Written by a Late Ingenious Physician, on the Disorders Incidental to Europeans at Gombroon in the Gulph of Persia; Illustrated with a Chart, Maps, and Other Copper-Plates.* London: Edward and Charles Dilly, 1773.

Jones, William. "The Third Anniversary Discourse on the Hindus." In idem, *The Works of Sir William Jones,* 3: 24–46. Delhi: Agam Prakashan, 1977.

Jones, William. *The Letters of Sir William Jones.* Edited by Garland Hampton Cannon. 2 vols. Oxford: Clarendon, 1970.

Kant, Immanuel. *Anthropology, History, and Education.* Translated by Günter Zöller and Robert I. Louden. Cambridge: Cambridge University Press, 2007.

———. *Gesammelte Schriften.* Edited by the Königliche Preussische (later Deutsche) Akademie der Wissenschaften. 29 vols. to date. Berlin: Georg Reimer (later Walter de Gruyter), 1900–.

———. *Lectures on Logic.* Translated by J. Michael Young. Cambridge; New York: Cambridge University Press, 1992.

———. *Lectures on Metaphysics.* Translated by Karl Ameriks and Steve Naragon. Cambridge; New York: Cambridge University Press, 1997.

———. *Prolegomena to Any Future Metaphysics.* Revised edition by Gary Hatfield. Cambridge: Cambridge University Press, 2004.

———. *What Real Progress Has Metaphysics Made in Germany since the Time of Leibniz and Wolff?* Translated by Ted Humphrey. New York: Abaris, 1983.

Lewes, George Henry. *A Biographical History of Philosophy.* London: Charles Knight & Co., 1845–6.

———. *The History of Philosophy from Thales to Comte.* 4th ed. London: Longmans, Green, 1871.

MacIntosh, William. *Travels in Europe, Asia, and Africa Describing Characters, Customs, Manners, Laws, and Productions of Nature and Art; Containing Various Remarks on the Political and Commercial Interests of Great Britain; and Delineating, in Particular, a New System for the Government and*

Improvement of the British Settlements in the East Indies; Begun in the Year 1777, and Finished in 1781. London: J. Murray, 1782.

———. *Voyages en Europe, en Asie et en Afrique, contenant la description des moeurs, coutumes, loix, productions, manufactures de ces contrées & l'état actuel des possessions angloises dans l'Inde; commencés en 1777, & finis en 1781, par M. Makintosh, suivis des voyages du Colonel Capper, dans les Indes, au travers de l'Egypte & du Grand Désert, par Suez & par Bassora, en 1779. Traduits de L'Anglois, & accompagnés de notes sur l'original & de cartes géographiques.* London; Paris: Regnaut, 1786; 2nd ed., 1788.

Majer, Friedrich. *Allgemeines mythologisches Lexikon.* 2 vols. Weimar, 1803–4.

———. *Brahma oder über die Religion der Indier als Brahmaismus.* Leipzig, 1818.

Meiners, Christoph. *Briefe über die Schweiz* 4 vols. Berlin: Spener, 1784–90.

———. *Geschichte des Ursprungs, Fortgangs und Verfalls der Wissenschaften in Griechenland und Rom.* 2 vols. Lemgo: Meyer, 1781.

———. *Grundriss der Geschichte der Menschheit.* Lemgo: Meyer, 1785; 2nd ed. 1793.

———. *Grundriss der Geschichte der Weltweisheit.* Lemgo: Meyer, 1786; 2nd ed. 1789.

———. *Geschichte der Ungleichheit der Stände unter den vornehmsten europäischen Völkern.* 2 vols. Hannover: Helwing, 1792.

———. *Histoire de l'origine, des progrès et de la décadence des sciences dans la Grèce,* 4 vols. Translated by J. Ch. Laveaux. Paris: Laveaux et Compagnie, 1799.

———. *Revision der Philosophie.* Göttingen; Gotha: Johann Christian Dieterich, 1772.

———. "Ueber die Natur der afrikanischen Neger." *Göttingisches historisches Magazin* 6 (1790): 385–456.

———. "Ueber die Ursachen des Despotismus." *Göttingisches historisches Magazin* 2 (1788): 193–229.

Meiners, Christoph, and Ludwig Timotheus Spittler, eds. *Göttingisches historisches Magazin.* Hannover: Helwing, 1787–94.

Michelis, Friedrich. *Geschichte der Philosophie von Thales bis auf unsere Zeit.* Braunsberg, 1865.

Morhof, Daniel Georg. *Polyhistor sive de notitia auctorum et rerum commentarii.* Lubecae: Petri Boeckmanni, 1688.

Morhof, Daniel Georg, Johannes Moller, Johann Frick, et alia. *Polyhistor literarius, philosophicus et physicus.* Lubecae: Petri Boeckmanni, 1747.

Nicolai, Friedrich. "Betrachtungen über die Frage: wie der mündliche Vortrag der Philosophie auf Universitäten eingerichtet werden sollte, um gemeinnütziger zu werden. Zwey Vorlesungen." In idem, *Philosophische Abhandlungen,* 2: 123–208. Berlin; Stettin, 1808.

Plessing, Friedrich Victor Lebrecht. *Historische und philosophische Untersuchungen über die Denkart, Theologie und Philosophie der ältern Völker vorzüglich der Griechen bis auf Aristoteles Zeiten.* Elbingen, 1785.

———. *Memnonium, oder Versuche zur Enthüllung der Geheimnisse des Alterthums.* Leipzig: Weygand, 1787.

———. *Osiris und Sokrates.* Berlin: Stralsund, 1783.

———. *Versuch zur Aufklärung der Philosophie des ältesten Alterthums.* Leipzig, 1788–90.

Régis, Pierre Sylvain. *Systême de Philosophie, contenant la logique, métaphysique, physique & morale.* Lyon: Anisson, Posuel & Rigaud, 1691.

Reinhardus, Laurentius. *Compendium historiae philosophiae.* Leipzig, 1725.

Reinhold, Karl Leonhard. "Ueber den Begrif der Geschichte der Philosophie." In *Beyträge zur Geschichte der Philosophie,* edited by Georg Gustav Fülleborn, 2nd ed., 1: 3–36. Züllichau; Freystadt: Friedrich Frommann, 1796.

Rixner, Thaddä Anselm. *Handbuch der Geschichte der Philosophie.* Sulzbach: Seidel, 1822–23; 2nd ed., 1829.

———. *Versuch einer neuen Darstellung der uralten indischen All-Eins-Lehre oder der Sammlung von Oupnek'haton: Erstes Stück Oupnek'hat Tschehandouk Genannt, nach dem Lat., der Pers. Uebersetzung Wörtlichgetreu nachgebildeten Texte des Herrn Anquetil du Perron frey ins Deutsche übers.* Nürnberg: Stein, 1808.

Schelling, Friedrich Wilhelm Joseph von. *Sämmtliche Werke.* Edited by Karl Friedrich August Schelling. 14 vols. Stuttgart; Augsburg: J. G. Cotta, 1856–61.

Schlegel, August Wilhelm. *Bhagavad-Gita: Id est Thespesion Melos, sive almi Crishnae et Arjunae colloquium de rebus divinis.* Bonnae: Academia Borussica Rhenana Typiis Regis, Prostat apud E. Weber, 1823.

Schlegel, Friedrich. *Friedrich Schlegels Briefe an seinem Bruder August Wilhelm.* Edited by Oskar F. Walzel. Berlin: Speyer & Peters, 1890.

———. *Kritische Friedrich-Schlegel-Ausgabe.* Edited by Ernst Behler, Jean Jacques Anstett, and Hans Eichner. 35 vols. München: F. Schöningh, 1958–.

———. *Philosophische Vorlesungen aus den Jahren 1804 bis 1806 nebst Fragmenten vorzüglich philosophisch-theologischen Inhalts.* 4 vols. Edited by C. J. H. Windischmann. Bonn: E. Weber, 1836–7.

———. *Ueber die Sprache und Weisheit der Indier.* Heidelberg: Mohr und Zimmer, 1808.

Schubert, Johann Ernst. *Historia philosophiae.* Ienae: Cröker, 1742.

Schwab, Johann Christoph, Karl Leonhard Reinhold, and Johann Heinrich Abicht. *Preisschriften über die Frage: Welche Fortschritte hat die Metaphysik seit Leibnitzens und Wolffs Zeiten in Deutschland gemacht?* Darmstadt: Wissenschaftliche Buchgesellschaft, 1971.

Schwegler, Albert. *Geschichte der Philosophie im Umriss: Ein Leitfaden zur Übersicht.* Stuttgart: Verlag der Franckh'schen Buchhandlung, 1848.

Sömmerring, Samuel Thomas. *Ueber die körperliche Verschiedenheit des Negers vom Europäer.* Frankfurt und Mainz: Varrentrapp Sohn und Wenner, 1785.

Sonnerat, Pierre de. *Reise nach Ostindien, und China, in den Jahren 1774 bis 1781, nebst dessen Beobachtungen über Pegu, Madagascar, das Cap, die Inseln France und Bourbon, die Maldiven, Ceylon, Malacca, die Philippinen und Molucken; aus dem Französischen.* Leipzig: Sommer, 1783.

———. *Voyage aux Indes orientales et à la Chine, fait par ordre du Roi, depuis 1774 jusqu'en 1781, dans lequel on traite des moeurs, de la religion, des sciences & des arts des indiens, des chinois, des pegouins & des madegasses; suivi d'observations sur le Cap de Bonne-Esperance, les isles de France & de Bourbon, les Maldives, Ceylan, Malacca, les Philippines & les Moluques, & de recherches sur l'histoire naturelle de ces pays.* Paris: chez l'auteur, Froule, Nyon, Barrois, 1782.

Stäudlin, Carl Friedrich. *Geschichte und Geist des Skepticismus, vorzüglich in Rücksicht auf Moral und Religion.* 2 vols. Leipzig: Crusius, 1794.

Stanley, Thomas. *The history of philosophy, containing the lives, opinions, actions and discourses of the philosophers of every sect.* 4 vols. London: Humphrey Moseley and Thomas Dring, 1655–62; subsequent editions of 1687, 1701, and 1743.

Stolle, Gottlieb. *Anleitung zur Historie der Gelahrheit.* Jena: Johann Meyer, 1718.

Tennemann, Wilhelm. *Geschichte der Philosophie.* 11 vols. Leipzig: Johann Ambrosius Barth, 1798–1819.

———. *Grundriss der Geschichte der Philosophie für den akademischen Unterricht.* Leipzig: Johann Ambrosius Barth, 1812; subsequent editions of 1816, 1820, 1825, and 1829.

———. "Übersicht des vorzügligsten, was für die Geschichte der Philosophie seit 1780 geleistet worden." *Philosophisches Journal einer Gesellschaft teutscher Gelehrten* 2, no. 4 (1795): 323–41.

Tholuck, August. *Blüthensammlung aus der morgenländischen Mystik, Nebst einer Einleitung über Mystik überhaupt und morgenländische insbesondere.* Berlin: Ferdinand Dümmler, 1825.

———. *Commentatio de VI guam graeca philosophia in theologiam tum Muhammedanorum tum Judaeorum exercuerit, Particula II: De orut Cabbalae.* Hamburgi: F. Perthes, 1837.

———. *Die Glaubwürdigkeit der evangelischen Geschichte, zugleich eine Kritik des Lebens Jesu von Strauss für theologische und nicht theologische Leser dargestellt.* Hamburg: F. Perthes, 1837.

———. *Die Lehre von der Sünde und vom Versöhner, oder Die wahre Weihe des Zweiflers.* Hamburg: Perthes, 1823; 2nd ed., 1825; 9th ed., 1871.

———. *Die speculative Trinitätslehre des späteren Orients, Eine religions-philosophische Monographie aus handschriftlichen Quellen der Leydener, Oxforder und Berliner Bibliothek.* Berlin: Ferdinand Dümmler, 1826.

———. *Ssufismus, sive, Theosophia Persarum pantheistica, quam e mss. bibliothecae regiae Berolinensis: persicis, arabicis, turcicis.* Berolini: Ferdinand Dümmler, 1821.

Tiedemann, Dieterich. *Geist der spekulativen Philosophie von Thales bis Sokrates.* 6 vols. Marburg: Neue akademische Buchhandlung, 1791–7.

———. *System der stoischen Philosophie.* 3 vols. Leipzig: Weidmanns Erben und Reich, 1776.

Ueberweg, Friedrich. *Grundriss der Geschichte der Philosophie von Thales bis auf die Gegenwart.* 3 vols. Berlin: E. S. Mittler, 1862–6.

Voltaire, François-Marie Arouet de. *Les oeuvres complètes de Voltaire/The Complete Works of Voltaire.* Edited by Theodore Bestermann. Geneva:

Institut et musée Voltaire; Toronto: University of Toronto Press; Banbury, Oxfordshire [etc.]: Voltaire Foundation, 1968–.

Vossius, Gerardus Joannes. *De philosophia et philosophorum sectis.* Hagae-Comitis: apud Adrianum Vlacq, 1657–8.

———. *De philosophorum sectis liber.* Lipsiae: Joh. Casp. Meyeri; Jenae: Henricus Beyerus, 1705.

Ward, William. *A View of the History, Literature and Religion of the Hindoos, including a minute description of their manners and customs, and translations from their principal works.* 3rd ed. London: Black, Parbury and Allen, 1817.

Weiss, Christian. *Über die Behandlungsart der Geschichte der Philosophie auf Universitäten.* Leipzig, 1799.

Secondary Literature

Allison, Henry E. *The Kant-Eberhard Controversy, an English Translation Together with Supplementary Materials and a Historical-Analytic Introduction of Immanuel Kant's On a Discovery According to Which Any New Critique of Pure Reason Has Been Made Superfluous by an Earlier One.* Baltimore; London: Johns Hopkins University Press, 1973.

Appel, Toby A. *The Cuvier-Geoffroy Debate: French Biology in the Decades before Darwin.* New York; Oxford: Oxford University Press, 1987.

Banton, Michael. *Race Relations.* New York: Basic Books, 1967.

Barck, Karlheinz. "Amerika in Hegels Geschichtsphilosophie." *Weimarer Beiträge* 38, No. 2 (1992): 274–78.

Behler, Ernst. "Das Indienbild der deutschen Romantik." *Germanisch-Romanische Monatsschrift* 49 (1968): 21–37.

———. *Friedrich Schlegel in Selbstzeugnissen und Bilddokumenten.* Reinbek bei Hamburg: Rowohlt, 1966.

Beiser, Frederick C. *The Fate of Reason: German Philosophy from Kant to Fichte.* Cambridge, MA; London: Harvard University Press, 1987.

———. *German Idealism: The Struggle against Subjectivism, 1781–1801.* Cambridge, MA; London: Harvard University Press, 2002.

———. *The Romantic Imperative: The Concept of Early German Romanticism.* Cambridge, MA; London: Harvard University Press, 2003.

Benfey, Theodor. *Geschichte der Sprachwissenschaft und orientalischen Philologie in Deutschland seit dem Anfange des 19. Jahrhunderts mit einem Rückblick auf die früheren Zeiten.* München: J. G. Cotta, 1869.

Bergmann, Julius. *Geschichte der Philosophie.* 2 vols. Berlin: Mittler, 1892–3.

Bernal, Martin. *Black Athena: The Afroasiatic Roots of Classical Civilization,* Vol. 1: *The Fabrication of Ancient Greece 1785–1985.* London: Free Association Books, 1987.

———. *Black Athena Writes Back: Martin Bernal Responds to His Critics.* Edited by David Chioni Moore. Durham, NC; London: Duke University Press, 2001.

Bernasconi, Robert. "Ethnicity, Culture and Philosophy." In *The Blackwell Companion to Philosophy*, edited by Nicholas Bunnin and E. P. Tsui-James, 567–81. Malden, MA: Blackwell, 2003.

———. "Hegel at the Court of the Ashanti." In *Hegel after Derrida*, edited by Stuart Barnett, 41–63. London: Routledge, 1998.

———. "Heidegger and the Invention of the Western Philosophical Tradition." *Journal of the British Society for Phenomenology* 26, no. 3 (1995): 240–54.

———. "'Ich Mag in Keinen Himmel, Wo Weisse Sind.' Herder's Critique of Eurocentrism." *Acta Institutionis Philosophiae et Aestheticae* 13 (1995): 69–81.

———. "Kant and Blumenbach's Polyps: A Neglected Chapter in the History of the Concept of Race." In *The German Invention of Race*, edited by Sara Eigen and Mark Larrimore, 73–90. Albany: SUNY Press, 2006.

———. "Kant as an Unfamiliar Source of Racism." In *Philosophers on Race: Critical Essays*, edited by Julie K. Ward and Tommy L. Lott, 145–66. Malden, MA: Blackwell, 2002.

———. "Kant's Third Thoughts on Race." In *Reading Kant's Geography*, edited by Stuart Elden and Eduardo Mendieta, 291–318. Albany: SUNY Press, 2011.

———. "Krimskrams: Hegel and the Current Controversy about the Beginnings of Philosophy." In *Interrogating the Tradition: Hermeneutics and the History of Philosophy*, edited by C. E. Scott and J. Sallis, 191–208. Albany: SUNY Press, 2000.

———. "On Heidegger's other sins of omission: his exclusion of Asian thought from the origins of Occidental metaphysics and his denial of the possibility of Christian philosophy." *American Catholic Philosophical Quarterly* 69, no. 2 (Spring 1995): 333–50.

———. "Philosophy's Paradoxical Parochialism: The Reinvention of Philosophy as Greek." In *Cultural Readings of Imperialism*, edited by Keith Ansell-Pearson, Benita Parry, and Judith Squires, 212–26. London: Lawrence & Wishart, 1997.

———. "Religious Philosophy: Hegel's Occasional Perplexity in the Face of the Distinction between Philosophy and Religion." *The Bulletin of the Hegel Society of Great Britain* 45/46 (2002): 1–15.

———. "Who Invented the Concept of Race? Kant's Role in the Enlightenment Construction of Race." In *Race*, edited by Robert Bernasconi, 11–36. Malden, MA: Blackwell, 2001.

———. "Will the Real Kant Please Stand Up: The Challenge of Enlightenment Racism to the Study of the History of Philosophy." *Radical Philosophy* 117 (2003): 13–22.

———. "With What Must the History of Philosophy Begin? Hegel's Role in the Debate on the Place of India within the History of Philosophy." In *Hegel's History of Philosophy: New Interpretations*, edited by David A. Duquette. Albany: SUNY Press, 2003.

———. "With What Must the Philosophy of World History Begin? On the Racial Basis of Hegel's Eurocentrism." *Nineteenth-Century Contexts* 22 (2000): 171–201.

Bernasconi, Robert, and Tommy L. Lott, eds. *The Idea of Race*. Indianapolis: Hackett, 2000.

Blackwell, Constance. "Jacob Brucker's Theory of Knowledge and the History of Natural Philosophy." In *Jacob Brucker (1696–1770), Philosoph und Historiker der europäischen Aufklärung*, edited by Wilhelm Schmidt-Biggemann and Theo Stammen, 198–217. Berlin: Akademie Verlag, 1998.

———. "Skepticism as a Sect, Skepticism as a Philosophical Stance: Johann Jacob Brucker Versus Carl Friedrich Stäudlin." In *The Skeptical Tradition around 1800*, edited by Johan van der Zande and Richard H. Popkin, 343–63. Dordrecht; Boston; London: Kluwer, 1998.

———. "Thales Philosophus: The Beginning of Philosophy as Discipline." In *History and the Disciplines: The Reclassification of Knowledge in Early Modern Europe*, edited by Donald R. Kelley, 61–82. Rochester, NY: University of Rochester Press, 1997.

Bödeker, Hans Erich, Philippe Büttgen, and Michel Espagne, eds. *Die Wissenschaft vom Menschen in Göttingen um 1800: Wissenschaftliche Praktiken, institutionelle Geographie, europäische Netzwerke*. Göttingen: Vandenhoeck und Ruprecht, 2008.

Bongie, Laurence L. "Hume and Skepticism in Late Eighteenth-Century France." In *The Skeptical Tradition around 1800*, edited by Johan van der Zande and Richard H. Popkin, 15–29. Dordrecht; Boston; London: Kluwer, 1998.

Braun, Lucien. *Histoire de l'histoire de la philosophie*. Paris: Ophrys, 1973.

Calton, Patricia Marie. *Hegel's Metaphysics of God: The Ontological Proof as the Development of a Trinitarian Divine Ontology*. Aldershot, UK; Burlington, VT: Ashgate, 2001.

Carhart, Michael C. "Polynesia and polygenism: the scientific use of travel literature in the early 19th century." *History of the Human Sciences* 22, no. 2 (2009): 58–86.

———. *The Science of Culture in Enlightenment Germany*. Cambridge, MA: Harvard University Press, 2007.

Chatelain, Jean-Marc. "Philologie, pansophie, polymathie, encyclopédie: Morhof et l'histoire du savoir global." In *Mapping the World of Learning: The Polyhistor of Daniel Georg Morhof*, edited by Françoise Waquet. Wiesbaden: Harrassowitz, 2000.

Clarke, J. J. *Oriental Enlightenment: The Encounter between Asian and Western Thought*. London; New York: Routledge, 1997.

Coleman, William. *Georges Cuvier, Zoologist: A Study in the History of Evolution Theory*. Cambridge, MA: Harvard University Press, 1964.

Cowan, Robert. *The Indo-German Identification: Reconciling South Asian Origins and European Destinies, 1765–1885*. Rochester, NY: Camden House, 2010.

Crowner, David, and Gerald Christianson. *The Spirituality of the German Awakening*. Mahwah, NJ: Paulist Press, 2003.

Davies, Anna Morpurgo. *Nineteenth-Century Linguistics*. New York: Longman, 1998.

Dilthey, Wilhelm. *Studien zur Geschichte des deutschen Geistes* (vol. 3 of idem, *Gesammelte Schriften*). Edited by Paul Ritter. Stuttgart: Teubner, 1959.

Dougherty, Frank W. P. "Christoph Meiners und Johann Friedrich Blumenbach im Streit um den Begriff der Menschenrasse." In *Die Natur des Menschen: Probleme der physischen Anthropologie und Rassenkunde (1750–1850)*, edited by Gunter Mann and Franz Dumont, 89–111. Stuttgart; New York: Gustav Fischer, 1990.

Eigen, Sara, and Mark Larrimore, eds. *The German Invention of Race*. Albany: SUNY Press, 2006.

Eze, Emmanuel Chukwudi. "The Color of Reason; the Idea of 'Race' in Kant's Anthropology." In *Postcolonial African Philosophy: A Critical Reader*, edited by Emmanuel Chukwudi Eze, 103–40. Cambridge, MA: Blackwell, 1997.

———. "Hume, Race, and Human Nature." *Journal of the History of Ideas* 61, no. 4 (2000): 691–98.

Frank, Manfred. *"Unendliche Annäherung": Die Anfänge der philosophischen Frühromantik*. Frankfurt am Main: Suhrkamp, 1997.

Fink, Karl J. "Storm and stress anthropology." *History of the Human Sciences* 6, no. 1 (1993): 51–71.

Figueira, Dorothy M. "Oriental Despotism and Despotic Orientalisms." In *Anthropology and the German Enlightenment: Perspectives on Humanity*, edited by Katherine M. Faull, 182–99. Lewisburg, PA: Bucknell University Press, 1995.

Freyer, J. *Geschichte der Geschichte der Philosophie im achtzehnten Jahrhundert*. Leipzig, 1912.

Jörn Garber, "Von der 'anthropologischen Geschichte des philosophierenden Geistes' zur Geschichte der Menschheit (Friedrich August Carus)." In *Zwischen Empirisierung und Konstruktionsleistung: Anthropologie im 18. Jahrhundert*, edited by Jörn Garber and Heinz Thoma, 219–61. Tübingen: Max Niemeyer, 2004.

Geiss, Immanuel. *Geschichte der Rassismus*. Frankfurt am Main: Suhrkamp, 1988.

Geldsetzer, Lutz. "Die Methodenstreit in der Philosophiegeschichtsschreibung, 1791–1820." *Kant-Studien* 56 (1966): 519–27.

———. *Die Philosophie der Philosophiegeschichte im 19. Jahrhundert, Zur Wissenschaftstheorie der Philosophiegeschichtsschreibung und -Betrachtung*. Meisenheim am Glan: Anton Hain, 1968.

Gérard, René. *L'Orient et la pensée romantique allemande*. Paris: M. Didier, 1963.

Germana, Nicholas A. *The Orient of Europe: The Mythical Image of India and Competing Images of German National Identity*. Newcastle upon Tyne: Cambridge Scholars Publishing, 2009.

Gierl, Martin. "Christoph Meiners, Geschichte der Menschheit und Göttinger Universalgeschichte: Rasse und Nation als Politisierung der deutschen Aufklärung." In *Die Wissenschaft vom Menschen in Göttingen um 1800: wissenschaftliche Praktiken, institutionelle Geographie, europäische Netzwerke*, edited by Hans Erich Bödeker, Philippe Büttgen, and Michel Espagne, 419–33. Göttingen: Vandenhoeck und Ruprecht, 2008.

Glasenapp, Helmuth von. *Das Indienbild deutscher Denker*. Stuttgart: K. F. Koehler, 1960.

Grafton, Anthony. "Polyhistor into *Philologe*: Notes on the Transformation of German Classical Scholarship, 1780–1850." In *History of Universities*, edited by Charles B. Schmitt, 3: 159–92. Amersham, UK: Avebury, 1983.

Guéroult, Martial. *Dianoématique, Livre I: Histoire de l'histoire de la philosophie*. 3 vols. Paris: Aubier Montaigne, 1984–8.

Halbfass, Wilhelm. *India and Europe: An Essay in Understanding*. Albany: SUNY Press, 1988.

Harten, Stuart Jay. *Raising the Veil of History: Orientalism, Classicism and the Birth of Western Civilization in Hegel's Berlin Lecture Courses of the 1820's*. Dissertation, Cornell University, 1994.

Hedrick, Todd. "Race, Difference, and Anthropology in Kant's Cosmopolitanism." *Journal of the History of Philosophy* 46, no. 2 (2008): 245–68.

Heidegger, Martin. *Was heisst Denken?* Tübingen: Max Niemeyer, 1954.

———. *What Is Philosophy?* Translated by William Kluback and Jean T. Wilde. London: Vision Press, 1956.

Herling, Bradley L. *The German Gītā: Hermeneutics and Discipline in the German Reception of Indian Thought, 1778–1831*. New York; London: Routledge, 2006.

Hess, Hans. "Das romantische Bild der Philosophiegeschichte." *Kant-Studien* 31, nos. 1–3 (1921): 251–85.

Hill, Thomas E., Jr., and Bernard Boxill. "Kant and Race." In *Race and Racism*, edited by Bernard Boxill, 448–71. New York: Oxford University Press, 2001.

Hirsch, Emanuel. *Geschichte der neueren evangelischen Theologie*. 4th ed. 5 vols. Gütersloh: Gerd Mohn, 1968.

Hoffheimer, Michael H. "Does Hegel Justify Slavery?" *Owl of Minerva* 25, no. 1 (Fall 1993): 118–19.

———. "Hegel, Race, Genocide." *Southern Journal of Philosophy* 39/Supp. (2001): 35–62.

———. "Race and Law in Hegel's Philosophy of Religion." In *Race and Racism in Modern Philosophy*, edited by Andrew Valls, 194–216. Ithaca, NY; London: Cornell University Press, 2005.

Hoffmann, Paul T. *Der indische und der deutsche Geist von Herder bis zur Romantik*. Dissertation, Tübingen, 1915(?).

Hulin, Michel. *Hegel et l'Orient*. Paris: J. Vrin, 1979.

Iggers, Georg G. "The University of Göttingen 1760–1800 and the Transformation of Historical Scholarship." *Storia della storiografia* 2 (1982): 11–37.

Ihle, Alexander. *Christoph Meiners und die Völkerkunde*. Göttingen: Vandenhoeck und Ruprecht, 1931.

Immerwahr, John. "Hume's Revised Racism." *Journal of the History of Ideas* 53, no. 3 (July–Sept. 1992): 481–86.

Jehl, Rainer. "Jacob Brucker und die 'Encyclopedie.'" In *Jacob Brucker (1696–1770), Philosoph und Historiker der europäischen Aufklärung*, edited by Wilhelm Schmidt-Biggemann and Theo Stammen, 238–56. Berlin: Akademie Verlag, 1998.

Kähler, Martin. "Tholuck, Friedrich August Gottreu." In *Realencyklopädie für protestantische Theologie und Kirche*, edited by J. J. Herzog, Albert Hauck, and Hermann Caselmann, 19: 695–702. Leipzig: J. C. Hinrichs, 1896–1913.

Kelley, Donald R. *The Descent of Ideas: The History of Intellectual History*. Aldershot, UK; Burlington, VT: Ashgate, 2002.

Kelley, Donald R., ed. *History and the Disciplines: The Reclassification of Knowledge in Early Modern Europe*. Rochester, NY: University of Rochester Press, 1997.

King, Richard. *Indian Philosophy: An Introduction to Hindu and Buddhist Thought*. Washington, DC: Georgetown University Press, 1999.

Kleingeld, Pauline. "Kant's Second Thoughts on Race." *Philosophical Quarterly* 57 (2007): 573–92.

Larrimore, Mark. "Antinomies of race: diversity and destiny in Kant." *Patterns of Prejudice* 42, nos. 4–5 (2008): 341–63.

———. "Race, Freedom and the Fall in Steffens and Kant." In *The German Invention of Race*, edited by Sara Eigen and Mark Larrimore, 91–120. Albany: SUNY Press, 2006.

———. "Sublime Waste: Kant on the Destiny of the 'Races.'" *Canadian Journal of Philosophy* 25/supp. (1999): 99–125.

Laursen, John Christian. "Skepticism and the History of Moral Philosophy: The Case of Carl Friedrich Stäudlin." In *The Skeptical Tradition around 1800: Skepticism in Philosophy, Science, and Society*, edited by Johan van der Zande and Richard H. Popkin, 365–78. Dordrecht; Boston; London: Kluwer, 1998.

Lefkowitz, Mary R., and Guy Maclean Rogers, eds. *Black Athena Revisited*. Chapel Hill: University of North Carolina Press, 1996.

Lotter, Friedrich. "Christoph Meiners und die Lehre von der unterschiedlichen Wertigkeit der Menschenrassen." In *Geschichtswissenschaft in Göttingen: eine Vorlesungsreihe*, edited by Hartmut Boockmann and Hermann Wellenreuther, 30–75. Göttingen: Vandenhoeck und Ruprecht, 1987.

Malter, Rudolf. "Der Rassebegriff in Kants Anthropologie." In *Die Natur des Menschen: Probleme der physischen Anthropologie und Rassenkunde (1750–1850)*, edited by Gunter Mann and Franz Dumont, 113–122. Stuttgart; New York: Gustav Fischer, 1990.

Marchand, Suzanne. *German Orientalism in the Age of Empire: Religion, Race, and Scholarship*. Washington, DC: German Historical Institute; Cambridge: Cambridge University Press, 2009.

Marchand, Suzanne, and Anthony Grafton. "Martin Bernal and His Critics." *Arion* 5, 2 (1997): 1–35.

Marchignoli, Saverio. "Canonizing an Indian Text? A. W. Schlegel, W. von Humboldt, Hegel, and the *Bhagavadgītā*." In *Sanskrit and 'Orientalism': Indology and Comparative Linguistics in Germany, 1750–1958*, edited by Douglas T. McGetchin, Peter K. J. Park, and D. R. SarDesai, 245–70. New Delhi: Manohar, 2004.

Marino, Luigi. *Praeceptores Germaniae: Göttingen 1770–1820*. Göttingen: Vandenhoeck und Ruprecht, 1995.

Martin, Seymour Guy, Gordon Haddon Clark, Francis P. Clarke, and Chester Townsend Ruddick. *A History of Philosophy*. New York: Crofts, 1941.

Maser, Peter. "Orientalische Mystik und evangelische Erweckungsbewegung: Eine biographische Studie zu Briefen von und an F. A. G. Tholuck." *Zeitschrift für Religions- und Geistesgeschichte* 33 (1981): 221–49.

McGetchin, Douglas T. *Indology, Indomania, and Orientalism: Ancient India's Rebirth in Modern Germany*. Madison, NJ: Fairleigh Dickinson University Press, 2009.

McGetchin, Douglas T., Peter K. J. Park, and D. R. SarDesai, eds. *Sanskrit and 'Orientalism': Indology and Comparative Linguistics in Germany, 1750–1958*. New Delhi: Manohar, 2004.

Meyer, Annette. *Von der Wahrheit zur Wahrscheinlichkeit: Die Wissenschaft vom Menschen in der schottischen und deutschen Aufklärung*. Tübingen: Max Niemeyer, 2008.

Michelis, Friedrich. *Geschichte der Philosophie von Thales bis auf unsere Zeit*. Braunsberg: Eduard Peter, 1865.

Millán-Zaibert, Elizabeth. *Friedrich Schlegel and the Emergence of Romantic Philosophy*. Albany: SUNY Press, 2007.

Moellendorf, Darrel. "Racism and Rationality in Hegel's Philosophy of Subjective Spirit." *History of Political Thought* 13, no. 2 (Summer 1992): 243–55.

Moravia, Sergio. *La scienza dell'uomo nel Settecento*. Bari: Laterza, 1970.

Morton, Eric. "Race and Racism in the Works of David Hume." *Journal of African Philosophy* 1, no. 1 (2002): 1–27.

Müller, G. M., ed. *Life and Religion: An Aftermath from the Writings of F. M. Müller*. New York: Doubleday, Page and Co., 1905.

Nelles, Paul. "Historia Litteraria and Morhof: Private Teaching and Professorial Libraries at the University of Kiel." In *Mapping the World of Learning: The Polyhistor of Daniel Georg Morhof*, edited by Françoise Waquet, 31–56. Wiesbaden: Harrassowitz, 2000.

Park, Peter K. J. "A Catholic Apologist in a Pantheistic World: New Approaches to Friedrich Schlegel." In *Sanskrit and 'Orientalism': Indology and Comparative Linguistics in Germany, 1750–1958*, edited by Douglas T. McGetchin, Peter K. J. Park, and D. R. SarDesai, 83–106. New Delhi: Manohar, 2004.

Parkinson, G. H. R. "Hegel, Pantheism, and Spinoza." *Journal of the History of Ideas* 38, no. 3 (July–Sept. 1977): 449–59.

Piaia, Gregorio. "Jacob Bruckers Wirkungsgeschichte in Frankreich und Italien." In *Jacob Brucker (1696–1770), Philosoph und Historiker der europäischen Aufklärung*, edited by Wilhelm Schmidt-Biggemann and Theo Stammen, 218–37. Berlin: Akademie Verlag, 1998.

Picavet, François. *Les Idéologues; Essai sur l'histoire des idées et des théories scientifiques, philosophiques, religieuses, etc. en France depuis 1789*. Reprint. New York: Burt Franklin, 1971.

Pöggeler, Otto. *Hegels Kritik der Romantik: Philosophie an der Jahrtausendwende*. München: Fink, 1998.

Polaschegg, Andrea. *Der andere Orientalismus: Regeln deutsch-morgenländischer Imagination im 19. Jahrhundert*. Berlin: Walter de Gruyter, 2005.

Poliakov, Léon. *The Aryan Myth: A History of Racist and Nationalist Ideas in Europe*. New York: Basic Books, 1974.

Pollock, Sheldon. "Deep Orientalism? Notes on Sanskrit and Power Beyond the Raj." In *Orientalism and the Postcolonial Predicament: Perspectives on South Asia*, edited by Carol A. Breckenridge and Peter van der Veer, 76–133. Philadelphia: University of Pennsylvania Press, 1993.

Popkin, Richard H. "Hume's Racism." In idem, *The High Road to Pyrrhonism*, edited by Richard A. Watson and James E. Force, 251–66. San Diego: Austin Hill, 1980.

———. "Hume's Racism Reconsidered." In idem, *The Third Force in Seventeenth Century Thought*, 64–75. Leiden: E. J. Brill, 1992.

———. "The Philosophical Bases of Modern Racism." In idem, *The High Road to Pyrrhonism*, edited by Richard A. Watson and James E. Force, 79–102. San Diego: Austin Hill, 1980.

———. "Some Thoughts about Stäudlin's 'History and Spirit of Skepticism.' " In *The Skeptical Tradition around 1800*, edited by Johan van der Zande and Richard H. Popkin. Dordrecht; Boston; London: Kluwer, 1998.

Popkin, Richard H., ed. *The Columbia History of Western Philosophy*. New York: MJF Books, 1999.

Querner, Hans. "Christoph Girtanner und die Anwendung des Kantischen Prinzips in der Bestimmung des Menschen." In *Die Natur des Menschen: Probleme der physischen Anthropologie und Rassenkunde (1750–1850)*, edited by Gunter Mann and Franz Dumont, 123–36. Stuttgart; New York: Gustav Fischer, 1990.

Rabault-Feuerhahn, Pascale. *L'archive des origines: Sanskrit, philologie, anthropologie dans l'Allemagne du XIXe siècle*. Paris: Cerf, 2008.

Reill, Peter Hanns. *The German Enlightenment and the Rise of Historicism*. Berkeley: University of California Press, 1975.

Rocher, Ludo. *Ezourvedam, a French Veda of the Eighteenth Century*. Amsterdam; Philadelphia: J. Benjamins, 1984.

Rothermund, Dietmar. *The German Intellectual Quest for India*. New Delhi: Manohar, 1986.

Rupp-Eisenreich, Britta. "Des choses occultes en histoire des sciences humaines: le destin de la 'science nouvelle' de Christoph Meiners." *L'Ethnographie* 90–91/special issue *Anthropologie: Points d'Histoire* edited by Britta Rupp-Eisenreich and Patrick Menget (1983): 131–83.

———. "C. Meiners et J. M. Gérando: un chapitre du comparatisme anthropologique." In *L'homme des Lumières et la découverte de l'autre: Études sur le XVIIIe siècle*, edited by Daniel Droixhe and Pol-Pierre Gossiaux, 21–47. Brussels: Université libre de Bruxelles, 1985.

Russell, Bertrand. *A History of Western Philosophy*. New York: Simon and Schuster, 1945.

Said, Edward W. *Orientalism*. New York: Pantheon, 1978.

Santinello, Giovanni, ed. *Storia delle storie generali della filosofia*. 5 vols. in 8. Brescia: La Scuola (later Padova: Editrice Antenore), 1979–2004.

Santinello, Giovanni, C. W. T. Blackwell, and Philip Weller. *Models of the History of Philosophy*, vol. 1: *From Its Origins in the Renaissance to the "Historia philosophica."* Dordrecht: Kluwer, 1993.

Scheidt, Walter. "The concept of race in anthropology." In *This is race: An anthology selected from the international literature on the races of man*, edited by E. W. Count, 354–91. New York: Schuman, 1950.

Schiebinger, Londa. *Nature's Body: Gender in the Making of Modern Science*. New Brunswick, NJ: Rutgers University Press, 1993.

Schings, Hans-Jürgen. *Melancholie und Aufklärung: Melancholiker und ihre Kritiker in Erfahrungsseelenkunde und Literatur des 18. Jahrhunderts.* Stuttgart: Metzler, 1977.

Schlitt, Dale M. *Hegel's Trinitarian Claim: A Critical Reflection*. Leiden: E. J. Brill, 1984.

———. "Trinity and Spirit." *American Catholic Philosophical Quarterly* 64, no. 4 (1990): 457–89.

Schmidt-Biggemann, Wilhelm, and Theo Stammen, eds. *Jacob Brucker (1696–1770), Philosoph und Historiker der europäischen Aufklärung.* Berlin: Akademie Verlag, 1998.

Schneider, Ulrich Johannes. *Die Vergangenheit des Geistes, eine Archaeologie der Philosophiegeschichte.* Frankfurt am Main: Suhrkamp, 1990.

———. *Philosophie und Universität: Historisierung der Vernunft im 19. Jahrhundert.* Hamburg: Felix Meiner, 1999.

Schulin, Ernst. *Die weltgeschichtliche Erschliessung des Orients bei Hegel und Ranke.* Göttingen: Vandenhoeck und Ruprecht, 1958.

Schwab, Raymond. *The Oriental Renaissance: Europe's Rediscovery of India and the East, 1680–1880.* Translated by Gene Patterson-Black and Victor Reinking. New York: Columbia University Press, 1984; French original, 1950.

Schwegler, Albert. *Geschichte der Philosophie im Umriss: ein Leitfaden zur Uebersicht.* 5th ed. Stuttgart: Franck, 1863.

Sengupta, Indra. *From salon to discipline: state, university and Indology in Germany, 1821–1914.* Würzburg: Ergon, 2005.

Serequeberhan, Tsenay. "Eurocentrism in Philosophy: The Case of Immanuel Kant." *The Philosophical Forum* 27, no. 4 (Summer 1996): 333–56.

Splett, Jorg. *Die Trinitätslehre G. W. F. Hegels.* München: Alber, 1965.

Taguieff, Pierre-André. *The Force of Prejudice: On Racism and Its Doubles.* Translated by Hassan Melehy. Minneapolis: University of Minnesota Press, 2001; French original, 1987.

Trautmann, Thomas R. *Aryans and British India.* Berkeley; Los Angeles: University of California Press, 1997.

Ueberweg, Friedrich, and Max Heinze. *Grundriss der Geschichte der Philosophie.* 8th ed. 4 vols. Berlin: E. S. Mittler, 1894.

Valls, Andrew. "A Lousy Empirical Scientist: Reconsidering Hume's Racism." In *Race and Racism in Modern Philosophy*, edited by Andrew Valls, 127–49. Ithaca, NY; London: Cornell University Press, 2005.

Valls, Andrew, ed. *Race and Racism in Modern Philosophy.* Ithaca, NY; London: Cornell University Press, 2005.

Vermeulen, Han. *Early History of Ethnography and Ethnology in the German Enlightenment: Anthropological Discourse in Europe and Asia, 1710–1808.* Dissertation, Leiden University, 2008.

———. "The German Invention of *Völkerkunde*: Ethnological Discourse in Europe and Asia, 1740–1798." In *The German Invention of Race*, edited by Sara Eigen and Mark Larrimore, 123–45. Albany: SUNY Press, 2006.

———. "Göttingen und die Völkerkunde: Ethnologie und Ethnographie in der deutschen Aufklärung, 1710–1815." In *Die Wissenschaft vom Menschen in Göttingen um 1800: Wissenschaftliche Praktiken, institutionelle Geographie, europäische Netzwerke*, edited by Hans Erich Bödeker, Philippe Büttgen, and Michel Espagne, 199–230. Göttingen: Vandenhoeck und Ruprecht, 2008.

Vetter, Sabine. *Wissenschaftlicher Reduktionismus und die Rassentheorie von Christoph Meiners: Ein Beitrag zur Geschichte der verlorenen Metaphysik in der Anthropologie.* Aachen: Mainz, 1996.

Viyagappa, Ignatius. *G. W. F. Hegel's Concept of Indian Philosophy.* Rome: Pontificia Universitas Gregoriana, 1980.

Vleeschauwer, H. J. de. *La déduction transcendentale dans l'oeuvre de Kant.* Antwerp: De Sikkel, 1934.

Walker, D. P. *The Ancient Theology: Studies in Christian Platonism from the Fifteenth to the Eighteenth Century.* Ithaca, NY: Cornell University Press, 1972.

Waquet, Françoise, ed. *Mapping the World of Learning: The* Polyhistor *of Daniel Georg Morhof.* Wiesbaden: Harrassowitz, 2000.

Wenz, Gunther. "'Gehe Du in Dich, Mein Guido': August Tholuck als Theologe der Erweckungsbewegung." *Pietismus und Neuzeit, Ein Jahrbuch zur Geschichte des neueren Protestantismus* 27 (2001): 68–80.

Wenzel, Herbert. *Christoph Meiners als Religionshistoriker, Inaugural-Dissertation zur Erlangung der Doktorwürde einer hohen philosophischen Fakultät der Universität zu Tübingen.* Frankfurt an der Oder: Paul Beholtz, 1917.

Willimszik, Klaus. *Friedrich Asts Geschichtsphilosophie, im Rahmen seiner Gesamtphilosophie.* Edited by Georgi Schieschkoff. Meisenheim am Glan: Anton Hain, 1967.

Willson, A. Leslie. *A Mythical Image: The Ideal of India in German Romanticism.* Durham, NC: Duke University Press, 1964.

Windelband, Wilhelm. "Die Geschichte der Philosophie." In *Die Philosophie im Beginn des 20. Jahrhunderts, Festschrift für Kuno Fischer*, edited by Wilhelm Windelband, 529–53 Heidelberg: C. Winter, 1904–5.

Windisch, Ernst. *Geschichte der Sanskrit-Philologie und indischen Altertumskunde.* Strassburg: K. J. Trübner, 1917.

Witte, Leopold. *Das Leben D. Friedrich August Gotttreu Tholuck's.* 2 vols. Bielefeld: Velhagen & Klasing, 1884–6.

Yates, Frances A. *Giordano Bruno and the Hermetic Tradition.* Chicago: University of Chicago Press, 1964.

Yerkes, James. *The Christology of Hegel.* Albany: SUNY Press, 1983.

Zammito, John H. *Kant, Herder, and the Birth of Anthropology.* Chicago; London: University of Chicago Press, 2002.

————. "Policing Polygeneticism in Germany, 1775: (Kames,) Kant, and Blumenbach." In *The German Invention of Race*, edited by Sara Eigen and Mark Larrimore, 35–54. Albany: SUNY Press, 2006.

Zande, Johan van der. "The Moderate Skepticism of German Popular Philosophy." In *The Skeptical Tradition around 1800: Skepticism in Philosophy, Science, and Society*, edited by Johan van der Zande and Richard H. Popkin, 69–80. Dordrecht; Boston; London: Kluwer, 1998.

————. "Popular philosophy and the history of mankind in eighteenth-century Germany." *Storia della storiografia* 22 (1992): 37–56.

Zande, Johan van der, and Richard H. Popkin, eds. *The Skeptical Tradition around 1800: Skepticism in Philosophy, Science, and Society*. Dordrecht; Boston; London: Kluwer, 1998.

Zantop, Susanne. "The Beautiful, the Ugly, and the German: Race, Gender, and Nationality in Eighteenth-Century Anthropological Discourse." In *Gender and Germanness: Cultural Productions of Nation*, edited by Patricia Herminghouse and Magda Mueller. Providence, RI: Berghahn, 1997.

————. *Colonial Fantasies: Conquest, Family, and Nation in Precolonial Germany, 1770–1870*. Durham, NC; London: Duke University Press, 1997.

Zeller, Edward. *Die Philosophie der Griechen in ihrer geschichtlichen Entwicklung*. 5th ed. 2 vols. Leipzig: O. R. Reisland, 1892.

Index

Abicht, Johann Heinrich: support for Kant, 22

Academics, 43

acosmism, 146

Adam, 2; as first philosopher, 70, 71, 72

Adelung, Johann Christoph: presentation of reason in humiliating light by, 100

Africa(ns): exclusion from histories of philosophy, xi, 1–9, 69–95; exclusion/inclusion in history of philosophy under Absolute Idealism, 97–131; presence of religion but not philosophy in, 1

Alcman, 107

Alexander the Great, 79, 80, 87

Alexander (Tsar), 77

Allgemeine Literatur-Zeitung (journal), 20

Alsted, Johann Heinrich, 16

Americans, Native, 94, 115, 116

Anaxagoras, 107, 128

Anaximander, 70, 72, 107

Anaximenes, 107

Anquetil du Perron, A. H., 66, 104

Anstett, Jean-Jacques, 53

Apollonius, 80

a priori construction, 7, 23, 24, 29, 98, 150

Arcesilas, 43

Archelaus, 107

Archytas, 107

Aristotle, 29, 61, 92, 109, 128, 137; logic of, 45

Asia: beginning of philosophy in, 2; beliefs not based in reason, 89; birth decisive in, 123; as center from which religion, art, and science flows, 103; emergence of pantheism in, 60; exclusion from histories of philosophy, xi, 1–9, 69–95; exclusion/inclusion in history of philosophy under Absolute Idealism, 97–131; mythosymbolic character of thought in, 89; origin of philosophy, 98; political conditions prevented development of philosophy in, 123; presence of religion but not philosophy in, 1

Asiatic Society of Bengal, 76

Ast, Friedrich, 8, 97; conceptualized circles, 101, 103, 107, 110, 120; differentiated between philosophy's eternal essence and forms, 42, 100; divided modern philosophy into epochs, 109–10; equated historical systems of philosophy to incarnations of the Spirit, 101; *Grundriss einer/der Geschichte der Philosophie*, 100, 101, 111, *112*, 131; idealism of, 98;

221